D1452382

RHODE ISLAND
IN THE
COLONIAL WARS

A List of Rhode Island
Soldiers & Sailors
in
King George's War
1740–1748

and

A List of Rhode Island
Soldiers & Sailors
in the
Old French & Indian War
1755–1762

By Howard M. Chapin

Two Volumes in One

Originally published: 1918, 1920
By the Rhode Island Historical Society
Reprinted, two volumes in one, by
Genealogical Publishing Co., Inc.
Baltimore, 1994
Library of Congress Catalogue Card Number 93-80413
International Standard Book Number 0-8063-1408-7
Made in the United States of America

Rhode Island in the Colonial Wars

A List of

Rhode Island

Soldiers & Sailors

IN

KING GEORGE'S WAR

1740 - 1748

BY

HOWARD M. CHAPIN

PROVIDENCE
PRINTED FOR THE SOCIETY
MCMXX

PUBLICATION COMMITTEE.

Rhode Island's Share in the War

The War of the Austrian Succession having broken out between England and Spain, the General Assembly of Rhode Island met in February,⁺1639-40 and made provision for putting the Colony in a state of defence. Rhode Island also sent two companies of volunteers under Capt. Hopkins in the unsuccessful expedition against Cartagena in 1740.

France entered the War in 1744 and the defences of the colony were on that account still further strengthened. A force of 150 men was raised in 1745 for Shirley's expedition against Louisbourg, but the Rhode Island contingent did not arrive until after that fortress had surrendered.* In the following year Rhode Island sent three more companies to Nova Scotia under Captains Sayer, Rice, and Cole.

By far the greater part of Rhode Island's effort in this conflict consisted in Privateering. A large number of these vessels were sent out each year and they inflicted great damage on the enemy's commerce. The Colony sloop of War Tartar was built during this war and was of much use as a scouting vessel and convoy guard.

This war, known in the Colonies as King George's War, came to an end in 1748 with the peace of Aix-la-Chapelle.

+For 1639 read 1739.

---

*Hutchison, Hist. of Mass. Bay, II, 371 and Winsor, Narr. & Ant. Hist. Vol. V, p. 410, and notes.

This list is compiled from the original manuscripts in the Rhode Island Historical Society and State Archives. A duplicate list on cards with references to the individual manuscripts is on file at the Rhode Island Historical Society.

Rhode Island Soldiers and Sailors in King George's War

1740 - 1748

AHORNEY, Isaac   An Indian apprentice of Newport.   Served in the expedition of 1746.

ALLEN, James   Commander of Privateer Revenge in 1741, 1742 and 1744, of Privateer Victory in 1742, of Privateer Prince William in 1744 and of the Colony Sloop Tartar in 1746.

James, Jr.   Captain.   Member of Council of War in 1743.

William   Commander of Privateer Prince William in 1743 and 1744, and of Privateer Brittania in 1744 and 1745.

William   Served in Capt. Rice's Co. in 1746.

ALLINGTON, John   Served in Capt. Rice's Co. in 1746.

AMORY, John   Captain's Quartermaster on Privateer Charming Betty in 1744, and Master on Privateer Prince Frederick in 1745.

ANGELL, James   Commissary of R. I. regiment at Louisbourg in 1745.

ARNOLD, Joseph of Smithfield   Second Lieut. on Privateer Reprisal in 1744 and 1745, First Lieut. on same in 1746, and Commander of same in 1747.

Nathaniel   Served in Capt. Rice's Co. in 1746.

William of Portsmouth.   Captain.   Summoned to Council of War in 1745.

ATKINSON, Joseph   Carpenter on Privateer Triton in 1744.

AUSTIN, Edward, Jr.   Served in Capt. Sheffield's Co. in 1740.

Thomas   Boatswain on Privateer Reprisal in 1744 and 1747 and on Privateer Prince Frederick in 1747.

AVERY, Jacob   Served in Capt. Sheffield's Co. in 1740.

AXTON, Young   Served at Fort George, Newport in 1743.

AYRAULT, Daniel of Newport Ensign, later Lieut. Member of
Councils of War in 1746 and 1747.
Elias Second Lieut. on Privateer Fame in 1744.
Stephen On guard duty at Newport in 1746.

BABCOCK, Amos Served in Capt. Sheffield's Co. in 1740.
Joshua Appointed to build watch house at Watch Hill in
1740.
BAILEY, John Gunner on Privateer Duke of Marlborough in
1745.
BAKER, Josiah Served in Capt. Sheffield's Co. in 1740.
Philip Served in Capt. Cole's Co. in 1746.
BARDINE, Charles On guard duty at Newport in 1746.
BARNET, William Served in Capt. Cole's Co. in 1746.
BARRON, Moses Served in Capt. Hopkins' Co. in 1740.
BASSILL, Francis Carpenter on Privateer Phenix in 1744.
BATTEY, John Master on Privateer Phenix in 1744.
BAXTER, William Served at Fort George, Newport in 1743.
BEALS, Thomas Boatswain on Privateer Triton in 1744.
BEARD, John Member of Committee on Transports in 1744.
BEAUCHAMP, John Captain's Quartermaster on Privateer King
George in 1745.
BEEBE, Daniel First Lieut. on Colony Sloop Tartar in 1740,
Second Lieut. on Privateer Defiance in 1744, First Lieut.
on Privateer Prince Frederick and on Privateer Prince
William in 1744, Quartermaster on Privateer Prince Fred-
erick in 1746, and Second Lieut. on same in 1747 and 1748.
BELITHO, John Captain. Member of Council of War in 1745 and
1746, and summoned to Council of War in 1747.
BELL, William Second Lieut. of Privateer Charming Betty in
1746.
BENJAMIN, Obed Served in Capt. Sheffield's Co. in 1740, and in
Capt. Cole's Co. in 1746.
BENNETT, Benjamin Sergeant in Capt. Rice's Co. in 1746.
Christopher Commander of Privateer Ranger in 1744 and
1745.
Elisha Served in Capt. Rice's Co. in 1746.
Job, Jr. On guard duty at Newport in 1746.

BENNETT,

> Jonathan   Corporal in Capt. Rice's Co. in 1746.
>
> Thomas   Corporal in Capt. Sayer's Co. in 1746.
>
> William   On guard duty at Newport in 1746.
>
> William, Jr.   Second Lieut. on Privateer Duke of Marlborough in 1744, and Commander of Privateer Duke of Cumberland in 1748.

BENNETLAND, William   Commander of Privateer Phenix in 1744.

BENSON, William   On guard duty at Newport in 1746.

BENTLEY, Edward   Gunner on Privateer Triton in 1744.

BILLINGTON, Joseph   Served in Capt. Sheffield's Co. in 1740.

BISSELL, Edward   Second Lieut. on Privateer Revenge in 1744.

> William   Served in Capt. Cole's Co. in 1746.

BLAKE, William   Surgeon on Privateer Revenge in 1741.

BLISS, Benjamin   Served in Capt. Rice's Co. in 1746.

BLOWEY, Alexander   Boatswain on Privateer Queen of Hungary in 1744.

BOAS, } Thomas   Boatswain on Privateer Fame in 1744.
BOAST, }

BOND, Henry   Served in Capt. Sayer's Co. in 1746.

BONFIELD, John   Carpenter on Privateer Prince Charles of Lorraine in 1744.

> William J.   Commander of Privateer Triton in 1741.

BOSTON, Matthew   Boatswain on Privateer Revenge in 1744.

BOURK   See Burke.

BOURNE, Thomas   Sergeant in Capt. Cole's Co. in 1746.

BOURNS

BOURS, Peter   Member of Committee to build Colony sloop in 1740, of Committee to fit out Colony sloop in 1741, of Committee to build magazine at Newport in 1741, of Council of War in 1743, and 1748, of Committee of War in 1746, and of Court Martial in 1749.

BOW, Roger   Captain's Clerk on Privateer Prince Frederick in 1748.

BOWLS, John   Served in Capt. Sayer's Co. in 1746.

BOYD, Robert   Lieut. on Privateer Defiance in 1746.

> William   Master on Privateer Prince Frederick in 1743.

BRADFORD, James   Served in Capt. Sheffield's Co. in 1740, and in Capt. Rice's Co. in 1746.

BRADSHAW, John   Served in Capt. Sayer's Co. in 1746.

BRAND, William Served in Capt. Sheffield's Co. in 1740.

BRENTON, Jahleel Captain. Member of Committee on Munitions in 1740. Summoned to Council of War in 1745, Member of Council of War, on guard duty at Newport, and on committee in charge of fortifications at Newport in 1746.

BREWER, Theo. On guard duty at Newport in 1746.

    Thomas Commander of Privateer Prince of Wales in 1745. Lost at sea.

BRIDGES, Robert First Lieut. on Privateer Prince William in 1744.

BROADFOOT, James (Indian) Served in the expedition of 1746.

BROOKS, John Served in Capt. Cole's Co. in 1746.

BROWN, Daniel Lieut. on Privateer Prince Charles of Lorraine in 1744.

    Eliphalet Carpenter on Privateer Patience in 1747.

    Henry Served in Capt. Sheffield's Co. in 1740.

    James Master's Mate on Privateer Brittania and Privateer Prince William in 1744, and Master on Privateer Lee Freggot in 1747. Perhaps Mate on Privateer Prince Frederick in 1747.

    John of Newport First Lieut. Summoned to Council of War in 1745, and on guard duty at Newport in 1746, and Member of Committee on Fortifications in 1746.

    John Lieut. on Privateer Patience in 1747.

    John Served in Capt. Cole's Co. in 1746.

    John, Jr. On guard duty at Newport in 1746.

    Josiah On guard duty at Newport in 1746.

    Obadiah Commander of Privateer Trembler in 1745.

    Peleg On guard duty at Newport in 1746.

    Peter Served in Capt. Sheffield's Co. in 1740.

    Robert Commander of Privateer Patience in 1747.

    William Second Lieut. on Privateer Reprisal in 1744 and 1747.

    William Second Lieut. on Privateer King George in 1745 and First Lieut. on same in 1747 and 1748.

    William Boatswain on Privateer Prince Charles of Lorraine in 1744.

    William Gunner on Privateer King George in 1747.

BROWN,

——————— Mate on Privateer Prince Frederick in 1747. Perhaps James, q. v.

BROWNELL, Stephen   Assistant Member of Council of War in 1746.

BRYANT, Anthony   Served in Capt. Sayer's Co. in 1746.

George   Mate on Privateer Hector in 1745, Master on Privateer King George in 1745 and 1747.

BULL, Joseph   Captain's Quartermaster on Privateer Duke of Marlborough in 1744.

Simon   Served in Capt. Sheffield's Co. in 1740.

BULLISON
BOLISON
BURLINGSON
BURLSON
} John   Served in Capt. Rice's Co. in 1746.

BURLINGAME, Joshua, Jr.   Served in Capt. Rice's Co. in 1746.

BURRIGE, William   Served in Capt. Rice's Co. in 1746.

BURKE, John   First Lieut. on Privateer King George in 1744.

BUTLER, John   Served in Capt. Rice's Co. in 1746.

BUTTON, Cyrus   Served in Capt. Sheffield's Co. in 1740.

BUTTS, William   Carpenter on Privateer Hector in 1745 and on Privateer Defiance in 1746.

CADMAN, William   Served in Capt. Sheffield's Co. in 1740.

CÆSAR, Joseph   Served in Capt. Sheffield's Co. in 1740, and in Capt. Rice's Co. in 1746.

Joshua   Served in Capt. Rice's Co. in 1746.

CAHOONE, John   Served in Campaign of 1740.

John   Lieut. on Colony Sloop Tartar in 1745.

CALDER, John   Captain's Quartermaster on Privateer Prince Frederick in 1743 and 1744, and on Privateer Defiance in 1744 and 1745.

CAMETT, Isaac   Served in Canadian expedition in 1746.

CAMPBELL, Charles   Served in Capt. Sheffield's Co. in 1740.

CANE, Briant   Served in Capt. Sayer's Co. in 1746.

John   Boatswain on Privateer King George in 1745 and 1747.

CANNIS, Edward   Served in Capt. Sayer's Co. in 1746.

Thomas   Served in Capt. Sayer's Co. in 1746.

CAPRON, Edward   Served in Capt. Cole's Co. in 1746.

CAPWELL, Peter   Served in Capt. Rice's Co. in 1746.

CARD, James   Served in Capt. Rice's Co. in 1746.

CARPENTER, Deliverance   Served in Capt. Rice's Co. in 1746.

> Hezekiah   Major, later Colonel.   Member of Councils of War in 1743 and 1745, and of Committee on Fortifications in 1741.

> Nathan   First Lieut. in Capt. Sayer's Co. in 1746 and Captain of Second Company, superseding Capt. Rice in May, 1747.

> William   Served in Capt. Rice's Co. in 1746.

CARR, Benjamin   Master on Privateer Duke of Marlborough in 1744 and perhaps in 1748.   Commander of same in 1745.

> Daniel   Master on Privateer Hector in 1745.

> Timothy   Served in Capt. Sayer's Co. in 1746.

CASWELL, Job   Captain.   Member of Council of War in 1743.

> Joseph   Served in Capt. Sayer's Co. in 1746.

CENERO, Antonio   Probably identical with Anthony Vigneron, q. v.

CHALONER, Walter of Newport.   Commissioned Officer in regiment which served at Carthagena in 1741, and Capt. at Fort George, Newport in 1748, and Member of Committee on Fortifications in 1746.

CHAMBERLAIN, William   Gunner on Privateer London in 1747 and 1748.

CHAMPLIN, Jeffrey   Ensign in Capt. Cole's Co. in 1746.

> Joshua   Captain of a Company in the Cape Breton expedition in 1745.

CHANNING, John   On guard duty at Newport in 1746.

CHASE, John   Served in Capt. Sayer's Co. in 1746.

CHEETS, Joseph   Served in Capt. Sheffield's Co. in 1740.

CHENEY, Thomas   Served in Capt. Sayer's Co. in 1746.

CHILD, Thomas   First Lieut. on Privateer Prince of Wales in 1745.

CLAPP, Edward   Served in Capt. Rice's Co. in 1746.

CLARK, Benjamin   Served in Capt. Sayer's Co. in 1746.

> Birt   Mate on Privateer Prince Frederick in 1744.

> Edward   Served in Capt. Sayer's Co. in 1746.

> James   Lieut on Privateer Charming Betty in 1744.

> Jeremiah   Appointed Master on Colony Sloop Tartar in 1740 but refused to serve.

CLARK,

> Jonathan   Captain.   Member of Council of War in 1743.
>
> Latham   Second Lieut. on Privateer King George in 1744.
>
> Michael   Commander of Privateer Hunter in 1743.
>
> Richard   Master's Mate on Privateer Prince Frederick in 1744.
>
> Simon   Served in Capt. Rice's Co. in 1746.

COBB, Josiah   Served in Capt. Rice's Co. in 1746.

CODDINGTON, William, Jr.   On guard duty at Newport in 1746.

COGGESHALL, Henry   On guard duty at Newport in 1746.

> John   Served in Capt. Cole's Co. in 1746.
>
> Joshua   Served in Capt. Sayer's Co. in 1746.

COHIES, Benjamin   Served in Capt. Cole's Co. in 1746.

> Zacharias   Gunner on Privateer Queen of Hungary in 1744.

COKER, Theodore   Surgeon on Privateer Duke of Marlborough in 1744.

COLE, Edward   Captain of Co. in expedition to Louisbourg in 1745, and Captain of 3rd Co. in 1746 and 1747, and Member of Committee on Fortifications in 1746.

> John   Served in Capt. Rice's Co. in 1746.

COLEGROVE, Nathan (Nathaniel)   Served in Capt. Rice's Co. in 1746.

> Stephen   Ensign in Capt. Rice's Co. in 1746.

COLLINGWOOD, James   Commander of Privateer Charming Betty in 1740.

COLLINS, James   On guard duty at Newport in 1746.

> Thomas   Served at Fort George, Newport in 1743.
>
> Thomas   Sergeant in Capt. Rice's Co. in 1746.
>
> Thomas, Jr.   Corporal in Capt. Rice's Co. in 1746.
>
> William   Served in Capt. Rice's Co. in 1746.

COMMET, Abraham   Served in Capt. Rice's Co. in 1746.

> Isaac   Served in Capt. Rice's Co. in 1746.

COMMOCK, Caesar   Served in Capt. Cole's Co. in 1746.

> Joseph   Served in Capt. Cole's Co. in 1746.

COMSTOCK, John   Assistant.   Member of Council of War in 1746.

CONKLING, Thomas   Commander of Privateer Queen of Hungary in 1744 and 1745.

CONVERSE, James   Served in Capt. Rice's Co. in 1746.

Cook, Anthony   Served in Capt. Sayer's Co. in 1746.

John   (Indian)   Served in Capt Sheffield's Co. in 1740.

John   Served in Capt. Sayer's Co. in 1746.

Peleg   Sergeant in Capt. Rice's Co. in 1746.

William   Master on Privateer Success in 1744.

Coon, Saunders   Served in Capt. Cole's Co. in 1746.

Cooper, Isaac   Boatswain on Privateer Prince William in 1744.

Samuel   Boatswain on Privateer Queen of Hungary in 1744, Second Lieut. on Privateer Defiance in 1746, and First Lieut. on same in 1747.

Corey, Caleb   Served in Capt. Sheffield's Co. in 1740.

Cornell, George, Jr., of Middletown.   Lieut.   Member of Council of War in 1748.

Gideon   Assistant.   Member of Council of War in 1745.

Cornish, James   Served in Capt. Cole's Co. in 1746.

Cottrell, George   Served in Capt. Cole's Co. in 1746.

Joshua   Served in Capt. Cole's Co. in 1746.

Couch, Ralph   Boatswain on Privateer Cæsar in 1743.

Cranston, Benjamin   Commander of Privateer King George in 1744 and of Privateer Duke of Cumberland in 1745.   Lost at sea.

Jeremiah   Captain's Quartermaster on Privateer King George in 1747.

John   Colonel.   Captain of Fort George, Newport, from 1739 to 1743, Commander of Colony Sloop Tartar in 1740, and Member of Councils of War in 1741, 1743, and 1746, of Committee on Munitions and Committee to build Colony sloop in 1740, Committee on Forts in 1741, Committee to fit out Colony sloop in 1741, and Committee of War in 1746.

Walter   Second Lieut, on Colony Sloop Tartar in 1740.

Cranwell, John   Quartermaster on Colony Sloop St. Andrew in 1741

Crossman, Seth   Sergeant in Capt. Cole's Co. in 1746.

Crow, George   Master on Privateer Reprisal in 1745 and 1746, and First Lieut. on same in 1747.

Cuchup, Simon   Served in Capt. Rice's Co. in 1746.

Culverson, John   First Lieut. on Privateer Hector in 1745.

CUNNINGHAM, —————— Commander of a Privateer in 1741.

CURREY, James   Mate on Privateer King George in 1745.

DAILEY, Henry   Mate on Privateer Defiance in 1748.
>   Jeremiah   Served in Capt. Rice's Co. in 1746.

DANES, Robert   Gunner on Privateer Patience in 1747.

DANES, see Daws or Dawes.

DARRACOTT, George   Commander of Privateer Mary Galley in
>   1745.

DAVENPORT, Charles   Mate on Privateer Phenix in 1744.

DAVIDSON, Charles   Commander of Colony Sloop St. Andrew in
>   1741 and Lieut. on Privateer Queen of Hungary in 1744.

DAVIS, Aaron   Served in Capt. Rice's Co. in 1746.
>   Guyas   Served in Capt. Hopkins' Co. in 1740.
>   John   Lieut. on Private Young Eagle of Boston in 1742.
>   John   Served in Capt. Rice's Co. in 1746.
>   Thomas   Served in Capt. Rice's Co. in 1746.
>   Thomas   Boatswain on Privateer Reprisal in 1744.
>   Zachariah   Served in Capt. Sayer's Co. in 1746.

DAVOE or DAVOL, John   Served in Capt. Sheffield's Co. in 1740.

DAWLEY, Samuel   Served in Capt. Cole's Co. in 1746.

DAWS, Robert—See DANES.

DENNIE, John   Served at Fort George, Newport in 1743.

DENNIS, James   Served in Capt. Sayer's Co. in 1746.
>   John   Commander of Privateer Prince Frederick in 1743,
>   1744 and 1746, of Privateer Defiance in 1744, 1745 and
>   1746, and of Privateer Jonathan in 1747.
>   Sampson   Served in Capt. Sayer's Co. in 1746.

DENTON, DANIEL   First Lieut. on Privateer Defiance in 1744 and
>   on Privateer Rebeccah in 1747 and 1748.

DEWOLF, Mark Anthony   Clerk on Privateer Prince Charles of
>   Lorraine in 1744 and Captains' Quartermaster, on Priva-
>   teer Prince Frederick in 1747.

DEXTER, John   Appointed to build watch house at Portsmouth in
>   1740.

DIAMOND James   Mate on Privateer Charming Betty in 1744.

DICK, Charles   Served in Capt. Sayer's Co. in 1746.

James   Served in Capt. Sayer's Co. in 1746.

DICKINSON, Robin   Served in Capt. Sheffield's Co. in 1740.

DODE or DODS, James   Chief Mate on Privateer Mary Galley in 1745.

William   Second Lieut. on Privateer Queen of Hungary in 1744.

DOLIFF, Jonathan   Served in Capt. Rice's Co. in 1746.

DOLIVER, Charles   Served in Capt. Sayer's Co. in 1746.

John   Served in Captain Sayer's Co. in 1746.

DOLLER, Jonathan   Served in expedition of 1746.

DOUBT, Isaac   Commander of Privateer Queen Elizabeth in 1744 and 1745.

DOUGLASS, William   Boatswain on Privateer Reprisal in 1747.

DOOLEY, } Michael.   Served in Capt. Rice's Co. in 1746.
DULIN,

DOUGHTY. Thomas   Quartermaster on Privateer Cæsar in 1744.

DOWNING, Valentine   Served in campaign of 1741.

DUNBAR, Henry   Quartermaster on Privateer Reprisal in 1744 and 1747.

DUNBAR, Robert   Steward on Privateer Duke of Marlborough in 1744, and Second Lieut. on same in 1745.

William   First Lieut. on Privateer Reprisal in 1744 and 1745 and Commander of same in 1746 and 1747.

DUNCAN, John   Served in Capt. Sayer's Co. in 1746.

DUNKIN, John   Served in Capt. Rice's Co. in 1746.

Samuel   Served in Capt. Rice's Co. in 1746.

DUNGRO, Abraham   Served in Capt. Cole's Co. in 1746.

DUNHAM, Daniel, Jr. of Newport   Captain.   Member of Councils of War in 1745, 1746, 1747 and 1748.

John   Lieut. on Privateer Ranger in 1744.

DUNWELL, John   Gunner on Privateer Reprisal in 1744 and 1746.

Samuel   Gunner on Privateer Reprisal in 1747.

DURFEE, Robert   Member of Committee on Transports in 1744.

DYER, Charles   Commander of Privateer Revenge in 1742.

John   Served at Fort George Newport in 1743.

EAST, Edward   Gunner on Privateer Defiance in 1747.

    John   Served in Capt. Rice's Co. in 1746.

EASTON, Moses   Served in Capt. Sayer's Co. in 1746.

    Samuel   Drew a plan of Fort George in 1745.

EDDY, Thomas   Carpenter on Privateer Reprisal in 1745.

EDMONDS, William   Gunner on Privateer Prince Frederick in 1743, on Privateer Brittania in 1744, on Privateer King George in 1744, and on Privateer Duke of Cumberland in 1745.

EDWARDS, Joseph   Served in Capt. Rice's Co. in 1746.

    Thomas   Served in Capt. Rice's Co. in 1746.

ELDRED, John   Second Lieut. on Privateer Cæsar in 1743.

    James   Served in Capt. Cole's Co. in 1746.

    Samuel   Served at Louisbourg in 1745, and as Lieut. in Capt. Cole's Co. in 1746.

ELDRIDGE, Elisha   Served in Capt. Hopkins' Co. in 1740.

    Randall   Member of Committee on Transports in 1744.

ELLERY, William   Assistant and Deputy Governor. Member of Council of War in 1743, summoned to Council of War in 1748, and Member of Committee on Fortifications in 1741.

ELLIS, John   Commander of Privateer Success in 1744.

ELLISON, John   Gunner on Privateer Cæsar in 1743 and on Privateer Fame in 1744.

ENGLISH, Alexander.   Master on Privateer London in 1747 and 1748.

ENOS, David   Served in Capt. Sheffield's Co. in 1740.

    Ichabod   Served in Capt. Cole's Co. in 1746.

EPHRAIM, Jonas   Served in Capt. Cole's Co. in 1746. Perhaps identical with Jonathan.

    Jonathan   Served in Canadian expedition. Perhaps the same as Jonas.

EWLING, Richard   Served in Capt. Rice's Co. in 1746.

FARS, John   Served in Capt. Coles' Co. in 1746.

FERROW, Joseph   Boatswain on Privateer Humming Bird in 1741.

FISH, Robert   Served in Capt. Rice's Co. in 1746.

    William   Served in Capt. Cole's Co. in 1746.

FISHER, Paul   Served in Capt. Rice's Co. in 1746.

FISHER, Richard   Captain's Quartermaster on Privateer Ranger in 1744.

FITON, Robert   Served in Capt. Sayer's Co. in 1746.

FLAGG, Ebenezer   On guard duty at Newport in 1746.

FLEMING, Arthur   Master and First Lieut. on Privateer Fame in 1744.

FLOYD, Joseph   Served in Capt. Sheffield's Co. in 1740.

FOAMS, John   Served in Capt. Hopkins' Co. in 1740.

FONES, Daniel   Commander of Colony Sloop Tartar in 1745, 1746, and 1747, and First Lieut. on Privateer Prince Frederick in 1748.

   John   Served in Capt. Sheffield's Co. in 1740.

FOSTER, Josiah   Served in Capt. Rice's Co. in 1746.

FOWLER, James   Served in Capt. Sayer's Co. in 1746.

   Robert   Privateer.   Commander of Sloop Bonita of St. Christopher in 1742.

Fox, Ezekiel   Captain's Quartermaster on Privateer Cæsar in 1743 and 1744.

   George   Commander of Privateer Revenge in 1741.

FREEBODY, John, Jr.   On guard duty at Newport in 1746.

   Thomas   On guard duty at Newport in 1746.

FREEBORN, John   Lieut. Col.   Member of Council of War in 1741 and summoned to Council of War in 1745.

FREET, Samuel   Sergeant in Capt. Cole's Co. in 1746.

FRETCHER, John   Served in Capt. Sayer's Co. in 1746.

FRIER, Samuel   Served at Fort George, Newport in 1743.

FROST, John   (Indian)   Served in Capt. Rice's Co. in 1746.

FRY, Daniel   Commander of Colony Sloop Tartar in 1741.

   Thomas   Commander of Privateer Molly in 1745 and of Privateer Charming Betty in 1746 and 1747.

FULLER, Jonathan   Surgeon on Privateer Prince Frederick in 1743.

GALE, John   Quartermaster and Master on Privateer Charming Betty in 1740.

GALLOP, Joseph   Served in Capt. Rice's Co. in 1746.

   Richard   Served in Capt. Cole's Co. in 1746.

   Richard, Jr.   Served in Capt. Cole's Co. in 1746.

GALLOWAY, Andrew   Master on Privateer Brittania in 1744.

GARDNER, Cato.   Served in Capt. Cole's Co. in 1746.

   Henry   Served in Capt. Cole's Co. in 1746.

GARDNER,

James of Newport   Captain.   Member of Council of War in 1745.

Job   Mate on Privateer Jonathan in 1747 and on Privateer Ranger in 1747 and 1748.

John   Colonel.   Member of Councils of War in 1741, 1743 and 1748, and of Committee on Fortifications in 1741 and 1746.

Peter   Served in Capt. Sayer's Co. in 1746.

Robert   Surgeon on Privateer Prince Frederick in 1744, and on Privateer Defiance in 1745.

Thomas   Served in Capt. Sayer's Co. in 1746.

GARRET, Philip   Mate on Privateer Queen of Hungary in 1744.

William   Captain's Quartermaster on Privateer Success in 1744.

GEERS, Zebulon   Carpenter on Privateer Defiance and Privateer Prince Frederick in 1744 and on Privateer King George in 1745.

GEORGE, Jacob   Served in Capt. Sayer's Co. in 1746.

GERSHOM, Aaron   Served in Capt. Sayer's Co. in 1746.

GERAN   See Goran.

GIBBS, John   Master on Privateer Prince Frederick in 1744.

John   Captain's Quartermaster on Privateer Brittania in 1744.

GIBBS, Robert   Assistant.   Member of Council of War in 1746.

Robert   Lieut. on Privateer Duke of Marlborough in 1744, First Lieut. on Privateer Jonathan in 1747, Lieut. on Privateer Ranger in 1747 and 1748, Commander of Privateer Rebecca in 1748.

William   Master on Privateer Revenge in 1742.

William   Steward on Privateer Prince Frederick in 1744.

GIBSON, John   Boatswain on Privateer Duke of Marlborough in 1745.

GICE, George   Served in Capt. Cole's Co. in 1746.

GLADDING, Joseph   Lieut.   Member of Council of War in 1743.

GLOVER, John   Served in Capt. Sayer's Co. in 1746.

GODFREY, John   Carpenter and Master on Colony Sloop Tartar in 1740 and Carpenter on Privateer Fame in 1744.

GODFREY, Robert   Served in Capt. Rice's Co. in 1746.

GOODMAN, John   Boatswain on Privateer London in 1747 and 1748
  Thomas   Boatswain on Privateer Prince Frederick in 1745.

GORAN or GERAN   Mate on Privateer Duke of Cumberland in
  1747.

GOULDING, George   Captain's Quartermaster on Privateer Prince
  William in 1744.
  George   Member of Committee to build Colony sloop in 1740,
  and of Committee to fit out Colony sloop in 1741.

GREENE, George   Served in Capt. Cole's Co. in 1746.
  Jeremiah   Served in Capt. Sayer's Co. in 1746.
  William   Governor. Member of Council of War in 1746.

GREENWOOD, Daniel   Served in Capt. Cole's Co. in 1746.
  Ephraim   Served in Capt. Cole's Co. in 1746.

GRIFFITH, John   Commander of Privateer Fame in 1742, and 1743
  of Privateer Cæsar in 1743 and 1744, same vessel in the
  Colony's service in 1744, and of Transport Success in
  1746.
  Thomas   Gunner on Privateer Prince Charles of Lorraine in
  1744.

GRIGG, Samuel   Master on Privateer Patience in 1747.

GRINNELL, Thomas   Gunner on Privateer Rebeccah in 1747 and
  1748.

GUST, Lewis   Lieut. on Privateer Henry in 1748.

HADREAL, Joseph   Served in Capt. Sheffield's Co. in 1740.

HALEY, Domini   Served in Capt. Sheffield's Co. in 1740.

HALFROD, James   Served in Capt. Sheffield's Co. in 1740.

HALL, Benjamin   Major, later Colonel. Member of Councils of
  War in 1743 and 1746.
  Job   Served in Capt. Sayer's Co. in 1746.

HAMBLETON, James   Corporal in Capt. Sayer's Co. in 1746.

HAMMOCK, Jeoffrey   Served in Capt. Sayer's Co. in 1746.

HAND or HANLEY, Godfrey   Gunner on Privateer Revenge in 1744,
  on Privateer Reprisal in 1745, on Privateer Prince Frederick and on Privateer Defiance in 1746 and on Privateer
  Reprisal in 1747.

HARDY, Robert   Served in Capt. Sheffield's Co. in 1740.

HARMON, Jeremiah   Master on Privateer Revenge in 1741.

HARRINGTON, Hezekiah   Served in Capt. Rice's Co. in 1746.

Isaac   Served in Capt. Cole's Co. in 1746.

Jabez   Served in Capt. Sayer's Co. in 1746.

HARRISON, Joseph   Drew plan of Fort George in 1745, and Member of Committee on Fortifictions in 1746.

Peter   Drew plan of Fort George in 1745, and Member of Committee on Fortifications in 1746.

HARRY, Benjamin   Served in Capt. Cole's Co. in 1746.

George   Served in Capt. Cole's Co. in 1746.

HARVEY, Seth   Served in expedition of 1745 and 1746. Master of Privateer Prince Frederick in 1747 and Lieut. on Privateer Duke of Cumberland in 1748.

HASSARD   See HAZARD.

HASTINGS, Benjamin   Served in Capt. Cole's Co. in 1746.

James   Gunner at Fort George, Newport in 1743.

John   Served in Capt. Sheffield's Co. in 1740, and in Capt. Cole's Co. in 1746.

HATCH, Ezekiel   Mate on Privateer Duke of Marlborough in 1744 and Master on Privateer Prince of Wales in 1745.

HATFIELD, Edward   Served in Capt. Sayer's Co. in 1746.

HAWLINGS, James   Served in Capt. Cole's Co. in 1746.

HAWES, Shubal   Sergeant in Capt. Sayer's Co. in 1746.

HAXTER, Benjamin   Carpenter on Privateer Charming Betty in 1746.

HAZARD, Anthony   Served in Capt. Cole's Co. in 1746.

Benjamin   Assistant. Member of Council of War in 1745 and summoned to Council of War in 1747.

Fones   Master on Privateer Jonathan in 1747.

HEATH, Jonathan of Newport. Captain. Member of Council of War in 1748.

HEFFERLAND, Anthony   Served at Fort George, Newport in 1745.

HELME, Silas   Lieut. in Capt. Cole's Co. in 1746.

HENNEBY, John   Boatswain on Privateer Mary Galley in 1745.

HERRICK, Wait   Served in Capt. Sheffield's Co. in 1740.

HIGGINS, William   Lieut. on Privateer Revenge in 1742 and Commander of Privateer Hector in 1745.

HILL, George   Served in Capt Rice's Co. in 1746.

HINCKLEY, Daniel   Served in Capt. Sayer's Co. in 1746.

HITT, John   Served in Capt. Cole's Co. in 1746.

HIX, James   Served in Capt. Rice's Co. in 1746.

HOLDEN, Anthony of Warwick   Mariner on H. M. S. Warwick in
   1747 and 1748.   His right arm was shot off during an
   engagement off Havana.

HOLMES, James   Commander of Privateer Endeavor in 1746, and
   of Colony Sloop Tartar in 1746, 1747 and 1748.

   John   Gunner on Privateer Duke of Cumberland in 1747.

   Nicholas   Surgeon on Privateer Revenge in 1744.

HOOD, Cambey   Lieut. on Privateer Triton in 1744.

HOOPER, Henry   Surgeon on Privateer Prince William in 1744.

HOPKINS, Esek   Commander of Privateer Wentworth in 1741.

   John   Commander of Privateer Reprisal in 1744 and 1745.

   William   Captain of one of the R. I. Companies in 1740, and
   Commander of Privateer Prince Frederick in 1743.

HORNY, Ebenezer   Served in Capt. Sayer's Co. in 1746.

HOUSE, Simon   Corporal in Capt. Sayer's Co. in 1746.

HOWARD, Edward   On guard duty at Newport in 1746.

   Martin   Gunner's Mate on Privateer Duke of Marlborough
   in 1744.

   Peter   Served in Capt. Rice's Co. in 1746.

HOYLE, Richard of Providence   Lieut. and Commissary in the
   expedition against Louisbourg in 1745.

HUBBARD, Ezekiel   Master on Privateer Revenge in 1744, and
   served in expedition of 1745 and 1746.

HUGH, John   Mate on Privateer Triton in 1744.

HULL, Samuel   Served in Capt. Cole's Co. in 1746.

HUMPHREYS, James   Served at Fort George, Newport, in 1743.

HUNT, Abraham   Served in Capt. Cole's Co. in 1746.

   Oliver   Mate on Privateer Reprisal in 1746, and Lieut. on
   same in 1747.

HUNTER, Andrew   On guard duty at Newport in 1746.

HURDELL, Edward   Served in Capt. Rice's Co. in 1746.

HUSTON, Robert   Served in Capt. Hopkin's Co. in 1740.

HUXFORD, Joseph   Served in Capt. Sayer's Co. in 1746.

HUXHAM, Jonathan   Mate on Privateer King George in 1747.

INGRAHAM, Benjamin   Master on Privateer Cæsar in 1743.

JACKSON, Andrew   Served in Capt. Cole's Co. in 1746.
    James   Carpenter on Privateer Queen Elizabeth in 1744.
    John   Served in Capt. Sayer's Co. in 1746.
    Richard   Served in Capt. Sayer's Co. in 1746.
    William   Boatswain on Privateer Defiance in 1746.
JACQUES, Ebenezer   Served in Capt. Sheffield's Co. in 1740.
JAMES, William   Mate on Privateer Queen Elizabeth in 1744.
JEFFRIES, Caleb   Gunner on Privateer Prince Frederick in 1745.
    Caleb   Captain.   Member of Council of War in 1741.
JENCKES, Jeremiah   Master on Privateer Reprisal in 1744 and
    1747.
JENNINGS, Josiah   Commander of Privateer Charming Betty in
    1744.
JOB, Samuel   Served in Capt. Cole's Co. in 1746.
JOHNSON, Edward   Second Lieut. on Privateer Hector in 1745 and
    First Lieut. on Privateer Duke of Cumberland in 1747.
    Elisha   Commander of Privateer Ranger in 1747, and 1748,
    and of Privateer Prince Frederick in 1749.
    Esek   Served in Capt. Rice's Co. in 1746.
    Gideon   Served in Capt. Sheffield's Co. in 1740.
    John Arthur   Gunner on Privateer Charming Betty in 1476.
    Richard   Served in Capt. Cole's Co. in 1746.
    Samuel   Served in Capt. Rice's Co. in 1746.
    William   Served in Capt. Rice's Co. in 1746.
JONES, Henry   Served in Capt. Hopkins' Co. in 1740.
    John   Served in the expedition of 1746.
    Richard   Lieut. on Privateer Defiance in 1747.
    Thomas   Boatswain on Privateer Queen Elizabeth in 1744.
    William   Served in Capt. Sayer's Co. in 1746.
    William   Master on Privateer Ranger in 1744.
    William   Boatswain and Master's Mate on Privateer King
    George in 1744, and Quartermaster and Second Lieut. on
    same in 1747.
JORDAN, Edmond   Served in Capt. Rice's Co. in 1746.
JOYCE, John   Served in Capt. Rice's Co. in 1746.
JUSTICE, Benjamin   Served in Capt. Cole's Co. in 1746.
    Thomas   Served in Capt. Cole's Co. in 1746.

KEACH, William   Served in Capt. Rice's Co. in 1746.

KENNEDY, John   Boatswain on Privateer Mary Galley in 1745.

KINNIMOUTH, Alexander   Second Lieut. and later First Lieut. on Privateer Queen of Hungary in 1744.

KETTLE, Thomas   Carpenter on Privateer Duke of Cumberland in 1747.

KIBBY, Robert   Commander of Privateer Three Brothers in 1747.

KING, Josias   Master on Privateer Duke of Cumberland in 1748.

KINNICUT, Edward   Lieut. Col. of R. I. Reg't, in 1746.

KINYON, Peter   Served in Capt. Cole's Co. in 1746.

KIP, William   Served on Privateer Prince Charles of Lorraine in 1744.

KIRBY, Edward   Served on a privateer.

KIRK, William   Boatswain's Mate on Privateer Duke of Marlborough in 1744.

LANE, John   Served in Capt. Sheffield's Co. in 1740.

LANGDEN, ————   Commander of a Privateer in 1741.

LANGWORTHY, Benjamin   Master on Privateer Cæsar in 1744, and on Privateer Duke of Cumberland in 1745.

LARKHAM, Thomas   Served in Capt. Cole's Co. in 1746.

LAWRENCE, Angle Brit (or Bris)   Carpenter on Privateer Prince Frederick in 1743.

LAWTON, Robert   Member of Council of War in 1746.

LEE, John   Sergeant in Capt. Sayer's Co. in 1746.

Richard   Served in Capt. Sheffield's Co. in 1740.

LEGG, Isaac   Carpenter on Privateer London in 1747 and 1748.

John   Boatswain on Privateer Duke of Cumberland in 1747.

LETSON, Robert   Served in Capt. Rice's Co. in 1746.

LEWIS, Samuel   Served at Fort George, Newport, in 1743.

LITTLEFIELD, Nathaniel   Member of Committee of Defence of Block Island in 1740.

LLOYD, John   Second Lieut. on Privateer Charming Betty in 1744.

LOGAN, Jonathan   Served in Capt. Rice's Co. in 1746.

LOUD, William   Master on Privateer Rebeccah in 1747 and 1748.

LOVEWCLE, John   Served in Capt. Rice's Co. in 1746.

LUTHER, Elisha   Lieut. on Privateer Revenge in 1744.

Philip   Served in Capt. Sayer's Co. in 1746.

LYON, ————— Quartermaster on Privateer Reprisal in 1747.

LYNDON, Josias On Committee on Fort George in 1745, and on guard duty at Newport in 1746.

Samuel Major, later Colonel. Member of Councils of War in 1745, 1747 and 1748.

MACCOON, John Served in Capt. Sheffield's Co. in 1740.

MACFARLAN, Thomas Commander of Privateer Triton in 1743 and 1744.

MADDOX, Michael Boatswain on Privateer Brittania in 1744.

MAGGOT, Thomas Boatswain on Privateer Cæsar in 1744.

MALBONE, Evan On guard duty at Newport in 1746.

Godfrey Colonel of R. I. Reg't in 1745, and Member of Committee on Fortifications in 1746.

MANTON, Edward Second Lieut. on Privateer Jonathan in 1747.

MARK, Job Served in Capt. Sayer's Co. in 1746.

MARSHALL, Peter Master's Mate on Privateer Victory in 1742 First Lieut. on Privateer Prince Frederick in 1743 and 1744, and on Privateer Phenix in 1744, Commander of Privateer Success in 1744 and 1745, of Privateer Prince Frederick in 1745 and 1746, of Colony Sloop Tartar in 1746 and of Privateer Duke of Cumberland in 1746 and 1747.

MARTIN, Andrew Surgeon's Mate on Privateer Revenge in 1744 and Master's Mate or Master on Privateer Defiance in 1745.

Edward Master on Privateer Defiance in 1747.

Isaac Second Mate on Privateer Duke of Marlborough in 1744.

James Corporal in Capt. Cole's Co. in 1746.

John Served in Capt. Hopkins' Co. in 1740.

John Served in Capt. Sayer's Co. in 1746.

John Sergeant in Capt. Cole's Co. in 1746.

William Drummer in Capt. Cole's Co. in 1746.

MARTINDALE, John Captain's Quartermaster and Carpenter on Privateer Queen of Hungary in 1744 and Carpenter on Privateer Prince Frederick in 1745, 1746 and 1747.

MASKEL, Samuel Boatswain on Privateer Defiance in 1747.

MATTHEWS, John   Boatswain's Mate on Privateer Duke of Marlborough in 1744.

MATTHEWSON, Benjamin   Served in Capt. Rice's Co. in 1746.

MAUDSLEY, John Master on Privateer Prince William in 1744, First Lieut. on Privateer Brittania in 1744, and on Privateer King George in 1745, Commander of Privateer King George in 1747 and 1748.

John   Master on Privateer Mary and Ann in 1747.   Perhaps error for 1744.

MAXFIELD, Gershom   Served in Capt. Sheffield's Co. in 1740.

Gershom   Served in Capt. Hopkins' Co. in 1740   (Probably transferred from Capt. Sheffield's Co.)

MAXSON, Jonathan   Served in Capt. Sheffield's Co. in 1740.

McCLANNING or McCLENNAN, Humphrey   Served in Capt. Rice's Co. in 1746.

McDANIEL, Archibald   Served in Capt. Sayer's Co. in 1746.

Peter   Gunner on Privateer Cæsar in 1744.

McDONALD, Alexander   Master on Privateer Queen of Hungary in 1744.   Second Lieut. on Privateer Prince William in 1744, on Privateer Prince Frederick in 1745 and 1746, and Lieut. on same in 1747.

McKUSICK, John of Portsmouth, N. H.   Quartermaster and Factor on Privateer Reprisal in 1744.

McLEOD, Roderick   Boatswain on Privateer Mary and Ann in 1747.

McLOVE, John   Carpenter on Privateer Reprisal in 1744.

MEDBERRY, John   Served in Capt. Hopkins' Co. in 1740.

MELVILLE, Thomas   Lieut.   Member of Council of War in 1745.

MERCHANT, Huxford   On guard duty at Newport in 1746 and Master on Privateer Duke of Cumberland in 1747.

MEW, George   Served in Capt. Cole's Co. in 1746.

MICHENER, Abel   Master on Privateer Charming Betty in 1746, and First Lieut. on Privateer Duke of Marlborough in 1748.

MILLER, Joseph   Carpenter on Privateer Success in 1744.

MITCHELL, Alexander   Gunner on Privateer Phenix in 1744.

Thomas   Served in Capt. Sheffield's Co. in 1740.

MOFFAT, Thomas   Surgeon of R. I. Reg't in 1746.

MOORE, Christopher   Served in Capt. Rice's Co. in 1746.
    Daniel   Served in Capt. Rice's Co. in 1746.
    David   On guard duty at Newport in 1746.
    John   Carpenter's Mate on Privateer Duke of Marlborough
        in 1744, and Carpenter on Privateer Reprisal in 1746 and
        1747.
MOREHEAD, Daniel   Gunner on Privateer Prince Frederick in
        1744, and on Privateer Defiance in 1744 and 1745.
    Ebenezer   Surgeon on Privateer Reprisal in 1746.
MORRILL, John A.   Quartermaster on Privateer Charming Betty
        in 1744.
MORRIS, Robert   Commander of Privateer Duke of Marlborough
        in 1744.
MORRISON, John   Boatswain on Privateer Reprisal in 1746.
MOSHER, Andrew   Master on Privateer Defiance in 1746.
    John   Served in Capt. Sheffield's Co. in 1740.
MOTT, John   Served in Capt. Sheffield's Co. in 1740.
MOWRY, Richard   Served in Capt. Sayer's Co. in 1746.
MOXLEY, John   Served in Capt. Sheffield's Co. in 1740.
MUDIE, Robert   Commander of Privateer London in 1747 and
        1748.
MUGGWORTH, William   Boatswain on Privateer Prince of Wales in
        1745.
MUMFORD, John   Boatswain on Privateer Phenix in 1744.
    William of Newport   Second Lieut., later Captain. Sum-
        moned to Council of War in 1745, on guard duty at
        Newport in 1746, and Member of Councils of War in 1747
        and 1748.
MUNDUN, John   Second Lieut. on Privateer Defiance in 1745,
        Mate on Privateer Prince Frederick in 1745, and Master's
        Mate on same in 1746.
MUNRO, Benjamin   Master on Privateer Prince Charles of
        Lorraine in 1744.
MURPHY, Nicholas   Served in Capt. Hopkins' Co. in 1740.
    Patrick   Cook on Privateer Duke of Marlborough in 1744.

NEWELL, Timothy   On guard duty at Newport in 1746.
NEWFIELD, Job, Jr.   (Indian)   Served in Capt. Rice's Co. in 1746.
NICHOLS, James   Served in Capt. Rice's Co. in 1746.
    Jonathan   Member of Committee of War in 1746.

NICHOLS,

    Joseph of Middletown. Captain. Summoned to Council of War in 1745.

    Samuel   Served in Capt. Sayer's Co. in 1746, and appointed Second Lieut. in that Company in May, 1747.

NILES, Jeremiah   Member of Council of War in 1745.

    Nathaniel   Appointed to build watch house at Point Judith in 1740.

NISBET, John   Master's Mate on Privateer Duke of Cumberland in 1745.

NIXON, Samuel   Surgeon on Privateer Cæsar in 1743, and on Privateer Fame in 1744.

NOIST, George   Boatswain on Privateer Duke of Marlborough in 1744.

NORTON, Benjamin   Commander of Privateer Revenge in 1741 and 1742.

NOXIT, Scipio   Served in Capt. Sayer's Co. in 1746.

OAKLEY, Jonathan   Served in Capt. Sayer's Co. in 1746.

O'NEAL, Henry   Served in Capt. Sayer's Co. in 1746.

ORIN, Robert   Served in Capt. Sheffield's Co. in 1740.

OSBORNE, Joseph   Served in Capt. Cole's Co. in 1746.

    Nathaniel   Served in Capt. Cole's Co. in 1746.

    William   Served in Capt. Sheffield's Co. in 1740.

PACHMAN, Isaac   Served in Capt. Cole's Co. in 1746.

PAINE, Lawrence   On guard duty at Newport in 1746.

PALMER, Christopher   Lieut. in Capt. Sheffield's Co. in 1740, and later served in Capt. Hopkins' Co. in 1740.

PARKE, Richard   Served in Capt. Sheffield's Co. in 1740.

PARLIAMENT, Paul   Gunner on Privateer Mary and Ann in 1747.

PARSONS, William   Mate on Privateer King George in 1748.

PARTRIDGE, Samuel   Served in Capt. Rice's Co. in 1746.

PAUL, John   Served in Capt. Sayer's Co. in 1746.

    William   On guard duty at Newport in 1746.

PEARCE, William   Served in Capt. Sayer's Co. in 1746.

PEASE, Simon   On guard duty at Newport in 1746.

PECKHAM, Jere   Served in campaign in 1740.

PECKHAM, Joseph   Served in Capt. Cole's Co. in 1746.

PELHAM, John   Mate on Privateer Fame in 1744, and Gunner on Privateer Prince of Wales in 1745.

PEMBERTON, Bryant   Served in Capt. Cole's Co. in 1746.

PENDLETON, Christopher   Served in Capt. Sheffield's Co. in 1740. James   Served in Capt. Sheffield's Co. in 1740.

PETEL, John   Second Lieut. on Privateer Duke of Cumberland in 1745.

PETERS, Benjamin   Served in Capt. Sayer's Co. in 1746.

PETTIES, Benjamin   Served in Capt. Sheffield's Co. in 1740.

PETTINGALL, Joseph   Served in Capt. Sayer's Co. in 1746.

PHILLIPS, Caleb   Captain's Quartermaster on Privateer Fame in 1744.

   Erasmus   Mate on Privateer Defiance in 1747.

   John   Served in Capt. Cole's Co. in 1746.

   Joshua   Served in Capt. Hopkins' Co. in 1740.

   Michael of Bristol.   Pilot and Mate on Privateer Prince of Lorraine in 1744.

PIERCE, William   Served in Capt. Sheffield's Co. in 1740.

PINNEGAR, William   Master on Privateer Queen of Hungary in 1744 and Lieut. on Colony Sloop Tartar in 1745.

PITCHER, Andrew   Served in Capt. Rice's Co. in 1746.

POKEAGE, John   Served in Capt. Cole's Co. in 1746.

POLLARD, John   Served in Capt. Sheffield's Co. in 1740.

POOL, Samuel   Carpenter on Privateer Mary Galley in 1745.

POOLE, Thomas   Second Mate on Privateer Prince of Wales in 1745.

POOR, Edward   Served in Capt. Sayer's Co. in 1746.

POTHAGE, Isaac   Served in Capt. Cole's Co. in 1746.

   Joseph   Served in Capt. Cole's Co. in 1746.

POTTER, David   Served in Capt. Sayer's Co. in 1746.

   Ichabod   Corporal in Capt. Rice's Co. in 1746.

   Jeffrey   Served in Capt. Sheffield's Co. in 1740, and on Privateer Prince Charles of Lorraine in 1744.

   Nathaniel   Lieut. on Colony Sloop Tartar in 1740, and Commander of Privateer Queen of Hungary in 1744.

   Simeon   Commander of Privateer Prince Charles of Lorraine in 1744.

   Thomas   Served in Capt. Cole's Co. in 1746.

POWER, Joseph   Commander of Privateer Victory in 1741 and 1742.

Oliver   Served in Capt. Sheffield's Co. and in Capt. Hopkins' Co., in 1740.

PRENTICE, John   Commander of the Guard Sloop Defence in 1745.

PRICE, Ephraim   Served in Capt. Rice's Co. in 1746.

PRIOR, Robert   Captain's Quartermaster on Privateer Charming Betty in 1746.

PROCTOR, James   Carpenter on Privateer Duke of Marlborough in 1745.

William   Carpenter on Privateer Defiance in 1745.

PUNCHARD, Thomas   Served in Capt. Cole's Co. in 1746.

QUONEL, Robin   Served in Capt. Sheffield's Co. in 1740.

QUONY, John   Served in Capt. Cole's Co. in 1746.

RANDALL, Stephen   Served in Capt. Sayer's Co. in 1746.

READ, Isaiah   Served in Capt. Sayer's Co. in 1746.

James   Served in Capt. Sheffield's Co. in 1740.

John   Served in Capt. Rice's Co. in 1746.

William   Member of Committee on Fortifications in 1746.

REDMOND, John   Second Mate on Privateer Mary Galley in 1745.

REDWOOD, Abraham   Member of Council of War in 1746, and of Committee of War in 1746.

REMINGTON, Josiah   Served in Capt. Cole's Co. in 1746.

RENNIS, Joseph   Served in Capt. Sheffield's Co. in 1740.

REYNOLDS, James   Served in Capt. Cole's Co. in 1746.

RHODES, Joseph   Served in Capt. Hopkins' Co. in 1740.

Simon   On guard duty at Newport in 1746.

RICE, William   Member of Committee on Fortifications in 1746 and Captain of 2nd R. I. Company in 1746.   Died January 22, 1746-7.

RICHARDS, Burnet   Lieut. on Privateer Mary and Ann in 1747.

William   Commander of Privateer Mary and Ann and of Privateer King George in 1747.

RICHARDSON, Barzillai   Served in Capt. Hopkins' Co. in 1740 perhaps transferred from Capt. Sheffield's Co.

Benjamin   Served in Capt. Sheffield's Co. in 1740, perhaps error for Barzillai.

RICHMOND, Thomas   Served at Fort George, Newport in 1743.

RIDER, Abraham   Served in Capt. Cole's Co. in 1746.

   Joseph   Mate on Privateer Charming Betty in 1746.

RILEY, Thomas   Served in Capt. Sayer's Co. in 1746.

ROBERTS, John   Served in Capt. Rice's Co. in 1746.

ROBINSON, Daniel   Boatswain's Mate on Privateer Prince Frederick in 1744.

   John   Lieut. on Privateer Charming Betty in 1740.

   Joseph   Served under Capt. Sheffield in 1740.

   William   Member of Council of War in 1748.

ROCKWELL, Joseph   Served in Capt. Sayer's Co. in 1746.

ROGERS, Edward   Served in Capt. Cole's Co. in 1746.

   Isaac   Captain's Quartermaster on Privateer Hector in 1745.

   James   On guard duty at Newport in 1746.

   John   Major. Member of Council of War in 1746.

   John   Carpenter on Privateer Revenge in 1744.

   Joseph   Captain's Quartermaster on Privateer Phenix in 1744

   William   On guard duty at Newport in 1746.

ROSS, John   Sergeant in Capt. Sayer's Co. in 1746.

   William, Jr.   Served in Capt. Sheffield's Co. in 1740.

ROWS, John   Commander of Bolinder Young Eagle of Boston in 1742.

RUSSELL, Daniel, Jr.   On guard duty at Newport in 1746.

SABIN, Benjamin   Boatswain on Privateer Hector in 1745.

SALISBURY, John   Served in Capt. Rice's Co. in 1746.

SAMBO, Samuel   Served in Capt. Cole's Co. in 1746.

SANDS, Edward   Member of Committee of Defence of Block Island in 1740, and Captain in Command on Block Island in 1744.

SANFORD, Benjamin   Served in Capt. Sayer's Co. in 1746.

   Edward   Pilot on Privateer Revenge in 1741.

   Esbon   Member of Committee on Munitions in 1740, and of Committee to build a magazine at Newport in 1741.

   Thomas   Second Lieut. on Privateer Brittania in 1744.

   William   Mate on Privateer Cæsar in 1743, and Second Lieut. on same in 1744.

SARGENT, Thomas Carpenter on Privateer Caesar in 1744.

William Gunner on Privateer Jonathan in 1747.

SAUNDERS, Philemon Captain's Quartermaster on Privateer Reprisal and Privateer Prince Frederick in 1744.

SAYER, Joshua Member of Committee on Fortifications in 1746, and Captain of 1st R. I. Co. in 1746 and 1747.

SCOTT, Hunter Served in Capt. Hopkins' Co. in 1740.

Joseph On guard duty at Newport in 1746.

SEXTON, Dennis Served in Capt. Hopkins' Co. in 1740.

SHADDOCK, James Served in Capt. Cole's Co. in 1746.

SHALER, Reuben of Middletown, Conn. Second Lieut. on Privateer Prince Charles of Lorraine, 1746.

SHANKS, Malatial Served in Capt. Sheffield's Co. in 1740.

SHARPE, Thomas Lieut. on Privateer London in 1747 and 1748.

SHAW, Francis Served in Capt. Cole's Co. in 1746.

SHEFFIELD, Joseph Captain of R. I. Company in 1740, later Lieut. in Capt. Hopkins' Co. in 1740, and on Committee on Fortifications in 1746.

SHELDON, James Served in Capt. Rice's Co. in 1746.

SHEPARD, James Served at Fort George, Newport, in 1743.

SHERBURN, Benjamin Captain. Member of Councils of War in 1746, 1747 and 1748.

SHERMAN, Edward Served in Capt. Sayer's Co. in 1746.

George Gunner on Privateer Success and on Privateer Prince William in 1744 and at Fort George, Newport, in 1745.

SHOLLEY, ⎱ John Second Lieut. on Privateer Prince Charles of
SHELLEY, ⎰   Lorraine in 1744.

SHORT, Samuel Served in Capt. Sayer's Co. in 1746.

SILLMAN, William Served in Capt. Sayer's Co. in 1746.

SILVESTER, Joseph of Newport Captain. Summoned to Council of War in 1745.

SIMSON, John Carpenter on Privateer Prince William in 1744.

SINEDOER, ⎱
             ⎰ Henry Boatswain on Privateer Reprisal in 1745.
SNIEDOER, ⎰

SKIFF, Jonathan Served in Capt. Sayer's Co. in 1746.

SLOCUM, Josh. (Indian) Served in Campaign in 1740.

Samuel of Jamestown Captain. Member of Council of War in 1748 and summoned in 1745.

SLYWOOD, Samuel (Indian) Served in Campaign of 1746. Probably identical with Samuel Spywood.

SMEDLEY, William Gunner on Privateer Queen of Hungary in 1744.

SMITH, Daniel Carpenter on Privateer Cæsar in 1743.

    John Carpenter on Privateer Brittania in 1744.

    John Gunner on Privateer Ranger in 1744.

    John Lieut. on Privateer Hunter in 1743.

    John Drummer in Capt. Sayer's Co. in 1746.

    Richard Lieut. at Cape Breton in 1745.

    Richard Gunner on Privateer Prince Frederick in 1747.

    Thomas Gunner on Privateer Charming Betty in 1744.

    William Boatswain on Privateer Lee Freggot in 1747.

    William Served in Capt. Sheffield's Co. in 1740.

    William Captain of R. I. Company at Louisbourg in 1745.

    William Sergeant in Capt. Rice's Co. in 1746.

    William Served in Capt. Cole's Co. in 1746.

SOUTHER, John Master on Privateer Duke of Marlborough in 1745.

SOWARD, Sampson Served in Capt. Sayer's Co. in 1746.

SOWLE, Henry On guard duty at Newport in 1746.

SPINNEY, Joseph Carpenter on Privateer Prince Charles of Lorraine in 1744.

    Zebenr Mate on Privateer Duke of Cumberland in 1748.

SPOONER, Wing of Newport Captain, later Major. Member of Councils of War in 1746, 1747 and 1748. Summoned in 1745.

SPRINGER, Joseph Served in Capt. Cole's Co. in 1746.

    Richard Served in Capt. Cole's Co. in 1746.

SPYWOOD, Samuel of Warwick Served in Capt. Rice's Co. in 1746

    Thomas Served in Capt. Hopkins' Co. in 1740.

STACY, Henry Served in campaign of 1740.

    Samuel Gunner on Privateer Lee Freggot in 1747.

STAFFORD, John Lieut. on Colony Sloop Tartar in 1745.

    Urial Served in Capt. Rice's Co. in 1746.

    William Drummer in Capt. Rice's Co. in 1746.

STANTON, Benjamin Served in Capt. Cole's Co. in 1746.

STANTON,

    Clement   First Lieut. on Privateer Cæsar in 1744 and on Duke of Cumberland in 1745.

    Latham   Commander of Privateer Lee Freggot in 1747.

STERRY, Cyprian   Served in Capt. Rice's Co. in 1746.

    Robert   Lieut. in Capt. Rice's Co. in 1746.

STEVENS, Robert   On guard duty at Newport in 1746.

    Robert   Sailor in H. M. Navy. Enlisted at Newport in 1746.

STEVENS, ————— Mate on Privateer Reprisal in 1747.

STEVENSON, Henry   Second Lieut. on Privateer Success in 1744, Master on Privateer Defiance in 1745, on Privateer Prince Frederick in 1746 and on Privateer Ranger in 1747 and 1748.

STEWARD, Joseph   Served in Capt. Cole's Co. in 1746.

STILL, Isaac   On guard duty at Newport in 1746.

STOCKARD, John   First Lieut. on Privateer Charming Betty in 1746.

STODDARD, Robert   Captain's Quartermaster on Privateer Queen of Hungary in 1744.

STONE, James   Carpenter on Privateer Reprisal in 1744.

STORY, Joseph   Served in Capt. Champlin's Co. in 1745.

STRAIGHT, Henry   Served in Capt. Rice's Co. in 1746.

    Samuel   Served in Capt. Rice's Co. in 1746.

    Thomas   Lieut. in Capt. Rice's Co. in 1746.

STRUM, Nathaniel   Served in Capt. Cole's Co. in 1746.

SUMMER, William   Served in Capt. Cole's Co. in 1746.

SUNDERLIN, Joseph   Corporal in Capt. Cole's Co. in 1746.

SWAN, George   Served in Capt. Sayer's Co. in 1746.

SWEET, Ebenezer   Served in Capt. Rice's Co. in 1746.

    Elnathan   Served in Capt. Cole's Co. in 1746.

    James   Gunner on Privateer King George in 1745.

    James   Served in Capt. Rice's Co. in 1746.

    John   Second Lieut. on Privateer Prince Frederick and on Privateer Prince William in 1744, Master on Privateer Defiance in 1744, First Lieut. on same in 1745 and Commander of same in 1746, 1747 and 1748.

    Philip   Served in Capt. Rice's Co. in 1746.

    Silvester   Mate on Privateer Reprisal in 1744 and 1747.

SWEET,
> William   Boatswain on Privateer Prince Frederick in 1744.
>
> William   First Lieut. on Privateer Success in 1744, and on Privateer Duke of Marlborough in 1745.

SWEETING. Nathaniel   Master on Privateer King George in 1744 and Commander of Privateer King George in 1745.

SWINBORN, Thomas   Carpenter on Privateer Charming Betty in 1744.

TARR, Othniel   Commander of Privateer Henry in 1747 and 1748.

TAYLOR, Joseph   Served in Capt. Sayer's Co. in 1746.
> William   Served in Capt. Cole's Co. in 1746.

TEW, Paul   Quartermaster on Privateer Revenge in 1744, and Captain's Quartermaster on Privateer Prince Frederick in 1745.

THING, Josias   Master on Privateer Duke of Cumberland in 1748.

THOMAS, Robert   Second Lieut. on Privateer Defiance in 1748.

THOMPSON, John   (Indian)   Served in campaign of 1746.
> John   Gunner on Privateer Hector in 1745 and Captain's Quartermaster on Privateer Reprisal in 1746.
>
> Richard   Quartermaster on Privateer Reprisal in 1746, and Second Lieut. on same in 1747.
>
> Thomas   First Lieut. on Privateer Cæsar in 1743, Commander of Privateer Fame in 1744 and 1745. The Fame was in the service of the Colony in these years.

THURSTON, Grindle   Carpenter on Privateer Duke of Marlborough in 1744.
> James   Commander of Privateer Hector in 1744.
>
> Jonathan   On guard duty at Newport in 1746.
>
> Jonathan, Jr.   Captain's Quartermaster on Privateer Duke of Marlborough in 1745 and on guard duty at Newport in 1746.
>
> Joseph   Captain's Quartermaster on Privateer Defiance in 1746 and 1747, and Quartermaster on same in 1748.
>
> Samuel   Second Lieut. on Privateer Phenix in 1744.
>
> William   Carpenter on Privateer Jonathan in 1747, and on Privateer Mary and Ann in 1747.

TIKIN See TYKEN

TILLINGHAST, John of Newport Ensign. Summoned to Council
of War in 1745, and on guard duty at Newport in 1746.
John Mate on Privateeer Reprisal in 1745.
Jonathan On guard duty at Newport in 1746.
Nicholas On guard duty at Newport in 1746.
Pardon On guard duty at Newport in 1746.

TISDALE, Henry Member of Committee on Munitions in 1740, and
on guard duty at Newport in 1746.

TOBEY, David Served in Capt. Cole's Co. in 1746.

TOKUS, Cæsar Served in Capt. Sheffield's Co. in 1740.

TOMAN, Thomas Master on Privateer Hunter in 1743.

TONQUOT, Solomon Served in Capt. Sayer's Co. in 1746.

TOSH, Aches Mate on Privateer Ranger in 1744, and on Privateer Defiance in 1746.

TOWN, Robert Served in Capt. Cole's Co. in 1746.

TOWNSEND, John Commander of Privateer Defiance in 1745.
Solomon On guard duty at Newport in 1746.

TREBY, Peter On guard duty at Newport in 1746.

TRIM, Benjamin Master's Mate on Privateer Revenge in 1744,
and served in Capt. Sayer's Co. in 1746.

TRIPP, Stephen Carpenter on Privateer King George in 1744.

TROWBRIDGE, Ebenezer Master on Privateer Charming Betty in
1744, First Lieut. on Privateer Prince Frederick in 1745
and 1746, and Commander of same in 1747 and 1748.

TRUMPETOR, John Served in Capt. Sayer's Co. in 1746.

TUCKER, Benjamin Member of Council of War in 1747.

TURNER, William Captain. Member of Council of War in 1741.

TURPIN, Joseph Served in Capt. Rice's Co. in 1746.

TWIST, George Boatswain on Privateer Duke of Marlborough in
1744.

TYKEN, } Aaron (Indian) Served in Capt. Sheffield's Co. in
TIKEN, } 1740, and in Capt. Hopkins' Co. in 1743.
Jack Served in Capt. Cole's Co. in 1746.
Toby Served in Capt. Cole's Co. in 1746.

TYLER, Anthony Gunner on Privateer Mary Galley in 1745.
Ebenezer Served in Capt. Rice's Co. in 1746.

UTTER, Samuel   Served in Capt. Sayer's Co. in 1746.

    Simeon   Served in Capt. Cole's Co. in 1746.

    Stephen   Served in Capt. Rice's Co. in 1746.

VARNO, Daniel   Surgeon's Mate on Privateer Duke of Marlborough in 1744.

VAUGHN, Daniel   Boatswain on Privateer Prince Frederick in 1743.

    Daniel   Boatswain on Privateer Jonathan in 1747.

    Daniel   Lieut. on Privateer Prince Charles of Lorraine in
1744 and on Colony Sloop Tartar in 1746, 1747 and 1748.

VERNON, Daniel   On guard duty at Newport in 1746.

    Thomas   Captain's Quartermaster on Privateer King George
in 1744, and on guard duty at Newport in 1746.

VIGNERON, Anthony   Surgeon on Privateer Cæsar in 1744, and
on Privateer Prince Frederick in 1746.

VOLKERS, William   Gunner on Privateer Duke of Marlborough in
1744.

WALDER, Samuel   Boatswain on Privateer Charming Betty in
1746.

WALL, William   Served in Capt. Sayer's Co. in 1746.

WALLACE, Adam   Mate on Privateer Prince of Wales in 1745.

WAMOGG, Thomas   Served in Capt. Rice's Co. in 1746.

WANTON, Edward   Second Lieut. on Private Jonathan in 1747.

    George   Member of Committee on Munitions in 1740, of Com-
mittee on Fort George in 1745, of Committee of War in
1746, and of Council of War in 1747.

    Gideon   Governor. Member of Councils of War in 1745,
1747 and 1748.

    William   Captain's Quartermaster on Privateer Duke of Cum-
berland in 1745.

WAPPY, Johnson   Served in Capt. Cole's Co. in 1746.

WARD, Patrick   Served in Capt. Cole's Co. in 1746.

    Richard   Governor. Member of Councils of War in 1741 and
1743.

    Samuel   On guard duty at Newport in 1746.

WARNER, William   Mate on Privateer Duke of Marlborough in
1745.

WARREN, Thomas   Boatswain on Privateer Success in 1744.

WATSON, Andrew   Captain's Quartermaster on Privateer Prince of Wales in 1745.

WATTS, Henry Christopher   Served in Capt. Sheffield's and Capt. Hopkins' Co. in 1740.

WEATHERHEAD, John   Sevred in Capt Rice's Co. in 1746.

WEBB, Jeremiah   Corporal in Capt. Rice's Co. in 1746.

    John   Mate on Privateer Revenge in 1741, Mate on Privateer Success in 1744, and Second Lieut. on Privateer Prince of Wales in 1745.

WEDGE, Moses   Served in Capt. Cole's Co. in 1746.

WEEDEN, Joseph   Ensign in expedition of 1745.

WEEKLY, William   Served in Capt. Sheffield's Co. in 1740.

WELLS, John   Served in Capt. Sheffield's Co. in 1740.

WELSH, ———   Sergeant in campaign of 1740.

WENTWORTH, Hugh   Commander of Privateer Castor in 1742.

WHAILS, Samuel   Served in Capt. Rice's Co. in 1746.

WHALEY, Theophilus   Served in Capt. Sheffield's Co. in 1740.

    Thomas   Served in Capt. Sheffield's Co. in 1740.

WHALING, James   Served in Capt. Rice's Co. in 1746.

WHENMAN, Richard   Served in Capt. Cole's Co. in 1746.

WHIPPLE, Hezekiah   Served in Capt. Rice's Co. in 1746.

    John   Served in Capt. Rice's Co. in 1746.

    Joseph   Deputy-Governor.   Member of Committee to build Colony sloop and Committee on Munitions in 1740, of Committee to fit out Colony sloop in 1741, of Councils of War in 1743 and 1746.

    Joseph, Jr.   On guard duty at Newport in 1746.

WHITE, Nicholas   Commander of Privateer Young Godfrey in 1743.

    William   On guard duty at Newport in 1746.

WHITEHORNE, John   On guard duty at Newport in 1746.

WHITFORD, James   Served in Capt. Cole's Co. in 1746.

WICKHAM, Benjamin   Commander of Colony's Sloop Tartar i n 1741 and 1746, Commander of Colony's squadron in 1741, and on guard duty at Newport in 1746.

    Charles   On guard duty at Newport in 1746.

WICKHAM,

    Samuel   Member of Committee of War in 1746, and on guard duty at Newport in 1746.

    Thomas   Ensign. On guard duty at Newport in 1746, and Member of Council of War in 1747.

WILCOX, John   Served in Capt. Cole's Co. in 1746.

WILKINSON, Philip of Newport   Second Lieut. in Capt. Sayer's Co. in 1746 and First Lieut. in 1747. Member of Council of War in 1746, and 1748. Summoned to Council of War in 1747. Member of Committee on Fortifications in 1746.

    Philip   Captain of Colony Sloop Tartar in 1744.

    Philip   On guard duty at Newport in 1746. All of these items may relate to one man.

    Philip, Jr.   On guard duty at Newport in 1746.

    Thomas   Master of Privateer Revenge in 1745.

    William   Commander of Privateer Mary in 1742 and 1743, and of Privateer Diana in 1746.

WILL, Wicked   Served in Capt. Cole's Co. in 1746.

WILLIAMS, John   Carpenter on Privateer Ranger in 1744.

    William   Master's Mate on Privateer Prince Frederick in 1743.

WILLIS, John   Served in Capt. Rice's Co. in 1746.

WILSON, Andrew   Captain's Quartermaster on Privateer Prince of Wales in 1745.

    Anthony   Served in Capt. Cole's Co. in 1746.

    John   Appointed to build watch house at Jamestown in 1740.

    Robert   Served in Capt. Hopkins' Co. in 1740.

    William   Served in Capt. Sayer's Co. in 1746.

WIMPLE, James   Commander of Privateer Victory in 1743.

WOOD, Jacob   Served in Capt. Sayer's Co. in 1746.

    John   Served in Capt. Champlin's Co. in 1745.

WOODWARD, William   Boatswain on Privateer Defiance in 1744. and 1745, Privateer Frederick in 1746, and Second Lieut. on Privateer Defiance in 1747.

WOOLFORD, Robert   Commander of Privateer Pullox in 1742.

WRIGHT, John   Served in Capt. Sayer's Co. in 1746.

WYATT, Benjamin   Boatswain on Privateer Ranger in 1744.

    William   Master's Mate on Privateer Defiance in 1744.

YEATS, Archibald   Master on Privateer Reprisal in 1744, Captain's
        Quartermaster on same in 1745, Second Lieut. on same in
        1746, and Master on same in 1747.

YEATS, John   Mate on Privateer Reprisal in 1744.

YORK, Stanton   Served in Capt. Sheffield's Co. in 1740.

Rhode Island in the Colonial Wars

A List of
Rhode Island
Soldiers & Sailors

IN THE

Old French & Indian War

1755-1762

BY

HOWARD M. CHAPIN

DULCE ET DECORUM EST PRO PATRIA MORI

PROVIDENCE
PRINTED FOR THE SOCIETY
MCMXVIII

Rhode Island's Share in the War

The conflict of French and English interests in the Ohio Valley served as the prelude, and Washington's defeat of Jumonville near Fort Du Quesne on May 27th 1754 as the spark, which ignited the fourth French war in which Rhode Island participated. This struggle called by European historians "The Seven Years War" is better known in America as "The Old French and Indian War." Military preparations were made in both England and France as well as in the Colonies.

On January 1st 1755 the Rhode Island General Assembly voted to raise a company of 100 men for the emergency. As is usual, the length and intensity of the impending struggle was underestimated. In February the number was increased to 113, apparently to allow for officers, some of whom were appointed. A committee of War of five men was established to manage the military affairs of the Colony.

In March 1755, before the 100 men had been enlisted, it was voted to raise four companies of 100 men each to take part in the secret expedition against Crown Point. The acts calling for 113 men were repealed and the officers transferred to the new companies. Christopher Harris was appointed Colonel of this expeditionary regiment.

Meanwhile Braddock had landed in Virginia and taken command of the English forces in America. He planned to strike the French at three points. The southern army, under his personal command, was to attack Fort Du Quesne, and the northern army was to assemble at Albany, whence one detachment under Governor Shirley was to attack Niagara, while the other, under Colonel (later Sir) William Johnson, was to move against Crown Point.

The Rhode Island regiment under Col. Harris marched to Green-Bush near Albany, where their boats were caulked and their guns cleaned and mended.

On August 8th, leaving the Rhode Island and New York regiments in camp, Johnson marched northward with the rest of the army. He left a garrison at Fort Lyman (afterwards called Fort Edward in honor of the Duke of York), and continuing northward encamped at the upper end of Lake George. The Rhode Island regiment was at Albany on August 24th, but soon followed the main army and reached the camp late in August or early in September.

Baron Dieskau, commander of the army, which had been sent over from France, and which had been augmented by Canadians and Indians, marched southward through the woods east of Lake George. Upon the news of the approach of the French, Johnson sent out Col. Ephraim Williams and the Indian Chief Hendricks with a scouting party in the direction of South Bay on September 8th. This force was surprised by Dieskau, and in the fighting which followed, both Williams* and Hendricks were killed. Re-enforcements under the command of Lt. Col. Edward Cole of the Rhode Island regiment arrived in time to rescue the remnant of Williams' force and to hold the French in check temporarily, thus giving Johnson time to strengthen the defences of the camp. Dieskau attacked the camp at 10 o'clock in the morning (September 8, 1755), and the fighting lasted until four in the afternoon, when the French force was dispersed. Both Johnson and Dieskau were wounded, the latter being taken prisoner. Johnson did not pursue the fugitives, but fortified the camp which he named Fort William Henry in honor of the Duke of Gloucester, the king's grandson.

Four Rhode Island companies took part in this battle of September 8, 1755, known as the Battle of Lake George. They were the companies commanded by Cole, Angell, Babcock and Francis.

On account of Braddock's defeat before Fort Du Quesne, The General Assembly voted on August 11th, to raise three more companies of fifty men each and to send them to re-enforce Col. Harris' troops, and thus strengthen the

*Williams College was founded by a bequest in Col. Williams' will.

Colonial Army against the added number of French troops, which being freed from service in the Monongahela Valley, would doubtless be rushed northward to Lake Champlain. This vote for additional companies was not passed without opposition, and seven deputies including the Speaker, had their dissent from the vote, recorded in the acts and resolves. John Whiting was ranking Captain of this detachment, which was recruited before September 8th, on which day the General Assembly ordered them to proceed to Albany by water and thence from Albany to the force under Col. Harris. Many of Col. Harris' troopers, disgusted by the hardships of the march overland and little realizing the scope and importance of the conflict had deserted. These men upon their return home were added to Capt. Whiting's command, and ordered to proceed subject to his orders until they should reach the camp and re-enter their respective companies.

In September Rhode Island voted to raise four more companies of 50 men each. Daniel Bosworth was appointed ranking Captain of this third detachment. Inasmuch as the war was not particularly popular in Rhode Island, and as the danger to the Colony was not imminent, volunteers were not forthcoming in numbers sufficient to fill the companies that had been authorized, although bounties had been offered to encourage enlistment. Hence the General Assembly at the September session found it necessary to pass an act authorizing conscription. Thenceforth during the war the Rhode Island regiments consisted partly of volunteers, many of whom were attracted by the bounties, and partly of conscripts. In 1755 Rhode Island put approximately 750 men in the field.

Late in November Johnson marched southward with the main part of the army, which either went into winter quarters or returned home. Seventy-two Rhode Islanders commanded by Capt. Whiting were left on garrison duty at the Forts near Lake George. The campaign of 1755 had been unfortunate in the Colonies. Braddock's expedition had been defeated, Shirley's expedition had done but little, and although Johnson

had repelled an attack, he had not even approached Crown
Point, his avowed objective. On December 22d the General
Assembly voted that 100 of the best men with (apparently
13) suitable officers be selected from the troops returned and
returning from the Expedition against Crown Point and that
the remainder be discharged. Besides this 100 men, 72, as
already noted, were detailed for garrison duty at Fort Edward
and Fort William Henry, under Capt. Whiting. The remainder of the troops were ordered discharged on or before
December 31st, 1755.

Shirley, chief commander of the English forces in
America determined on a vigorous campaign for 1756. He
planned to move against Niagara with one part of his force
and to send the other part commanded by (Gen.) John
Winslow against Lake Champlain. In February Rhode Island
voted to raise a force of 500 men (including those still in
service) for the reduction of the French forts on Lake
Champlain. Col. Harris was given command of this regiment,
which consisted of 10 companies.

The Rhode Island troops went by water, touching at
New York, and arriving at Albany on Friday evening, May
14th, 1756, according to a letter of George Hopkins. The
regiment moved to Camp Half Moon before June 29th where
all the Rhode Island companies, except two, Major Babcock's
and Capt. Bozerd's (Bosworth), had arrived by June 11th.
The Rhode Islanders were soon scattered, some being at Fort
William Henry, and Edward, while others were at Stillwater,
Camp Half Moon, and Albany. Many were still at Camp
Half Moon on July 11th but the bulk soon moved up to Fort
Edward, where they were on July 22d and had been four
weeks on August 14th, according to Hopkins.

Meanwhile preparations for the campaign had been
pushed in Europe. Louis XV sent the Marquis of Montcalm to command his forces in America and George II
sent the Earl of Loudon. On May 17th, 1756, two years
after the defeat of Jumonville by Washington, England
formally declared war against France. Prussia under

Frederick the Great had made an alliance with England, and Austria had made an alliance with France. Europe was to be a more bloody battlefield than America. Sweden, Russia and Poland soon joined France and Austria.

The Earl of Loudon reached New York in July and relieved Shirley of the chief command. This change together with Loudon's inefficiency doomed the campaign of 1756 to failure. On July 24th Col. Angell of the Rhode Island regiment commanded a scouting party of 300 men that went out from Fort Edward towards South Bay and Wood Creek.

The Rhode Island General Assembly, expecting a vigorous campaign ordered two additional companies of 50 men each, exclusive of officers, in June. These troops were commanded by Captains Jenckes and Fry, and joined the force under Harris.

In August Montcalm attacked and captured the English forts on the Oswego River and then returned to check any advance which might be attempted by the English at Lake George.

Conditions rapidly became more threatening for the English colonies. Another company of 60 men and officers was authorized by the General Assembly in September and Joseph Windsor was given the command, but this company was merged in the new regiment of 400 men, (eight companies) which was ordered in October. The Governor, Stephen Hopkins was chosen Colonel of this, the 2nd Regiment, known as "The 400 men," but on October 27th the General Assembly met and ordered them not to march on account of the fact that Small Pox was rife at Albany. By orders from Loudon this regiment was discharged on or before Nov. 8th 1756.

Some of the Rhode Island troops at Fort Edward had been sent up to Fort William Henry where Quarter-Master Shehan was located on Nov. 9th, 1756. The companies commanded by Harris, Angell, Potter and Jenckes, returned to Providence in December and were paid off in December and January. The other companies may have been discharged at the same time but their pay rolls have not been located.

The defeat of the English at Oswego was the only noteworthy feature of the campaign of 1756. Several Newport shipwrights who were on special construction service at Oswego were captured by the French.

In February 1757 Rhode Island ordered a five company regiment of 450 men to assist Loudon in the ensuing campaign. Samuel Angell was appointed "Chief Officer" (i. e. Colonel) of this force which in May proceeded to Albany. Meanwhile in March the French under Rigaud attempted unsuccessfully to surprise Fort William Henry, and Loudon prepared his futile expedition against Louisburg.

In May an act for raising 150 more men was passed by the Rhode Island General Assembly at its May session, but was repealed in August before the companies were raised. Some of the Rhode Islanders under Angell were stationed at Fort Edward, while others were at Fort William Henry.

Montcalm had not been idle during the spring, but had collected a large force with the main part of which he sailed up Lake George, while the balance of the force under De Levis marched along the west shore of the Lake. Fort William Henry was surrounded by the French but held out until word was received from Gen. Webb, who was stationed at Fort Edward, that he would not send assistance. Munro, the commander of Fort William Henry was therefore obliged to surrender on August 9th, 1757. A large number of the English soldiers were massacred by the Indians on August 10th, although about 600 refugees succeeded in reaching Fort Edward.

Col. Angell who was at Fort Edward wrote to Governor Greene on August 14th and described the attack on Fort William Henry in the following words:

"On the 3d inst., at five o'clock, in the morning, the fort and camp were invested by Canadians and Indians; and at the same time, a large body of boats and canoes appeared on the lake near, while our camp was attacked by a superior number of the enemy. They landed their artillery the same day. Our rangers brought in one of their lieutenants prisoner, who gave account of their strength consisted of three thousand regulars, five thousand Canadians, and three thousand five hundred savages, thirty-six cannon, and four mortars.

"The siege continued obstinate till the ninth day at six o'clock in the morning, when all the cannon, bigger than twelve pounders, were broken; the men in camp and garrison, spent with fatigue. They capitulated on honorable terms, viz.: that they should march to this place with a brass twelve pounder in the front, and their fire-locks clubbed, and colors flying, with all their baggage. This was agreed to, and articles signed. General Montcalm and other principal officers of his army, expressed and acknowledged that they had made a defence beyond expectation, and for those reasons, he allowed them as good terms as General Blakeney had. The articles obliged our men not to bear arms till eighteen months were expired.

"The morning following, our men were to march with a strong guard of regulars, to keep the savages from insulting them. When our people began to draw up for a march, the horrible scene of massacre then began, by the savages scalping our sick and wounded men; next, by their drawing out all the black men, scalping the Indians and keeping the negroes for slaves. All this did not satisfy them; but they went to stripping and scalping without distinction; which put our men to the flight, each man for himself—having no protection agreeably to the articles. They all scattered in the woods; the Indians following them several miles. Our men have been coming in since eleven o'clock, that day, till this morning, by single persons and small parties; not a man but is stripped; some, quite naked.

"There are yet behind several hundred; many of whom, it is known, are sick, and many, it is thought, will perish in the woods. This minute, a deserter from the French says that above two hundred of our men went back to the French for protection.

"By our parties just came in, we have certain accounts that the fort is destroyed; and that the enemy are drawing off. We have about four thousand militia here, and two thousand troops."

The danger by which Fort William Henry was threatened greatly alarmed the Colony. The General Assembly met on August 10th, and not as yet having heard of the loss of Fort William Henry, passed an act which drafted one sixth of the militia of the colony, probably about 1000 men, for service in the relief of Fort William Henry. Col. John Andrews was given the command of this regiment. On August 15th thirty-four prominent men of Providence who were not subject to the draft volunteered their services and signed a paper of that import. Of a muster roll of 113 men who marched out of Newport County in answer to this call, 21 were volunteers.

This Second Rhode Island regiment went no farther than Connecticut, when news was received that Fort William Henry had fallen. The men returned home and the October Assembly after regulating their pay for this service, voted to re-enlist 250 men for service in the army during the pleasure of the General Assembly.

Ninety of these did garrison service at Saratoga. Capt. Ebenezer Whiting was given the command of those who were garrisoned at Fort Edward during the winter.

If the campaign of 1756 had disheartened the English, that of 1757 was still more discouraging. The expedition against Louisburg had come to naught, Fort William Henry had been lost, and from Europe came the still more discouraging news that the Duke of Cumberland had been decisively defeated by D'Estrees.

As well as sending the quota to the Colonial contingent, Rhode Island had strengthened and garrisoned Fort George at Newport, and had also equipped and sent forth many privateers which had made severe and telling inroads upon the enemy's maritime commerce.

The following letter gives a concise description of the conditions in the Colony in 1758;

II

"We the Commissioners from the Government of Rhode Island, being ordered to lay before your Lordship, an exact State of the Colony, with Regard to its Fortifications and Military Stores, the Number of Inhabitants, the State of the Treasury, and Funds for supplying the same, beg Leave to represent to your Lordship, that there is only one Fortification in the Colony, called Fort George, very conveniently situated for the Defence of the Town and Harbour of Newport, which is the Metropolis of the Colony. But as there are in the Fort only twenty-six Carriage Guns fit for Service, and a few other Military Stores, it is to be feared the Town might be entirely destroyed by a very small Force, and the Colony thereby disabled from raising any more Men for the common Cause. And of what fatal Consequence it might be to His Majesty's Interest, to have the Enemy in Possession of so fine a Harbour and Island, situate in the Midst of New England, we leave your Lordship to judge.

"By an Account of the Number of Men in the Colony, taken the 24th of December, One Thousand Seven Hundred and Fifty-five, it appears, my Lord, there were then in the Colony, Eight Thousand Two Hundred and Sixty-two Men, able to bear Arms. But as we have since lost many Men by the War, and near Fifteen Hundred Men are out in our Privateers, we imagine there is not near that Number now left in the Colony."

In March, 1758, the General Assembly voted to raise a regiment of 1000 men. Col. Malbone was given the command of this regiment, which was to consist of nine new companies and the company under Capt. Ebenezer Whiting, which was in garrison service at the Forts. Malbone was succeeded by Henry Babcock as Colonel, before the regiment moved. The troops went to Albany by water. During March and April a detachment of 1853 of His Majesty's regulars were quartered at Providence before being sent against Louisburg. In May, Amherst, with the northern army, supported by the fleet, marched on Louisburg; in June, Forbes, with the southern army, proceeded against Fort Du Quesne; and on July 5th Abercrombie, with 15,000 English and Colonials, including the

Rhode Island companies, except those under Potter and Wall, moved against Ticonderoga. Col. Babcock's description of the Battle of Ticonderoga, being that of an eye witness and important officer, follows:

"Lake George, 10th July, 1758.

"Honored Sir:—The 5th inst., the army consisting of fifteen thousand men, proceeded down the lake, in batteaux, with thirty days' provision. The 6th, in the morning, half after eight, we landed at the advance guard; who were very easily driven from their post, with no loss on our side, and but four on theirs. About two o'clock, P. M., the whole army marched, saving a battalion of the York regiment, who were posted as a guard on our batteaux. About three o'clock we were attacked by a party of the enemy, in which engagement, we unfortunately lost the brave Lord Howe. There were taken of the enemy one hundred prisoners, eight of whom were officers; our army was much scattered by reason of the firing in the woods, and it was thought advisable to return that evening to our batteaux.

"The next day Col. Broadstreet was ordered with fifteen hundred batteaux men, and two regular regiments, with five of the Massachusetts regiments, to take possession of the saw mill, which we did, without the loss of a man. The same evening, the whole marched up to the saw mill.

"The 8th, (the fatal 8th,) were ordered to proceed in the following manner: the batteaux men, light armed infantry, and the rangers, were ordered to form a line about two hundred yards from the French entrenchments; which extended from Lake George to Lake Champlain; the regulars were to form a line behind the first line; who, after they were formed were to pass through the first line, they making avenues for them; after that, they were to form the line again. A captain and fifty men, out of the line, were detached for picket, who were to form in front; the grenadiers were to form behind them; and in this manner, they were to attack the trenches, and were to march with shouldered firelocks, till they should get on top of the trenches.

"They accordingly marched on with great intrepidity, but

were received so warmly, that they were obliged to give ground, after making most vigorous efforts; they even went up to the breast-work, but were knocked down so fast, that it was very difficult for those behind to get over the dead and wounded. But before the attack of the regulars, the enemy began with firing upon the Yorkers. In the rear of the regulars, the Connecticut, New Jersey and Rhode Island troops were ordered to form about three hundred yards behind, who were to support them, if necessary.

"About an hour after the attack, I was ordered to march with the regiment, to relieve those that had been engaged. We went up within about forty yards of the breast-work. Soon after I got up, in posting my regiment to the best advantage I could, I received a shot in my left knee; after that, finding myself of no advantage, I ordered two men to carry me off, and left the regiment warmly engaged. We have lost no officers. Capt. John Whiting, Lieuts. Russell and Smith are slightly wounded. The return of the killed and wounded, Your Honor has enclosed.

"The same evening, to my great surprise, the whole army was ordered to return to the batteaux, to the great mortification of chief of the officers; and the next evening we arrived here.

"Never did an army gain more advantage in so little time, whilst the late Lord Howe was alive; but soon after that, we became a confused rabble. We have lost a great many brave officers; in Lord Howe's regiment, all the field officers were killed.

"Sir William Johnson joined us four hours before the engagement; but the Indians not being used to attack trenches, soon came off."

Lord Howe, the brains of the English army, was killed in this fight, and the incompetent Abercrombie retreated to Fort William Henry, turning a potential victory into an unnecessary defeat. In August Col. Bradstreet marched to Oswego with 3000 men, of whom 312 were Rhode Islanders under Lt. Col. Potter and Major Wall. This expedition captured Fort Frontenac on August 25th, destroyed the French naval power on Lake Ontario, and cut the communication between Fort Du Quesne and Canada, thus materially assisting the southern army under Forbes, which so seriously threatened Fort Du Quesne in November, that the garrison destroyed the fortress and retreated. Meanwhile, in the North, Amherst had taken Louisburg.

Some of the Rhode Island soldiers were retained in service for the campaign of 1759, and a call for new enlistments was made in December, 1758.

On February 26th, 1759, the Colony voted to furnish 1000 men for the ensuing campaign, and later the Assembly ordered the thirteen companies already raised to proceed to Albany. Some were sent by boat, while others marched overland, the rendezvous being ordered for April 10th. The quota of 1000 men was not easily raised, and in May a bonus of two months' pay was offered for enlistments. Bonuses were also offered to seamen who should enlist in H. M. navy.

In June a second detachment was sent, and an act to raise 115 men to complete the regiment was ordered. Amherst spent the summer and autumn in preparations, and when he was ready to move northward, the season had become too cold. A small English force under Prideaux drove the French from Niagara, but the remainder of the army operating in the Colonies accomplished nothing. Meanwhile in Canada Wolfe had brilliantly defeated Montcalm on September 18th, Quebec became English.

In February, 1760, the Colony voted to raise 1000 men for the Canadian Expedition. Christopher Harris was made Colonel, and proceeding to Albany, joined the force under Lord Amherst. Many of the soldiers, fearing the hardships of a campaign against so distant a place as Montreal, deserted on the way to Albany. Amherst advanced with his main force through Oswego, across Ontario and down the St. Lawrence. Murray came up the river from Quebec, while Haviland with many Colonials, including the Rhode Island contingent, approached down Lake Champlain. On Sept. 8th, 1760, Montreal surrendered to the English, and immediately many of the Colonial troops "demobilized themselves" and returned home.

The Rhode Islanders were very weary of the war, whose military campaign had made heavy levies of both men and money, and although adding Canada to the English domain had been of scant benefit to the Colony. The war itself, on account of the enormous profits made by the privateering enterprises, was rather popular with the maritime interests.

In March, 1761, the General Assembly voted to raise 666 men for the ensuing campaign. These men were to serve until November first unless the campaign ended previously. John Whiting was made Colonel. The commissioned officers, as was the custom, had to enlist a certain number of men in order to qualify for their commission. The campaign was for the most part garrison duty. In October Col. Whiting and a company of 66 men were detailed to garrison Fort Stanwix, and the rest of the Rhode Islanders returned to Albany and thence by water to Providence.

In February, 1762, the Colony voted to raise 666 men for the year's campaign. In March an act was passed to raise 178 men for H. M. regular army. Samuel Rose was made Colonel of the Rhode Island regiment. The first detachment was hurried to New York in May and shipped to Cuba. The Rhode Island contingent was commanded by Lt. Col. Hargill and consisted of (187 or, as some accounts say, 210 men), being the first detachments of the companies under Hargill, Fry, and Russell. The remainder of the regiment, the second detachment, went to Albany under Col. Rose. Havana was captured by the Colonial and Regular troops on August 13th, 1762, and the Rhode Islanders returned home in November, having lost about half their number through sickness and battle. Another 179 men enlisted in H. M. regular army during the latter part of 1762 and early part of 1763. Capt. Cornell with 66 men served at Fort Stanwix during the winter of 1762-63, but were disbanded in July, 1763.

In the later years of the war the English arms had been successful not only in Canada and the West Indies, but also in India, where Clive was laying the foundations for a large empire. On the European battlefield, too, England and her allies had finally obtained the ascendency, Sweden and Russia having withdrawn from the conflict. These conquests had but little effect upon Rhode Island, who found herself, upon the declaration of peace, facing the problems of reorganization with her chief source of income (privateering) abruptly cut off, and her population and wealth sorely depleted by the late war.

On Tuesday, February 8th, 1763, the King's Proclamation of Peace was publicly read in Rhode Island.

*　　*　　*

In February, 1755, a Committee of War consisting of five members was constituted, and given the control and direction of the military activities of the Colony. The membership of this board was augmented from time to time, and continued to exercise its important functions throughout the war, although subject to the resolutions of the General Assembly, which created it.

Councils of War were held occasionally but were of local rather than of general importance. They consisted of the Governor and Deputy Governor, the Assistants from the town, and the Colonels, Lieutenant-Colonels, Majors, and Captains or those acting as such, of the militia companies of the County in which the Council was held. When at Newport the Captain of Fort George was also included.

The size of the companies varied from fifty to one hundred men, and the regiments from five to thirteen companies, as the exigencies of the situation demanded. Each regiment was commanded by a Colonel, with his staff, consisting of a Lieutenant-Colonel, a Major, and an Adjutant. Usually each regiment had a Chaplain, a Commissary, and a Surgeon. In some campaigns a Deputy-Commissary, a Quartermaster, a Sutler, an Assistant Surgeon, and an Armorer were attached to the regiment. In no campaigns did two Rhode Island regiments operate in the same expedition. In the campaign of 1762 the Rhode Island regiment was divided into two detachments, the one operating about Albany being under the Colonel, and the one taking part in the siege of Havana being under the Lieutenant-Colonel.

Each company had a Captain, a Lieutenant and an Ensign and in some campaigns a Second Lieutenant also. The first, second and third companies were (except in the campaign of 1755) under the command of the Colonel, the Lieutenant-Colonel and the Major, respectively. The First Lieutenant of each of these three companies was often styled Captain-Lieutenant and drew a Captain's pay. The regiment's Adjutant was chosen from the company Lieutenants and acted in both capacities. The non-commissioned officers were Sergeants and Corporals and usually two drummers were considered as necessary for each company.

OUTLINE SUMMARY OF THE COMPANIES OF THE RHODE ISLAND REGIMENTS, 1755 TO 1762

Enlisted   1755

COL. CHRISTOPHER HARRIS' Regt.

March	1st Co.	Capt.	Cole
	2	" "	(Sterry) Angell
	3	" "	Babcock
	4	" "	Francis
August	5	" "	J. Whiting
	6	" "	Hammond
	7	" "	Bradford
September	8	" "	Bosworth
	9	" "	Potter
	10	" "	Hopkins
	11	" "	Richmond

Winter of 1755-6
1st Co. Capt. J. Whiting

Enlisted   1756

COL. CHRISTOPHER HARRIS' Regt.

February	1st Co.	Col.	Harris
	2	"	Lt. Col. Champlin
	3	"	Maj. Angell
	4	"	Capt. Gardner
	5	" "	Babcock
	6	" "	Richmond
	7	" "	Potter
	8	" "	Bosworth
Continuous service	9	" "	J. Whiting
	10	" "	Hammond (Sept. Burkett)
June	11	" "	Fry
	12	" "	Jenckes

COL. HOPKINS' Regt. called "The 400 Men."

October	1st Co.	Col. Hopkins
2	"	Lt. Col. Wickham
3	"	Major Champlin
4	"	Capt. Belcher
5	"	" Richmond
6	"	" Windsor
7	"	" Coggeshall

Enlisted   **1757**

COL. SAMUEL ANGELL'S Regt.

February	1st Co.	Capt. (Gardner) E. Whiting
2	"	" (Potter) Jenckes
3	"	" J. Whiting
4	"	" Greene
5	"	" Wall

August   COL. JOHN ANDREWS' Regt.

Marched on the alarm of August 1757, known as the 10 days' expedition.

Winter Service 1757-8
1st Co. Capt. E. Whiting

Enlisted   **1758**

COL. (GODFREY MALBONE) HENRY BABCOCK'S Regt.

March	1st Co.	Col. (Malbone) Babcock
2	"	Lt. Col. (Babcock) Potter
3	"	Major Wall (Brown)
4	"	Capt. J. Whiting
5	"	" Jenckes (Burkett)
6	"	" Tew
7	"	" Rose
8	"	" Peck
9	"	" (Potter) Hacker
Continuous service 10	"	" E. Whiting

Enlisted   1759
COL. HENRY BABCOCK's Regt.

February   1st Co. Col. Babcock

2	"	Lt. Col. (Wall) J. Whiting	
3	"	Major (J. Whiting) E. Whiting	
4	"	Capt. Burkett	
5	"	"	Tew
6	"	"	Rose
7	"	"	Peck
8	"	"	Fry
9	"	"	Eddy
10	"	"	Hargill
11	"	"	Brown
12	"	"	Tripp
13	"	"	Palmer

Enlisted   1760
COL. CHRISTOPHER HARRIS' Regt.

February   1st Co. Col. Harris

2	"	Lt. Col. Whiting	
3	"	Major Burkett	
4	"	Capt. Rose	
5	"	"	Hargill
6	"	"	Peck
7	"	"	Fry
8	"	"	Russell
9	"	"	Tew
10	"	"	Brown

Enlisted   1761
COL. JOHN WHITING's Regt.

March   1st Co. Col. J. Whiting

2	"	Lt. Col. Rose	
3	"	Major Hargill	
4	"	Capt. Kimball	
5	"	"	Peck
6	"	"	Hopkins
7	"	"	Russell

Winter Service 1761-2
1st Co. Col. Whiting

1762

COL. SAMUEL ROSE'S Regt.

1st Co. Col. Rose
2 " Lt. Col. Hargill
3 " Major Peck
4 " Capt. Hawkins
5 " " Fry
6 " " Tew
7 " " Russell

Winter service 1762-63
1st Co. Capt. Geo. Cornell

TABLE SHOWING THE YEARS OF SERVICE OF THE MEMBERS
OF THE COMMITTEE OF WAR OF THE COLONY
OF RHODE ISLAND.

Appointed		Name	
February	1755	Daniel Jenckes	1755—56—57—58—59—60
"	"	Thomas Cranston	1755—56—57—58—59—60—61—62
"	"	Peter Bours	1755—56—57—58—59—60—61 died
"	"	Stephen Hopkins	1755—56—57
"	"	Jonathan Nichols	1755—56—died
September	1756	John Gardner	....1756—57— —59—60
May	1757	Robert Potter	........1757—58—59— —61—62
March	1758	Nathan Rice	...........1758—59—60
May	"	Abraham Smith	...........1758—59—60
December	"	Thomas Greene	...........1758—59—60
February	1759	Nicholas Gardner	..............1759—60—61
"	1760	Gideon Comstock	.... 1760—61—62
May	"	Joseph Hazard	 1760
June	1761	John Jepson	.....................1761—62
"	"	Elisha Brown	.....................1761—62
"	"	Thos. Casey	.....................1761—62
"	"	Shearjashub Bourn	.....................1761—62
October	"	John Bours	.....................1761—62
	1762	George Jackson	1762
	"	Thomas Potter, Jr.	1762

This list is compiled from the original manuscripts in the Rhode Island Historical Society and the State Archives. A duplicate list on cards with references to the individual manuscripts is on file at the Rhode Island Historical Society.

———

ABBREVIATIONS

(Sh)= Sheffield's "Privateersmen of Newport."
(Sm)= Smith's "Civil and Military Lists."

A List of
Rhode Island Soldiers and Sailors

––––––

AARON, Joseph   Served in Capt. Kimball's Co. in 1761.

ABBY, Felix   Served in campaigns of 1757 and 1760.

    Peleg   Served in campaigns of 1760, 1761 and 1762.

ABORN, James of Warwick   Commander of Privateer King
        Frederick in 1758.

ABRAHAMS, Ephraim   Served in Capt. J. Whiting's Co. in 1757.

ACKLIN, Francis   Enlisted in H. M. regular army in 1762.

ADAMS, Ebenezer   Served in campaign of 1760.

AGEDT, Peter   Gunner on Privateer Blackbird in 1762.

ALBRO,

ALSBRO, James   Served in campaign of 1762.

    Job   Served in 1762 at Albany in Lt. Col. Hargill's Co.

    John   Served in campaign of 1762.

    Maturin of Newport   Served at Fort George in 1757 and
        in campaign of 1762.

    Peter of Exeter   Marched on alarm of Aug. 1757, and
        served in campaign of 1760.

    Philip   Served on Privateer Defiance of Newport in 1756.

    Robert   Served in campaign of 1762.

    Stephen of Exeter   Marched as Lieutenant on alarm of
        Aug. 1757.

    William of North Kingstown   Marched on alarm of Aug.
        1757.

ALDRICH, Abel   Served in Major Burkett's Co. in 1760. Taken
        sick with small-pox in Jan. 1761 at Charlestown, N. H.

    Abner   Lieutenant in Capt. Jenckes' Co. in 1756.

    Caleb of Smithfield   Marched on alarm of Aug. 1757.

    Daniel   Served in campaign of 1762.

    Ezra   Served in Capt. Jenckes' Co. in 1757.

    James   Served in campaign of 1760 and in Capt. Kim-
        ball's Co. in 1761.

    Joseph   Served in Lt. Col. Angell's Co. in 1756.

ALDRICH

Philip   Served in the campaign of 1761.

Reuben of Smithfield   Marched on alarm of Aug. 1757.

Simon   Served in campaign of 1760.

ALEXANDER, Richard of Cumberland   Marched on alarm of Aug. 1757, and enlisted for campaign of 1758.

ALGER, Josiah   Served in Lt. Col. Angell's Co. in 1756 and in campaign of 1757.

ALISON, David   Served in Capt. Kimball's Co. in 1761.

ALLEN, Amos of Providence   Marched on alarm of Aug. 1757.

Augustus of Providence   Served in Capt. Potter's Co. in 1756, in Capt. Jenckes' Co. in 1757, and as Ensign in Capt. Jenckes' Co. in 1758.

Barnabas   Served in Major Peck's Co. in 1762.

Benjamin of Newport   Drafted and marched on alarm of Aug. 1757.

Caleb   Served under Col. Rose in 1762.

Gabriel   Served in Major Peck's Co. in 1762.

James   Served in Capt. Fry's Co. at Havana in 1762.

Jeremiah   Private in Capt. Peck's Co. in 1761.

Joseph   Served in Capt. J. Whiting's Co. in 1757.

Joshua of Portsmouth   Marched as Captain on alarm of Aug. 1757; appointed 1st Lieut. of Capt. Peck's Co. in March 1758, but refused to serve.

Nathanial of Portsmouth   Marched on alarm of Aug. 1757.

Peter   Served in Capt. Potter's Co. in 1756, and in Capt. Jenckes' Co. in 1757.

Peter   Served in Capt. J. Whiting's Co. in 1757.

Seth   Served in 1762.

Sylvester   Served in Major Peck's Co. in 1762.

Timothy Henry of Newport   Volunteered and marched on alarm of Aug. 1757.

William of Newport   Marched on alarm of Aug. 1757, served in Capt. Rose's Co. in 1758, enlisted for campaign of 1762, and in H. M. regular Army on Jan. 9, 1763.

Zachariah of Providence   Marched on alarm of Aug. 1757.

ALMY, Benjamin of Newport   Commander of Privateer General Johnston of Newport in 1756 (Sh), and 1760.

Benjamin of Newport   Drafted in August 1757.

ALSBRO, see ALBRO.

ALSWORTH, see AYLSWORTH.

ALVERSON, David of Providence   Marched on Alarm of Aug. 1757, and served in campaign of 1762.

Simeon or Simon   Served in the campaign of 1761. Served in Major Peck's Co. in 1762.

Thomas   Served in Col. Rose's Regt. in 1762.

AMBROSE, Israel   Served on Privateer George of Newport in 1757.

AMOS, Samuel of Newport   Enlisted for campaign of 1762.

William   Enlisted in H. M. regular Army in 1762.

AMY, William   Served on Privateer Defiance of Newport in 1756.

ANDERSON, Alexander   Master on Privateer General Johnston in 1757.

James of Newport   Marched on alarm of Aug. 1757.

ANDREWS, Benjamin   Served in Col. Harris' Regt. in 1760.

Benoni   Served in campaign of 1758.

David   Served as A. B. seaman on H. M. S. Pembroke in 1759 and 1760.

James   Served on Privateer George of Newport in 1758.

Jonathan   Appointed Ensign of Capt. Bradford's Co. in Aug. 1755.

John   Appointed Colonel of Regt. raised on alarm of Aug. 1757. Appointed commissioner to wait upon the Earl of Loudon, Feb. 14, 1758, and in Dec. 1758 a member of the court-martial to inquire into the conduct of the officers in the last campaign.

John   Served in campaign of 1759.

Joshua   Served in Col. Harris' Regt. in 1760, and in Capt. Tew's Co. in 1762.

Philip   Served in Col. Harris' Regt. in 1760, and in Capt. Tew's Co. in 1762.

Timothy of Coventry   Marched on alarm of Aug. 1757. Served in Capt. Jenckes' Co. in 1758 and 1759. Died.

ANDREWS

 William Served in Col. Harris' Regt. in 1760, and in Major Peck's Co. in 1762.

 Zepheniah of Gloucester Served in Capt. Jenckes' Co. in 1756, and marched on alarm of Aug. 1757.

ANGELL, Christopher of Smithfield Marched on alarm of Aug. 1757.

 James Appointed 1st Lieutenant of Col. Hopkins' Co. in Oct. 1756.

 James of Providence Marched on alarm of Aug. 1757, and served in campaigns of 1760 and 1761.

 John Served in Col. Harris' Regt. in 1760.

 Negro of Providence Marched on alarm of Aug. 1757.

 Samuel Succeeded Sterry as Captain of 2nd Co. in Col. Harris' Regt. in 1755, appointed Major of Col. Harris' Regt. in Feb. 1756, and succeeded Champlin as Lieutenant Colonel; appointed Colonel and so served in campaign of 1758.

 Samuel Commander of Privateer Jolly Bachellor of Newport in 1758 (Sh).

 Thomas of Providence Marched as hostler on alarm of Aug. 1757.

ANTHONY, Philip of South Kingstown Marched on alarm of Aug. 1757. Served in Capt. Brown's Co. in 1759 and in campaign of 1762.

ANTUOMPT, John Served in Major Babcock's Co. in 1755,
ANTIUM, and in Capt. Brown's Co. in 1759.

ARMINGTON, Josiah Served in Major Peck's Co. in 1762.

 William Served in Major Peck's Co. in 1762.

ARMSTRONG, Nathan Served in campaign of 1759.

ARNOLD, Benedict Served in Capt. Fry's Co. at Havana in 1762.

 Caleb of Smithfield Marched on alarm of Aug. 1757.

 David of Gloucester Marched on alarm of Aug. 1757.

 Isaac Served in Capt. Jenckes' Co. in 1757, and in Col. Harris' Regt. in 1760.

 Joseph of Newport Commander of Privateer Polly in 1759.

ARNOLD

Joseph of Providence Volunteered on alarm of Aug. 1757.

Josiah of Warwick Marched on alarm of Aug. 1757.

Philip of Smithfield Marched on alarm of Aug. 1757.

Stephen of Smithfield Appointed Lieutenant of Capt. Hammond's Co. in Aug. 1755; 1st Lieutenant in Capt. Windsor's Co. in Oct. 1756, and marched as Captain on alarm of Aug. 1757.

William of Warwick Marched as Private on alarm of Aug. 1757.

(———) Served on Privateer Providence in 1758. Made Prizemaster 25 May 1758.

ARTHUR, William Served in Lt. Col. Cole's Co. in 1755 and
ARTER, appointed Armorer to Col. Harris' Regt. upon their arrival at Green-Bush.

ASH, John Served in campaign of 1762.

(———) Gunner on Privateer Duke of Marlborough in 1758.

ASHPO, John Served in Capt. Russell's Co. at Havana in 1762.

ASHWORTH, Robert Served on Privateer George of Newport in 1758.

ASPELL, Nicholas Served on Privateer Blackbird in 1762.

ASTEN, See AUSTIN.

ATES, William Served in campaign of 1761 and as Private in Capt. Hawkins' Co. in 1762.

ATHERTON, Solomon Enlisted for campaign of 1758.

ATWOOD, Anthony Served on Privateer George of Newport in 1757. Enlisted for campaign of 1762.

Benjamin of Newport Enlisted for campaign of 1762.

Scipio (colored) Served on Privateer George of Newport in 1757.

AUCHMUTY, John Served in Capt. Brown's Co. in 1758 and 1759, and served in campaign of 1760.

AUSTIN,
ASTEN,
ASTON, Benjamin Served in Col. Harris' Regt. in 1760.

AUSTIN

Benoni of West Greenwich   Served in Capt. Fry's Co. in 1756.

David   Served in Capt. Russell's Co. in 1760.

James   Served on Privateer George of Newport in 1758.

James of North Kingstown   Marched on alarm of Aug. 1757, and served in Capt. Fry's Co. in 1762.

Jeremiah   Served in Capt. Wall's Co. in 1757, and in campaign of 1758.

Jeremiah, Jr. of Exeter   Marched on alarm of Aug. 1757.

John   Served in Capt. Potter's Co. in 1756, in Capt. J. Whiting's Co. in 1757, and in Col. Rose's Regt. in 1762.

John   Enlisted as a seaman in 1756 and went to Oswego, where he was captured by the French.

Joseph   Enlisted as a sawer-a-top in 1756, and went to Oswego where he was captured by the French.

Joseph of Jamestown   Marched on alarm of Aug. 1757.

Parismus   Served in Col. Rose's Regt. in 1762.

Peres alias Pyerus   Served in Col. Rose's Regt. in 1762.

William   Enlisted in H. M. regular army in 1762.

AVERY, Thomas of Coventry   Served in Capt. Jenckes' Co. in 1756, marched on alarm of Aug. 1757, served in campaigns of 1758, 1759 and 1760.

AXTON, Young   Served as soldier at Fort George, R. I., from 1755 to 1763.

AYLSWORTH, Anthony   Served in campaign of 1756.

Benjamin   Served in Capt. Wall's Co. in 1757.

Christopher   Served in Col. Rose's Regt. in 1762.

John, Jr. of Coventry   Marched on alarm of Aug. 1757, served in Capt. Jenckes' Co. in 1758, and in campaigns of 1759, 1760 and 1761, and in Capt. Fry's Co. at Havana in 1762.

Josiah   Served in Col. Hopkins' Regt. in 1756.

Philip   Served in Col. Harris' Regt. in 1760.

Robert   Served in Capt. Wall's Co. in 1757, in Capt. Russell's Co. in 1760, and in Col. Rose's Regt. in 1762.

AYLSWORTH

Robert, Jr.   Served in Capt. Russell's Co. in 1760.

Thomas   Appointed Ensign of the 9th Co. (Potter's, later Hacker's Co.) in March 1758, became Lieutenant before June, transferred and served as Lieutenant of Capt. Jenckes' Co. in 1758.

AYRAULT, Daniel, Jr.   Member of Councils of War in 1757, 1758, 1759, and 1762.

BABCOCK, Abel   Served in Col. Babcock's Co. in 1758.

Amos   Served in Capt. J. Whiting's Co. in 1757, and in campaign of 1762.

Andrew   Served in Col. Babcock's Co. in 1758 and 1759, and in Capt. Russell's Co. in 1760.

Henry   Appointed Captain of 3rd Co. in Col. Harris' Regt. March 6, 1755; and served in campaign of 1755, becoming Major before Nov. 27.   He commanded the 2nd Co. in the campaign of 1756.   He was appointed 2nd Lieutenant-Colonel in Col. Andrews' Regt., which marched on the alarm of Aug. 1757.   He was appointed Lieutenant-Colonel in March 1758, and succeeded Malbone as Colonel in May 1758.   He served as Colonel and Commander of the Rhode Island forces in campaigns of 1758 and 1759.

Ichabod, Jr.   Appointed Ensign of Capt. Babcock's Co. in March 1755.

Job of Hopkinton   Marched on alarm of Aug. 1757, and served in campaign of 1762.

John of Hopkinton   Marched on alarm of Aug. 1757.

Joshua   Served in Col. Babcock's Co. in 1759.

Luke   Served as Commissary in campaign of 1759.

Oliver   Served in Col. Rose's Regt. in 1762.

William   Enlisted in H. M. regular army in 1762.

BACK, Daniel   Served in Lt. Col. Hargill's Co. at Havana in 1762.

John   Served in Capt. Rose's Co. in 1758, and in Lt. Col. Hargill's Co. at Havana in 1762.

BACKIER, John   Private in Capt. Hawkins' Co. in 1762.

BACON, Henry of Providence   Marched on alarm of Aug. 1757.

BAGLEY, Joseph of Smithfield   Marched on alarm of Aug. 1757.

BAILEY, Bennett of Tiverton   Marched on alarm of Aug.
BALES,   1757.
    Oliver   Served in Lt. Col. Hargill's Co. at Havana in 1762.

    Samuel   Served in Capt. Rose's Co. in 1758.

BAKER, Benjamin of Warwick   Marched on alarm of Aug. 1757.

    Benjamin of South Kingstown   Marched on alarm of Aug. 1757.

    Elisha of Newport   Marched on alarm of Aug. 1757.

    Elisha of Exeter   Marched on alarm of Aug. 1757.

    Elisha   Served in campaign of 1758.

    Ephraim   Served in campaigns of 1758 and 1762.

    Jeremiah of North Kingstown   Marched on alarm of Aug. 1757.

    Jonathan   Served in Col. Harris' Regt. in 1760.

    Joshua   Served in Capt. J. Whiting's Co. in 1757.

    Philip   Appointed 2nd Lieutenant of Capt. Wall's Co. in March 1758, and served in Col. Rose's Regt. in 1762.

    Samuel   Served in Capt. Russell's Co. in 1760.

    William   Served in Capt. Greene's Co. in 1757, and in Col. Rose's Regt. in 1762.

BALCH, Timothy of Newport   Drafted and marched as Ensign on alarm of Aug. 1757.   Member of Council of War in 1761 and 1762.

BALES, See BAILEY.

BALL, Thomas   Enlisted at Newport as a seaman and was sent to New York in Aug. 1762.

BALLARD,

BOLLARD, Jeremiah   Private in Capt. Hawkins' Co. in 1762.

    Jonathan   Served in campaign of 1758.

BALLOU, Daniel   Served in campaign of 1760.

    Elisha of Cumberland   Appointed Lieutenant in Col. Harris' Regt. in 1756, but did not march.

BALLOU

Jonathan of Providence   Volunteered on alarm of Aug. 1757.

Stephen   Served in Capt. Jenckes' Co. in 1758, and in campaign of 1762, and enlisted in H. M. regular army in 1762.

BARBER, Daniel   Served in Capt. Rose's Co. in 1758.

John of Hopkinton   Marched on .larm of Aug. 1757, and served in Col. Rose's Regt. in 1762.

Zebulon of Exeter   Marched on alarm of Aug. 1757, and served in Capt. Russell's Co. in 1760.

BARDINE,

BOARDWINE, Nathan   Served in Capt. Wall's Co. in 1757.

Prince of North Kingstown   Served in Capt. Wall's Co. in 1757.

BARKER, Edward of Middletown   Marched on alarm of Aug. 1757.

Edward of Portsmouth   Marched on alarm of Aug. 1757.

Joseph of North Kingstown   Marched on alarm of Aug. 1757.

BARNES, John   Served in Col. Harris' Regt. in 1756.

(son of Thomas of Gloucester)   Marched on alarm of Aug. 1757.

BARNEY, Israel, Jr. of Newport   Drafted and marched on alarm of Aug. 1757.

BARTHOLOMEW, Caesar of Newport   Marched on alarm of Aug. 1757.

BARTLETT, Charles   Served in Capt. Jenckes' Co. in 1758.

Christopher of Cumberland   Marched on alarm of Aug. 1757, and served in campaign of 1760.

David   Served in Capt. Hawkins' Co. in 1762.

Daniel, Jr.   Served in Capt. Kimball's Co. in 1761.

Israel   Served in campaign of 1760.

Thomas   Served in Capt. Greene's Co. in 1757.

BARTON, Anthony of Warwick   Marched on alarm of Aug. 1757, and served in campaign of 1758, in Capt. Kimball's Co. in 1761, and in Capt. Fry's Co. at Havana in 1762.

BARTON
Rufus, Jr.   Served in Col. Harris' Regt. in 1760.
BASS, John of Providence   Volunteered on alarm of Aug.
1757.   Appointed Chaplain and Surgeon's Mate of
Col. Babcock's Regt. in May 1758.
BATES, David   Served in campaign of 1761.
Ebenezer   Enlisted in H. M. regular army in 1762.
John of South Kingstown   Marched on alarm of Aug.
1757.
Oliver   Served in campaign of 1761, and in Capt. Fry's
Co. at Havana in 1762.
Robert   Served in Capt. J. Whiting's Co. in 1757.
BATTY, Benjamin   Served in Capt. Jenckes' Co. in 1756.
BAXTER, Thomas   Served in campaign of 1762.
BEARD, John   Lieutenant at Fort George, R. I., in 1759, 1760
and 1761.
BEVERLY, Gideon   Enlisted in H. M. regular army in 1762.
Jesse   Served in campaign of 1756.
John   Served in Capt. Jenckes' Co. in 1757, in campaign
of 1758, and as Ensign in Capt. Brown's Co. in 1759.
BEERS, Stephen   Served in Capt. Belcher's Co. in 1756.
BELCHER, Joseph of Newport   Appointed Captain of the 4th
Co. in the 2nd (Col. Hopkins') Regt. in Oct. 1756,
and served as Lieutenant on alarm of Aug. 1757.
BELKNAP, Benjamin   Served in campaign of 1760.
BELL, Edmund of Newport   Served in Capt. Belcher's Co. in
1756, on Privateer George of Newport in 1758, and
in campaign of 1762.
Edmund, Jr. of Newport   Served in campaign of 1762.
James   Served in Capt. J. Whiting's Co. in 1757.
Robert   Served as boy on Privateer George of Newport
in 1758.
Thomas   Served on Privateer George of Newport in
1758.
BENNETT, Ezekiel   Served in Capt. Wall's Co. in 1757.
Henry   Enlisted in H. M. regular army in 1762.
Job, Jr.   Member of Councils of War in 1756, 1757,
1758, 1759, 1760, 1761, and 1762.

BENNETT

John of Little Compton   Marched on alarm of Aug. 1757, served in campaign of 1758, and in Col. Harris' Regt. in 1760.

Jonathan   Served in Capt. Potter's Co. in 1756.

Joseph   Served in Capt. Jenckes' Co. in 1758, and died.

Joseph of Scituate   Served in Col. Harris' Regt. in 1760, in campaign of 1762, and in Capt. Cornell's Co. at Fort Stanwix in 1762 and 1763.

Judah   Served in Capt. Jenckes' Co. in 1758.

Samuel   Served in Capt. Potter's Co. in 1756, in Capt. E. Whiting's Co. in 1757, in Capt. Jenckes' Co. in 1758, and in Col. Harris' Regt. in 1760.

Samuel of Coventry   Marched on alarm of Aug. 1757.

Timothy   Served in campaign of 1761, and in Capt. Fry's Co. at Havana in 1762.

William   Served in Capt. Brown's Co. in 1758; appointed and served as Ensign of Col. Babcock's Co. in 1759, and succeeded Byrn as 2nd Lieutenant of Lt. Col. Whiting's Co. in 1760.

(son of Benjamin)   Served in campaign of 1760.

BENSON, Isaac   Served in Capt. Jenckes' Co. in 1757.

Jacob   Served in Capt. Jenckes' Co. in 1758.

BENTLEY, Benjamin   Served in Col. Harris' Regt. in 1760.

Caleb   Served in Capt. Russell's Co. at Havana in 1762.

Greene   Served in campaign of 1762.

James   Served in Capt. Greene's Co. in 1757.

Joseph   Served in Capt. Rose's Co. in 1758, and in Capt. Russell's Co. in 1760.

Thomas of Jamestown   Marched as Ensign on alarm of Aug. 1757.

Thomas (perhaps same as above)   Served in Col. Harris' Co. in 1760, and in campaign of 1761 at Fort Stanwix.

BERRY, Charles   Served in Capt. Fry's Co. in 1760, and in Col. Rose's Regt. in 1762.

Elisha   Served in Lt. Col. Angell's Co. in 1756.

Robert of Smithfield   Served in Capt. Jenckes' Co. in 1756 and 1757, in campaigns of 1758 and 1759, and in Capt. Hawkins' Co. in 1762.

BERRY

    Simeon   Served in Col. Babcock's Co. in 1759.

BILL, Joshua   Appointed Ensign of 1st Co. in Feb. 1755, but company was not raised. Appointed Ensign of Capt. Cole's Co. 6 March 1755.

BILLINGS, Daniel   Served in Capt. Russell's Co. in 1762, and died at Havana 25 Aug. 1762.

    Fellows   Served in campaign of 1760.

    Jabez   Served in Capt. Russell's Co. at Havana in 1762.

BILLINGTON, Daniel   Served in Capt. Rose's Co. in 1760. and in Col. Rose's Regt. in 1762.

    Elisha   Served in Col. Rose's Regt. in 1762.

    Joseph   Served in campaign of 1758.

BISHOP, Abner of Smithfield   Served in Capt. Jenckes' Co. in 1757, and in campaign of 1758.

    Ebenezer   Served in Major Peck's Co. in 1762.

    Ezekiel   Served in Capt. Jenckes' Co. in 1757, and in 1758.

    John   Served in Capt. Peck's Co. in 1761, and as Corporal in Major Peck's Co. in 1762.

    William of Gloucester   Marched on alarm of Aug. 1757.

BLACKMAR, Abner   Served in campaign of 1762.

    Ezekiel   Served in campaign of 1760.

    John of Gloucester   Marched on alarm of Aug. 1757.

BLACKMORE, James, Jr.   Served in campaigns of 1758 and 1759.

BLANCHARD, Isaac   Served in Capt. Fry's Co. at Havana in 1762.

    James   Served in Col. Harris' Regt. in 1756.

    Jeremiah   Served in Col. Harris' Regt. in 1756, in Capt. Jenckes' Co. in 1758, and in campaign of 1759.

    Joseph   Served in Major Burkett's Co. in 1760.

    Moses   Served in Major Peck's Co. in 1762.

    Simon   Served in Col. Harris' Regt. in 1755.

    William   Served in campaign of 1762.

BLAR, Manuel (colored) Served on Privateer Providence
BLAIR,   in 1757. Killed Dec. 21, 1757, off Porte Plate.

BLEU, John   Enlisted at Newport and served as seaman in 1762.

BLISS, George   Served in campaign of 1755.

James   Served in Capt. Russell's Co. in 1760.

William   Served in Capt. Fry's Co. at Havana in 1762.

William   Member of Councils of War in 1756 and 1757.

BLIVEN, James   Served in campaign of 1762.

Nathan   Served in Capt. Brown's Co. in 1758, and as Ensign in Capt. Tripp's Co. in 1759.

BOARDMAN, Jacob of North Kingstown   Marched on alarm of Aug. 1757.

Israel of Newport   Commander of Privateer General Webb of Newport in 1758.

BOID, Andrew   Served as Quartermaster of regiment in 1760,

BOYD,   2nd Lieutenant of Col. Whiting's Co. in 1761, and 2nd Lieutenant commanding second detachment of Capt. Fry's Co. at Albany in 1762.

BOISE, see BOYCE.

BOISS,

BOLLARD, see BALLARD.

BOLSTER, Isaiah   Served in campaign of 1761.

BOND, William   Served in Capt. Russell's Co. in 1760.

BOOTES, Joseph   Served in Capt. E. Whiting's Co. in 1757.

BOOTH, William of Newport   Served as a seaman in 1762.

BORDEN, Benjamin   Served in Capt. Belcher's Co. in 1756.

Thomas   Served on Privateer George of Newport in 1757.

BOSWORTH, Benjamin   Appointed Ensign of Capt. Whiting's Co. in Aug. 1755, and 2nd Lieutenant of Lt. Col. Champlin's Co. in Feb. 1756.

Daniel   Appointed Captain of the 8th Co. in Sept. 1755, and Captain of 8th Co. in Feb. 1756.

Joseph   Served in Col. Rose's Regt. in 1762.

Nero of Bristol (colored)   Marched on alarm of Aug. 1757.

BOURGET, Daniel   Enlisted in H. M. Regular Army in 1762.

BOURK, see BURKE.

BOURN, Michael   Served in Capt. Belcher's Co. in 1756.

Shearjashub   Member of Committee of War in 1761 and 1762.

BOURS, Peter   Member of Committee of War from 1755 to 1761 ; and appointed on committee to prepare a plan of the harbor of Newport and a profile of Fort George in Dec. 1755.

John, son of Peter   Succeeded his father as Member of Committee of War in 1761.

BOWDITCH,   Asa   Served in Capt. Brown's Co. in 1758,
BOWDISH,   Ensign of Capt. Fry's Co. in 1759, 2nd Lieutenant of Capt. Fry's Co. in 1760, 1st Lieutenant of Capt. Hopkins' Co. in 1761, and 1st Lieutenant of Lt. Col. Hargill's Co. in 1762. Died at Havana in 1762.

Moses   Served in Capt. Jenckes' Co. in 1758, and as 2nd Lieutenant of Capt. Burkett's Co. in 1759.

Nathaniel   Served in Capt. Jenckes' Co. in 1756, and as Ensign of Capt. Wall's Co. in 1758.

William   Served in Lt. Col. Hargill's Co. at Havana in 1762.

BOWDOWN   John   Soldier at Fort George, R. I., in 1755 and
BOWDOIN   1756.

BOWEN, Amos   Served in Capt. Jenckes' Co. in 1757.

Amos   Served on Privateer Providence in 1757, and was wounded Dec. 21.

Charles   Served in Capt. Brown's Co. in 1759.

Ebenezer of Providence   Marched on alarm of Aug. 1757.

Ephraim, Surgeon of Providence   Volunteered on alarm of Aug. 1757.

Fortin of Smithfield (colored)   Marched on alarm of Aug. 1757.

Jabez, Jr.   Served in campaign of 1762.

Thomas   Served in Major Peck's Co. in 1762.

Vinton   Served in Capt. Fry's Co. at Havana in 1762.

BOWERS, James   Enlisted at Newport for campaign of 1762.

BOWLER, Adam   Served on Privateer George of Newport in 1758.

BOWLER

Jack Served on Privateer George of Newport in 1758.

Metcalf Member of Councils of War in 1756, 1757, and 1762.

BOWLES, John of Newport Marched on alarm of Aug. 1757.

BOYCE, Daniel Served in campaign of 1758.

Paul of Smithfield Marched on alarm of Aug. 1757.

BRADBOAR, Henry Enlisted at Newport as a seaman in
BRADBURY, 1762.

BRADFORD, William Appointed Captain of 7th Co. in Aug. 1755.

BRAGG, Benjamin Served in Col. Harris' Regt. in 1760.

James Enlisted in H. M. regular army in 1762.

Nicholas of Warwick Served as hostler on alarm of Aug. 1757.

See **BRIGGS**.

BRAMAN, John Served in Capt. Brown's Co. in 1759, and
BRAYMAN, in campaign of 1762.

Josiah Served as 2nd Lieutenant in Capt. Kimball's Co. in 1761.

BRAND, Amos Served in Capt. E. Whiting's Co. in 1757.

John Served in Capt. Greene's Co. in 1757, and in Capt. Brown's Co. in 1758.

Thomas Served in Capt. E. Whiting's Co. in 1759.

Samuel Served in Capt. E. Whiting's Co. in 1757.

Samuel of Hopkinton Marched on alarm of Aug. 1757.

BRATTLE, Robert of Newport Marched on alarm of Aug. 1757.

BRAYTON, Gideon Served in Capt. Tew's Co. in 1762.

BRENAN, Laurence Served on Privateer Blackbird in 1762.

BRENTON, Benjamin Served at Louisburg in campaign of 1759.

Samuel Member of Council of War 28 April 1762.

BRETT, Richard Served on Privateer George of Newport in 1757.

BRIDGE, John Enlisted at Newport for campaign of 1762.

BRIGGS, Allenton Served in Col. Hopkins' Regt. in 1756.

Caleb Served in Col. Harris' Regt. in 1760.

BRIGGS

David   Served in campaigns of 1761 and 1762.

Jeremiah   2nd Lieutenant in Capt. Richmond's Co. in 1756.

Jeremiah of Scituate   Served in Capt. Jenckes' Co. in 1757, and in campaign of 1758.

John of E. Greenwich   Served in Capt. Wall's Co. in 1757, and in campaigns of 1758, 1759, and 1760.

Nathan   Served in Col. Harris' Regt. in 1760. Died.

Nathan   Served in Col. Rose's Co. in 1762.

Nathaniel   Served in Capt. J. Whiting's Co. in 1757.

Quacko   Served in Capt. J. Whiting's Co. in 1757.

Richard   Served in Capt. Rose's Co. in 1758.

Thomas of E. Greenwich   Marched on alarm of Aug. 1757.

Townsend   Served in campaigns of 1760 and 1762.

William   Served in campaigns of 1758 and 1759.

BRIGHTMAN, William   Served in Capt. E. Whiting's Co. in 1757.

BROADFOOT, Isaac   Served in Capt. Potter's Co. in 1756.

BROADLICK, John   Enlisted in H. M. regular army in 1762.

BROADWAY, Jeremiah   Served in campaigns of 1758, 1759, 1761, and in Capt. Hawkins' Co. in 1762.

BROCK, Amos   Served in Capt. Wall's Co. in 1757, as Corporal in campaign of 1759, in campaign of 1760, and as Corporal in Capt. Hawkins' Co. in 1762.

Ezekiel   Served in Capt. Potter's Co. in 1756.

George   Served in Capt. Wall's Co. in 1757, and in Capt. Hawkins' Co. in 1762.

Nicholas of Scituate   Served in Capt. Potter's Co. in 1756, in Capt. Jenckes' Co. in 1757, and in campaign of 1759.

BROMLEY, Nathan   Served in Capt. Russell's Co. at Havana in 1762, and died Oct. 13, 1762.

BROOKS, John   Enlisted at Newport for campaign of 1762.

BROUGHTON, John of Newport   Commander of Privateer Providence in 1760.

BROWN, Allen of Providence   Volunteered on alarm of Aug.
 1757, and served in campaign of 1758.

Alexander, Jr.   Served as Ensign in Lt. Col. Hargill's Co.
 in 1762.

Amos   Served in Capt. Jenckes' Co. in 1756, and in campaign of 1762.

Benajah   Served in Col. Babcock's Co. in 1759.

Benjamin of Cumberland   Marched on alarm of Aug.
 1757.

Benjamin   Served in Capt. Rose's Co. in 1758.

Benjamin   Served in Col. Babcock's Co. in 1758.

Benjamin   Served in campaigns of 1760 and 1762.

Benjamin   Surgeon's Mate of Col. Babcock's Regt. in
 1759, and Surgeon of Col. Rose's Regt. in 1762.

Chad of Gloucester   Marched as Captain on alarm of
 Aug. 1757.

Christopher   Served in Col. Harris' Co. in 1760.

Daniel   Enlisted in H. M. regular army in 1762.

Elisha   Member of Committee of War in 1761 and 1762.

Elisha   Served in Col. Babcock's Co. in 1759, and in Capt.
 Russell's Co. at Havana in 1762.

George   Commissioner to wait upon the Earl of Loudon
 in 1757, and member of committee to build sloop of
 war in 1757.

George of Newport   Marched on alarm of Aug. 1757.

Hugh   Enlisted in H. M. regular army in 1762.

Ichabod   Served in Capt. Jenckes' Co. in 1756.

James   Enlisted at Newport for campaign of 1762.

James   Served on Privateer Blackbird in 1762.

Jeremiah   Served in Capt. E. Whiting's Co. in 1758 and
 1759, and in Col. Harris' Regt. in 1760.

Jesse of Smithfield   Marched on alarm of Aug. 1757.

John of Newport   Volunteered and marched on alarm of
 Aug. 1757.

John   Served in campaign of 1760.

John of Newport   Commander of Privateer Mars of
 Newport in 1758.

BROWN

John   Served on Privateer Defiance of Newport in 1756, and on Privateer George of Newport in 1757.

Joseph of Providence   Volunteered on alarm of Aug. 1757.

Joseph   Served in Capt. E. Whiting's Co. in 1757.

Joseph of Middletown   Marched on alarm of Aug. 1757.

Joshua   2nd Lieutenant of Capt. Whiting's Co. in winter service 1755-6, and in 1756, 1st Lieutenant of Capt. Wall's Co. in 1758, succeeded Wall as Captain in 1758, and served as Captain in 1759 and 1760.

Joshua of Hopkinton   Marched on alarm of Aug. 1757.

Nathaniel   Served on Privateer Blackbird in 1762.

Nicholas of Providence   Volunteered on alarm of Aug. 1757.

Nicholas of Smithfield   Served in Col. Harris' Regt. in 1756, marched on alarm of Aug. 1757, and served in Capt. Jenckes' Co. in 1758.

Obadiah of Providence   Appointed on committee to build sloop of war in 1757, and volunteered on alarm of Aug. 1757.

Obadiah of Gloucester   Marched on alarm of Aug. 1757, and served in campaign of 1758.

Richard   Mate on Privateer Blackbird in 1762.

Roger   Served on Privateer George of Newport in 1757, and as Boatswain on Privateer George of Newport in 1758.

Stephen   Enlisted in H. M. regular army Jan. 13, 1763.

Thomas   Served in Capt. Belcher's Co. in 1756.

BROWNELL, Joseph   Served in Capt. E. Whiting's Co. in 1757, in campaign of 1760, and as Ensign of Capt. Hopkins' Co. in 1761.

BRUMMINGHAM, Richard   Served in campaign of 1758.

BRUCE, Robert   Served in Capt. Cornell's Co. in 1763 at Albany.

BRUSHEL,   Thomas   Served in Capt. Greene's Co. in 1757,
BRUSSILL,   and in Capt. Fry's Co. at Havana in 1762.

William of Warwick   Served in Lt. Col. Angell's Co. in 1756, and in Capt. Wall's Co. in 1757.

BRYANT, John Enlisted in H. M. regular army Jan. 6, 1763.
> Nicholas of Newport Marched on alarm of Aug. 1757.
> William Served in campaign of 1756.

BUCKLEY, Roger Enlisted at Newport for campaign of 1762.

BUCKLIN, Joseph of Providence Volunteered on alarm of
> Aug. 1757.

BUCKMASTER, Thomas Served in Capt. J. Whiting's Co. in
> 1757, and enlisted at Newport for campaign of 1762.

BUFFET, Thomas Served in Capt. Wall's Co. in 1757.

BUFFILL, Thomas Served in Capt. Potter's Co. in 1756, and
> in campaign of 1758.

BUFFUM, Walter of Newport Commander of Privateer
> Triton of Newport in 1758 (Sh), and 1759.

BULL, John Served on Privateer George of Newport in 1757,
> and as 2nd Lieutenant on Privateer George of New-
> port in 1758.

> Tom Served on Privateer George of Newport in 1758.

BULLOCK, Jonathan Served in Capt. Jenckes' Co. in 1757.

BUNDY, Jonathan Served in Capt. Greene's Co. in 1757.

BURDEN, John of Tiverton Marched on alarm of Aug. 1757.

BURDICK, Benjamin Served in Capt. Brown's Co. in 1758.
> Elias Ensign of Capt. Russell's Co. in 1761.
> Ezais Served in Capt. Brown's Co. in 1758 and 1759.
> Ichabod Served in Capt. Brown's Co. in 1758 and 1759.
> Jesse Served in campaign of 1762.
> John of Charlestown Marched on alarm of Aug. 1757.
> Jonathan of Newport Commander of Privateer Molly of
>   Newport in 1760, and of Privateer Sarah in 1761
>   (Sh.).
> Oliver of Westerly Served in Capt. Russell's Co. at
>   Havana in 1762, and died 22 Aug. 1762.
> Robert of Westerly Marched on alarm of Aug. 1757.
> Thomas of Stonington and Westerly Served in campaign
>   of 1755, and was killed.
> Thomas Served in campaign of 1762.
> Zaccheus Served in Capt. Greene's Co. in 1757.
> Zebediah Served in campaign of 1762.

BURGEN, Thomas Steward on Privateer Defiance of Newport in 1756.

BURGESS, Benjamin Served in campaign of 1762.

Edward Served in campaign of 1755.

Lewis Enlisted at Newport for campaign of 1762.

BURKE, John Served on Privateer George of Newport in 1758.

BURKETT, Thomas of Providence Ensign of Capt. Sterry's Co. in 1755, 1st Lieutenant of Col. Harris' Co. in 1756, succeeded Hammond as Captain of 10th Co. Sept. 1, 1756, Captain in campaign of 1758, probably succeeding Jenckes in 1758, Captain in 1759, and Major of Col. Harris' Regt. in 1760.

BURLESON, Edward of Coventry Marched on alarm of Aug. 1757.

BURLINGAME, David of Gloucester Marched on alarm of
BURLINHAM, Aug. 1757.

Jeremiah Served in Col. Harris' Regt. in 1760.

John Served in Capt. Potter's Co. in 1756.

Joshua of Cranston Marched on alarm of Aug. 1757.

Josiah Served at Fort George, R. I., from 1755 to 1759.

Peter of Cranston Marched on alarm of Aug. 1757.

Roger Served in campaign of 1761.

Stukeley Served in campaign of 1758, and in Capt. Kimball's Co. in 1761.

BURNHAM, Jacob of Gloucester Served in Capt. Jenckes' Co. in 1757.

BURR, Ezekiel of Providence Marched on alarm of Aug. 1757.

John Served in Capt. J. Whiting's Co. in 1757.

BURRINGTON, Peter of Portsmouth Marched on alarm of Aug. 1757.

BUSH, Bowen Served in Capt. Hawkins' Co. in 1762.

BUSSENBERGER, Christanus of Jamestown Marched on alarm
BUSSENBURY, of Aug. 1757.

BURT, John of Gloucester Marched on alarm of Aug. 1757.

BUSHEE, James of Warren Marched on alarm of Aug. 1757.

BUSEY, John M. Served on Privateer Defiance of Newport in 1756.

BUTLER, Benjamin of Cumberland   Marched on alarm of **Aug.** 1757.

    Benjamin   2nd Lieutenant of Capt. Windsor's Co. in 1756.

    Joseph of Hopkinton   Marched on alarm of Aug. 1757.

BUTTERWORTH, Benjamin   Served in Capt. J. Whiting's Co. in 1757.

BUTTON, Amos   Served in Capt. Brown's Co. in 1759, and in campaign of 1762.

    Charles   Served in Capt. Rose's Co. in 1758.

    Daniel   Served in Col. Babcock's Co. in 1759.

    (son of Mathias)   Served in Capt. Rose's Co. in 1758.

    Elisha   Served in Col. Babcock's Co. in 1759.

    Isaiah   Served in Col. Babcock's Co. in 1758 and 1759, and in campaign of 1762.

    Nathan   Served in Col. Babcock's Co. in 1758 and 1759.

    Rufus   Served in Capt. Brown's Co. in 1759.

BYRN, Daniel   2nd Lieutenant of Major Whiting's Co. in 1759, and 2nd Lieutenant of Lt. Col. Whiting's Co. in 1760. Died in 1760.

    Michael   Enlisted at Newport for campaign of 1762.

    Thomas   Enlisted at Newport for campaign of 1762.

    William   Served as gunner on Privateer Defiance of Newport in 1756.

CADY, Benjamin of Providence   Marched on alarm of Aug. 1757.

CAESAR, Charles   Served in campaign of 1762.

    Carder   Served in Capt. Wall's Co. in 1757.

    Ebenezer   Served on Privateer George of Newport in 1758.

    Jacob of Warwick   Served in Capt. Wall's Co. in 1757.

    Josiah   Served in campaigns of 1758 and 1762.

    Joseph   Served in Capt. Fry's Co. at Havana in 1762.

    Obediah of N. Kingstown (colored)   Served in Capt. Greene's Co. in 1757.

    Obediah   Served on Privateer George of Newport in 1758.

CAESAR
> Thomas   Served in Capt. J. Whiting's Co. in 1757.

CAHOONE, Benjamin   Served in Capt. Potter's Co. in 1756, in Capt. Wall's Co. in 1757, in campaign of 1758, Sergeant in campaign of 1759, and in Col. Harris' Regt. in 1760.
> Ebenezer   Lieutenant of Capt. Hopkins' Co. in 1755.
> James   Member of Council of War in 1762.
> John   Served on Privateer George of Newport in 1758, and at Fort George, R. I., in 1760.
> Thomas   Served in campaign of 1761, and in Capt. Fry's Co. in 1762.

CALLAHAN, Michael   Linguister on Privateer George of Newport in 1758.

CALLENDER, Ellis   Marched on alarm of Aug. 1757, and enlisted at Newport for campaign of 1762.

CALLUM, John   Served in Capt. Jenckes' Co. in 1758.

CALVER, William   Served in Capt. Wall's Co. in 1757.

CAMMETT, Abraham   Served in Col. Hopkins' Regt. in 1756.
> Isaac   Served in Capt. Fry's Co. at Havana in 1762, and enlisted in H. M. regular army 10 Jan. 1763.

CAMP, John   Served in campaign of 1760.

CAMPBELL, Henry   Served on Privateer George of Newport in 1758.
> John of Newport   Volunteered and marched on alarm of Aug. 1757.
> Tamberlin   Served in Capt. J. Whiting's Co. in 1757, Ensign of Capt. J. Whiting's Co. in 1758, 2nd Lieutenant of Capt. Hargill's Co. in 1759, and appointed Ensign of Capt. Peck's Co. in 1760, but did not serve.

CANE, John   Served on Privateer George of Newport in 1757.

CAPRON, Charles of Cumberland   Marched on alarm of Aug. 1757.
> Edward of Warwick   Served in Capt. Potter's Co. in 1756, marched on alarm of Aug. 1757, and served in Capt. Fry's Co. in 1761 and 1762.
> Oliver   Served in Capt. Jenckes' Co. in 1756.

CAPWELL, Amos   Served in campaign of 1761, and in Capt.
Fry's Co. at Havana in 1762.

Benjamin of Coventry   Served in Col. Hopkins' Regt. in
1756, in Capt. Wall's Co. in 1757, in campaign of
1759, and in Capt. Fry's Co. at Havana in 1762.

CARD, Benjamin   Served in Capt. J. Whiting's Co. in 1757.

Peleg   Served in campaign of 1761.

CARELL, see CAROLL.

CARNEY, Thomas   Served as A. B. seaman on H. M. S. Pembroke in 1759 and 1760.

CARPENTER, Beloved   Served in campaign of 1761.

Benjamin   Served in campaigns of 1758 and 1759.

Comfort   Served at Fort George, R. I., in 1757, in Col.
Harris' Regt. in 1760, and as Ensign in Capt. Peck's
Co. in 1761.

Edward   Served at Fort George, R. I., in 1757.

Ezekiel   Served in Major Peck's Co. in 1762.

Joseph of Cranston   Marched as Lieutenant on alarm of
Aug. 1757.

Joseph of E. Greenwich   Marched as Captain on alarm of
Aug. 1757.

CARR, Benjamin   2nd Lieutenant of Lt. Col. Wall's Co. in
1759.

Caleb, Lieutenant of Fort George, R. I., in 1756, 1757,
1758, 1759, 1761, and 1762.

Caleb of Warwick   Served in Capt. Wall's Co. in 1757.

Esek   Served in Capt. E. Whiting's Co. in 1757, and as
Ensign of Col. Babcock's Co. in 1758.

James   Gunner at Fort George in 1762.

John   Served on Privateer Defiance of Newport in 1756.

John   Served in Capt. E. Whiting's Co. in 1757.

Michael of N. Kingstown   Served in Capt. Greene's Co.
in 1757.

Patrick   Enlisted at Newport for campaign of 1762.

Samuel   Appointed Captain of Fort George, R. I., in
May 1763.

CARROLL, David   Served in Capt. J. Whiting's Co. in 1757.

CARROLL

James   Served in Major Peck's Co. in 1762.

Lawrence   Served in Capt. J. Whiting's Co. in 1757.

CARTER, William of Newport   Marched on alarm of Aug. 1757.

CARTY, Benjamin   Served in campaign of 1757.

CAREY, Elias of S. Kingstown   Marched on alarm of Aug.
CARY,   1757, served in Capt. Rose's Co., in 1758, and in
CARRY,   Capt. Russell's Co. in 1760.

Thomas   Served in Capt. Russell's Co. at Havana in 1762.

CASE, Carder   Served in Col. Hopkins' Regt. in 1756, and in
      Capt. Wall's Co. in 1757.

Immanuel   Served in Col. Rose's Regt. in 1762.

Israel   Served in Capt. Fry's Co. at Havana in 1762.

Mitchell of Warwick   Marched as Captain on alarm of
      Aug. 1757, served as Ensign in Capt. Potter's Co. in
      1758, as 1st Lieutenant in Capt. Tripp's Co. in 1759,
      as 2nd Lieutenant in Capt. Brown's Co. in 1760, as
      Ensign in Lt. Col. Rose's Co. in 1761, and as 2nd
      Lieutenant on Privateer Blackbird in 1762.

Nathan   Served at Fort George, R. I., in 1756.

Peter of S. Kingstown   Marched on alarm of Aug. 1757.

Sanford of S. Kingstown   Served in Capt. Greene's Co.
      in 1757.

CASEY, Silas of E. Greenwich   Served as hostler on alarm of
      Aug. 1757.

Thomas   Member of Committee of War in 1761 and
      1762.

CASS, Benjamin   Served in Col. Harris' Regt. in 1760.

Joseph   Served in Capt. Jenckes' Co. in 1758.

Oliver   Served in campaign of 1760.

CAST, Joseph   Served in Capt. Jenckes' Co. in 1756.

CATIAN, William   Served on Privateer George of Newport in
      1757 and 1758.

CAUHIES, see COHEIS.

CHACE, see CHASE.

CHADWICK, George   Served on Privateer George of Newport
      in 1757.

CHADWICK

Thomas   Served on Privateer Defiance of Newport in 1756.

CHAFFEE, Shuball   Served as Corporal in Major Peck's Co. in 1762.

CHALLIS, James   Enlisted at Newport for campaign of 1762.

CHALONER, Walter   Commander of Privateer Defiance of Newport in 1757.

CHAMPLIN, Christopher, Jr.   Commissary and Major of Col. Harris' Regt. in 1755, and on Special Investigating Committee in Oct. 1755.   Appointed Lieut. Colonel of Col. Harris' Regt. in 1756.

Dereck   Served in Col. Babcock's Co. in 1759.

Elias   Served on Privateer George of Newport in 1758.

Jabez   Member of Councils of war in 1760 and 1761.

Joseph   Major of Col. Hopkins' Regt. in 1756.

Peter   Served in Capt. Russell's Co. in 1760, and in Capt. Russell's Co. at Havana in 1762.

Samuel   1st Lieutenant in Capt. Hammond's Co. in 1756, and 2nd Lieutenant in Capt. Brown's Co. in 1759.

Thomas   Error for Samuel q. v.

Trumpeter   Served in Capt. J. Whiting's Co. in 1757.

CHANDLER, William of Newport   Volunteered and marched on alarm of Aug. 1757.

CHANNING, Shar'pr   Served as cook on Privateer George of Newport in 1758.

CHAPMAN, Alexander   Enlisted at Newport as a seaman in 1762.

Stephen   Served in Capt. Potter's Co. in 1756, and in Capt. Jenckes' Co. in 1757.

CHAPPELL, Stephen   Served in Col. Rose's Regt. in 1762.

CHASE,   Abner   Served in Capt. Russell's Co. in Havana in
CHACE,   1762.

Abraham of Coventry   Marched on alarm of Aug. 1757.

Benjamin   Enlisted in H. M. regular army Jan. 9, 1763.

Comfort   Served in Capt. Russell's Co. at Havana in 1762.

John   Served on Privateer George of Newport in 1757.

CHACE

John   Served in Col. Rose's Regt. in 1762.

Samuel   Served in Capt. Jenckes' Co. in 1757.

Seth   Served in Capt. Russell's Co. at Havana in 1762.

Zacheus   Drafted on alarm of Aug. 1757.

CHASE, see CHEESE.

CHEATS, William   Served in Capt. Belcher's Co. in 1756.

CHEESE, Joseph   Served in campaign of 1761, and in Capt. Fry's Co. at Havana in 1762.

Peter of Warwick   Served in Capt. Potter's Co. in 1756, and in Capt. Wall's Co. in 1757.

Thomas   Served in Capt. Potter's Co. in 1756.

CHENEY, Oliver   Served in campaign of 1762.

CHESEBOROUGH, David   Enlisted at Newport for campaign of 1762.

James   Served in Capt. E. Whiting's Co. in 1757, 1758, and 1759.

CHESNUT, Samuel   Enlisted at Newport for campaign of 1762.

CHICHESTER, Jeremiah   Served in campaign of 1761.

CHILD, Henry   Served in campaign of 1761.

CHIPMAN, John   Enlisted at Newport for campaign of 1762, and in H. M. regular army Jan. 1, 1763.

CHRISTIAN, John   Enlisted at Newport as a seaman in 1762.

CHURCH, Benedict   Served in Col. Rose's Regt. in 1762.

Charles of Newport   Marched on alarm of Aug. 1757.

David   Served in Capt. E. Whiting's Co. in 1758 and 1759.

Edward of Little Compton   Marched on alarm of Aug. 1757.

Edward   Commander of Privateer Charming Betty of Newport in 1757.

Isaac   Served in Capt. E. Whiting's Co. in 1757, in Capt. Russell's Co. in 1760, and enlisted in H. M. regular army in 1762.

Joshua   Served in Capt. Greene's Co. in 1757, in Capt. Brown's Co. in 1758 and 1759, and in campaign of 1762.

Church

Rufus   Served as a carpenter at Oswego in 1756, and was taken prisoner by the French.

Rufus of Newport   Marched on alarm of Aug. 1757.

Samuel   Served in campaign of 1762.

Thomas of Little Compton   Marched as Captain on alarm of Aug. 1757.

Clannel, see Clanning, Clouner.

Clarke, Amos   Served in Col. Babcock's Co. in 1758.

Caleb, Jr.   Served in Capt. Russell's Co. at Havana in 1762, and died Nov. 16, 1762.

Crawford   Served in Capt. J. Whiting's Co. in 1757.

Edward   Served in Capt. E. Whiting's Co. in 1757, in Col. Babcock's Co. in 1759, and in Capt. Russell's Co. at Havana in 1762, and died Nov. 1, 1762.

Elisha of Charlestown   Marched as Ensign on alarm of Aug. 1757.

Hutchinson   Served in Capt. Fry's Co. at Havana in 1762.

Jabez   Served in campaign of 1762.

James of Newport   Marched on alarm of Aug. 1757.

John   Served at Fort George, R. I., in 1761.

John, Jr. of Newport   Marched on alarm of Aug. 1757.

John of Smithfield   Marched on alarm of Aug. 1757, and served in Capt. Brown's Co. in 1758 and 1759.

Jonathan of Providence   Volunteered on alarm of Aug. 1757.

Joseph, Jr.   Served in campaign of 1762.

Latham   Served as Captain in Col. Hopkins' Regt. in 1756.

Reuben   Served on Privateer George of Newport in 1758.

Robert   Served in Capt. Russell's Co. at Havana in 1762, and died 6 Sept. 1762.

Stephen   Served in Capt. Russell's Co. at Havana in 1762, and died 22 Aug. 1762.

Thomas   Served in Capt. Rose's Co. in 1758.

Walter   Commander of Privateer Bearer of Newport in 1762.

CLARKE

Walter   Served as Lieutenant in Capt. Tew's Co. in 1760.

Weston   Served in Col. Babcock's Co. in 1759.

CLEMENCE,   John of Smithfield   Served in Col. Harris' Regt.
CLEMENTS,   in 1756, and marched on alarm of Aug. 1757.

John   Enlisted at Newport as a seaman in 1762.

Richard of Providence   Marched on alarm of Aug. 1757.

CLEVELAND, John   Served in Col. Rose's Regt. in 1762.

CLOIS, Thomas   Served in Capt. Jenckes' Co. in 1757, and was
transferred to Capt. Wall's Co.

CLOSSON, Ichobod   Served in campaign of 1762.

Richard   Served in Capt. Greene's Co. in 1757, and in
Capt. Brown's Co. in 1759.

CLOUNER,   Edward   Served as caulker and sawer at Oswego
CLANNEL,   in 1756, and was taken prisoner by the French.
CLANNING,

COATES, David   Served in Col. Babcock's Co. in 1758 and
1759.

John   Enlisted at Newport as a seaman in 1762.

John   Enlisted in H. M. regular army in 1762.

COBB, Benjamin   Served in Col. Rose's Regt. in 1762.

Daniel   Served in Capt. Rose's Co. in 1758, and in Col.
Rose's Regt. in 1762.

Freeman   Served on Privateer Defiance of Newport in
1756.

James   Served as A. B. seaman on H. M. S. Pembroke
in 1759 and 1760.

John   Served in campaign of 1758.

COBURN, James   Served on Privateer George of Newport in
1758.

CODDINGTON, Francis of Newport   Commander of Privateer
Britannia in 1762.

James   Commander of Privateer Wolf of Newport in
1762.

Nathaniel   Prize Master on Privateer George of Newport
in 1758.

CODNER, David   Served in Capt. Greene's Co. in 1757.

George of Warren   Marched on alarm of Aug. 1757.

CODNER

Ishmael   Served in Capt. Greene's Co. in 1757, and in Capt. Brown's Co. in 1759.

John   Served in Lt. Col. Hargill's Co. at Havana in 1762.

Samuel   Served in Capt. Rose's Co. in 1758, and in Col. Rose's Regt. in 1762.

Stephen   Served in Lt. Col. Hargill's Co. in 1762.

COFFERE, James   Served in Major Peck's Co. in 1762.

COGGESHALL, Daniel, Jr.   Ensign in Col. Rose's Co. in 1762.

Giles of Portsmouth   Marched on alarm of Aug. 1757, and enlisted for campaign of 1762.

James   Enlisted at Newport for campaign of 1762.

Joseph of North Kingstown   Captain of 7th Co. of Col. Hopkins' Regt. in 1756, and Commissary of Col. Babcock's Regt. in 1758.

Joseph of Warwick   Marched on alarm of Aug. 1757.

John   Served in Col. Babcock's Co. in 1759.

Joshua   Served at Fort George, R. I., in 1755.

Joshua, Jr., of Middletown   Marched as officer on alarm of Aug. 1757.

Nicholas of Newport   Served on Privateer George of Newport in 1757 and 1758, and as A. B. seaman on H. M. S. Pembroke in 1759.

Solomon (Indian)   Served on Privateer Providence in 1759.

COYHIS, COHEIS, COYEES, CAUHIES.

Charles   Served in Capt. Greene's Co. in 1757.

Edom of Charlestown   Marched on alarm of Aug. 1757.

Ephraim, Jr., of Richmond   Marched on alarm of Aug. 1757.

Thomas   Served in Capt. J. Whiting's Co. in 1758, and in Capt. E. Whiting's Co. in 1759.

COLE, Constant   Served in Lt. Col. Angell's Co. in 1756, and in Capt. Wall's Co. in 1757.

Edward   Captain of 1st Co. and Lt. Col. of Col. Harris' Regt. in 1755, and in command of the reinforcements that rescued the remnants of Col. Williams' force on Sept. 8, 1755.

COLE

George   Served in Capt. Peck's Co. in 1761, and in Major Peck's Co. in 1762.

Hugh   Served in campaign of 1762.

Isaac of Warren   Marched on alarm of Aug. 1757.

John of Scituate   Served in Capt. Jenckes' Co. in 1757, in campaigns of 1758 and 1760, and in Capt. Kimball's Co. in 1761.

John of Providence   Volunteered on alarm of Aug. 1757.

Joseph of Providence   Volunteered on alarm of Aug. 1757.

Nathan of Warren   Marched on alarm of Aug. 1757.

Richard   Served as Corporal in Capt. Peck's Co. in 1761, and as drummer in Major Peck's Co. in 1762.

Spencer   Served on Privateer George of Newport in 1757 and 1758.

Thomas of Warren   Marched as Lieutenant on alarm of Aug. 1757.

COLEGROVE, Benjamin   Served in Capt. Wall's Co. in 1757.

Isaac   Served in Capt. Jenckes' Co. in 1757 and was transferred to Capt. Wall's Co.

Jeremi'y   Served in Capt. Russell's Co. in 1760.

COLLER, Daniel of Cumberland   Served in Capt. Angell's Co. in 1755, in Capt. Whiting's Co. in winter of 1755-56, and in 1756. Captured by the French in May 1756.

Daniel   Served in campaign of 1762.

Jonathan of Cumberland   Marched on alarm of Aug. 1757, and served in campaign of 1760.

COLLINS, James   Served in Capt. Russell's Co. in 1760.

Jedediah, Jr.   Served in Capt. Russell's Co. at Havana in 1762.

Nathan   Served in Col. Harris' Regt. in 1760.

Thomas of Newport   Marched on alarm of Aug. 1757, served in Capt. Jenckes' Co. in 1758, as 2nd Lieutenant in Capt. Eddy's Co. in 1759, and as 2nd Lieutenant in Col. Harris' Co. in 1760.

COLVER, Stephen, Jr., of Coventry   Marched on alarm of Aug. 1757.

COLVER

William of West Greenwich   Served in Capt. Wall's Co.
in 1757.

COLVIN,   Luther   Served in Col. Harris' Regt. in 1760.

COLVILL,

COMAN, Benjamin   Served in campaign of 1761.

COMSTOCK, Aaron   Served in campaigns of 1760 and 1761.

Abner   Served in campaigns of 1760 and 1761.

Abraham of Smithfield   Marched on alarm of Aug. 1757.

Azariah of Smithfield   Marched on alarm of Aug. 1757.

Gideon   Member of committee of war in 1760, 1761 and
1762.

Jeremiah of Gloucester   Marched on alarm of Aug. 1757.

Moses of Smithfield   Marched on alarm of Aug. 1757,
and served in Capt. Kimball's Co. in 1761.

Nathan   Served in Major Angell's Co. in 1756.

Samuel of Smithfield   Served in Col. Harris' Co. in 1756,
and marched on alarm of Aug. 1757.

CONGDON, Charles   Served in Capt. Rose's Co. in 1758, and in
Col. Harris' Regt. in 1760.

Christopher   Served in Capt. Russell's Co. in 1760.

John   Enlisted in H. M. regular army in 1762.

Robert   Served in Capt. Russell's Co. in 1760, and in Col.
Rose's Regt. in 1762.

CONIE, John   Served as boatswain's mate on Privateer George
of Newport in 1758.

CONNER, Joseph   Served in Col. Harris' Co. in 1756.

Michael   Served in campaign of 1755.

CONNOLLY, John   Enlisted in H. M. regular army in 1762.

CONVERSE, Asa   Served in campaign of 1761.

James of Warwick   Marched on alarm of Aug. 1757.

COOK, Aaron   Served in Capt. Jenckes' Co. in 1758.

Charles of Newport   Served in Capt. Belcher's Co. in
1756, and marched on alarm of Aug. 1757.

Gregory   Served in Capt. Rose's Co. in 1758, and in Col.
Rose's Regt. in 1762.

Jeremiah   Served at Fort Stanwix during winter of 1761-
62.

COOK

John of Tiverton   Served in Capt. Belcher's Co. in 1756, and marched on alarm of Aug. 1757.

Nicholas of Providence   Volunteered on alarm of Aug. 1757.

Samuel of Smithfield   Marched on alarm of Aug. 1757.

Silas   Served, probably as an officer, in campaign of 1755, and as 1st Lieutenant of Major Angell's Co. in 1756.

Silas of Providence   Commander of Privateer Providence in 1758 and 1759, and was taken prisoner by the French April 20, 1759; Commander of Privateer Roby in 1760.

COONE, Amos   Served in campaign of 1762.

Benjamin of West Greenwich   Served in Capt. Wall's Co. in 1757.

John of Hopkinton   Marched as Captain on alarm of Aug. 1757.

Nathan of Hopkinton   Marched on alarm of Aug. 1757, and served in campaign of 1762.

Nathan, Jr.   Served in campaign of 1762.

Peleg   Served in Capt. Russell's Co. at Havana in 1762.

Thomas   Served in Capt. Brown's Co. in 1759.

William of Hopkinton   Marched on alarm of Aug. 1757.

COOPER, Adam   Served in Capt. Fry's Co. in 1762.

Thomas   Served on Privateer George of Newport in 1757.

William   Served in Capt. Greene's Co. in 1757.

William of Newport   Marched on alarm of Aug. 1757.

CORBIN, Edward   Served in Capt. Jenckes' Co. in 1757.

CORY, Benjamin   Served in Col. Rose's Regt. in 1762.

Caleb   Served in Col. Rose's Regt. in 1762.

Oliver   Served in Col. Rose's Regt. in 1762.

CORNELL, Benjamin of Portsmouth   Member of Council of War in 1757, and marched as Captain on alarm of Aug. 1757.

George of Newport   Marched on alarm of Aug. 1757.

George (son of Clarke)   Ensign in Capt. Tew's Co. in 1759, 2nd Lieutenant in Capt. Hargill's Co. in 1760, 1st Lieutenant in Capt. Russell's Co. in 1761, Lieutenant at Fort Stanwix during winter of 1761-62, 1st Lieutenant in Capt. Hawkins' Co. in 1762, and Captain of R. I. Co. at Fort Stanwix from Nov. 1762 to July 1763.

Jonathan of Portsmouth   Marched on alarm of Aug. 1757.

CORNISH, William   Served in Capt. E. Whiting's Co. in 1758.

CORPS, Jeremiah   Served in campaign of 1758.

COTTRELL, Nathan   Served in Col. Babcock's Co. in 1758 and 1759, and in Capt. Russell's Co. in 1760.

Stephen, Jr.   Served in Col. Rose's Co. in 1762.

Sylvester   Served in Col. Babcock's Co. in 1758 and 1759.

Thomas   Served in Capt. Greene's Co. in 1757, and as 1st Lieutenant in Capt. Tew's Co. in 1762.

COTTOR, Jonathan of Cumberland   Marched on alarm of Aug. 1757.

COUCHUP, see TOCKCUP.

COUSIN, John of South Kingstown   Marched on alarm of Aug. 1757.

COUSIN, see COZZENS

COVELL, Peter   Served in campaign of 1760.

COVEY, James   Served in Capt. Brown's Co. in 1759.

COWEN, John   Served in Major Peck's Co. in 1762.

COWLEY, Joseph of Newport   Volunteered and marched on alarm of Aug. 1757.

COX, Benjamin of Cumberland   Marched on alarm of Aug. 1757.

Charles of Newport   Marched on alarm of Aug. 1757.

COY, Benjamin   Served in campaign of 1762.

COZZENS, Joseph   Served in Capt. Russell's Co. in 1760 and in campaign of 1761.

COZZENS, see COUSIN.

CRANDALL, Benjamin   Served in campaign of 1758.

Eber   Served in Col. Babcock's Co. in 1759.

Jeremiah   Served in Capt. Brown's Co. in 1759, and in campaign of 1762.

Jonathan   Served in Capt. Brown's Co. in 1758 and 1759.

CRANDALL

    Peter   Served in Capt. Rose's Co. in 1758, in Capt. Russell's Co. in 1760, and in Capt. Russell's Co. at Havana in 1762. Died 9 Nov. 1762.

CRANSTON, Benjamin   2nd Lieut. on Privateer Roby in 1759.

    Caleb of Warren   Commander of Privateer Polly in 1759, of Privateer Roby in 1759, and of Privateer Polly in 1762 (Sh).

    Jeremiah of Newport   Commander of Privateer Catherine in 1757, and 1761.

    Richmond   Served on Privateer George of Newport in 1757, and as sailmaker on same vessel in 1758.

    Thomas   Member of committee of war from 1755 to 1762.

CRARY, Oliver   Served in Capt. Belcher's Co. in 1756.

CROCKER, Amaziah   Served in Capt. Brown's Co. in 1759.

    George   Served in Capt. J. Whiting's Co. in 1757, and in Capt. Hargill's Co. in 1760.

CROOKSHANKS, Peter   Enlisted at Newport as a seaman in 1762.

CROSS, Benjamin   Served in Capt. Brown's Co. in 1759.

    Edward   Served in Capt. Greene's Co. in 1757, as Ensign in Capt. Russell's Co. in 1760, as Ensign in Major Hargill's Co. in 1761, and as 2nd Lieutenant in Capt. Russell's Co. in 1762.

    Gideon   Served in Capt. Russell's Co. in 1760.

    James   Served on Privateer George of Newport in 1758.

    John   Enlisted at Newport as a seaman in 1762.

    Samuel   Served in campaigns of 1758 and 1760.

CROSSMAN, Abiel   Served in campaign of 1761.

CROSSWELL, George   Commander of Privateer Triton of Newport in 1756.

CRUMB, Daniel   Served in Col. Babcock's Co. in 1759.

    Samuel   Served in Col. Babcock's Co. in 1759.

    Waite   Served in Capt. Russell's Co. in 1760, and in Capt. Russell's Co. at Havana in 1762.

CULLESSON, John   Served as Master on Privateer Defiance of Newport in 1756.

CUMMINS, Benjamin of Cumberland Marched on alarm of
Aug. 1757, and served in campaigns of 1758 and 1759.
John Served in Capt. Jenckes' Co. in 1757, and in cam-
paign of 1762.
Joseph Served in Capt. Jenckes' Co. in 1757.
CUNDEL, Benjamin Served in Capt. Jenckes' Co. in 1757.
CUNNINGHAM, John Served at Fort George, R. I., in 1755,
1756 and 1757.
CURRELL, Thomas Served in Capt. Rose's Co. in 1758, and
campaign of 1762.
CURTIS, Ebenezer of Gloucester Served in Capt. Jenckes' Co.
in 1757, and in campaign of 1758.
Nathaniel Served in Major Peck's Co. in 1762.
Simeon Served in Capt. Peck's Co. in 1761, and in Major
Peck's Co. in 1762.
CUTIPH, James Served in Col. Harris' Regt. in 1760, and in
Capt. Kimball's Co. in 1761.
CUTLER, Samuel Served in Capt. Jenckes' Co. in 1756.
CUZZENS, see COZZENS.

DAILEY, Carder Served in Capt. Wall's Co. in 1757.
David Served in Col. Harris' Regt. in 1760, and in cam-
paign of 1762.
James Served in Col. Harris' Regt. in 1760.
Jonathan Served in Capt. Jenckes' Co. in 1758.
Pardon Served in Capt. Wall's Co. in 1757.
Samuel Served in Col. Harris' Regt. in 1760.
Timothy Served in Capt. Potter's Co. in 1756.
DAMON, Ezekiel of Newport Marched on alarm of Aug. 1757.
DARLING, Ebenezer of Gloucester Marched on alarm of Aug.
1757.
DARNLY, John Served in campaigns of 1758 and 1759.
DAVIS, Bell of Warwick Served in campaign of 1760.
George Served as boatswain of Privateer Defiance of
Newport in 1756.
John Commander of a privateer between 1755 and 1758.
John of Newport Drafted and marched on alarm of Aug.
1757.

DAVIS

Joseph of Cumberland   Appointed Ensign of Capt. Hammond's Co. in 1755, and 1st Lieutenant of Capt. Richmond's Co. in 1756.

Joseph   Served in Capt. Jenckes' Co. in 1756.

Mark   Served on Privateer Defiance of Newport in 1756.

May of Newport   Marched on alarm of Aug. 1757.

Nathaniel   Served in Capt. Russell's Co. in 1760.

Samuel of Warwick   Marched on alarm of Aug. 1757.

William of North Kingstown   Marched on alarm of Aug. 1757, and served in Capt. Fry's Co. at Havana in 1762.

William   Served on Privateer George of Newport in 1758.

DAWLEY, Ephraim of North Kingstown   Marched on alarm of Aug. 1757, and served in campaign of 1761.

Michael   Served in Capt. Rose's Co. in 1758.

Peleg   Served in Lt. Col. Hargill's Co. at Albany in 1762.

DAY, Ezra   Served in campaigns of 1758 and 1759.

Joseph   Served in Capt. Kimball's Co. in 1761.

Nathan   Served in Capt. Jenckes' Co. in 1757.

DELAPE, James   Enlisted at Newport in H. M. regular army in Aug. 1762.

DENNIS, James   Served in campaign of 1759, and in Major

DENNIE,   Peck's Co. in 1762.

John of Newport   Commander of Privateer Foye of Newport in 1756.

DENNISON, Joseph of Stonington   Commander of Privateer Dolphin of Westerly in 1762.

DENTERY, Joseph   Served in Capt. Belcher's Co. in 1756.

DERRICK, John   Served in Capt. Brown's Co. in 1759, in Capt. Russell's Co. in 1760, and in campaign of 1762.

DE WOLF, Mark Anthony of Bristol   Commander of Privateer Rhoba of Warren in 1757, and 1758 (Sh).

DEXTER, Andrew   Served in campaigns of 1759, 1760 and 1761.

David   Appointed Lieutenant of Capt. Sterry's Co. in 1755.

Gideon of Providence   Marched on alarm of Aug. 1757.

James of Cumberland   Marched on alarm of Aug. 1757.

DEXTER

Knight of Providence   Marched as Ensign on alarm of
Aug. 1757.

DICKERSON, Christopher   Served in Col. Harris' Regt. in 1756.

DIKES, Francis   Served on Privateer Defiance of Newport in
1756.

DILLINGHAM, Elisha   Served in campaign of 1760.

DIMAN, Benjamin   Served in Col. Rose's Regt. in 1762.

Jeremiah, Jr., of Bristol   Served in campaign of 1760 and
died at Albany.

(———, son of Jeremiah of Bristol)   Served in campaign of 1761.

DIMPSEY, Edward   Served in Capt. Brown's Co. in 1759.

DIXSON,

DICKSON, Francis   Served in Lt. Col. Hargill's Co. in 1762.

Thomas   Enlisted in H. M. regular service in 1762.

DOBSON, John   Enlisted at Newport for campaign of 1762.

DOCCARTY, William   Enlisted at Newport for campaign of
1762.

DOGGETT, Israel   Served in Major Peck's Co. in 1762.

DOLBEAR, John   Served in campaign of 1762.

DOLIVER, Joseph   Served in Capt. Potter's Co. in 1758, and as
Sergeant in Col. Harris' Regt. in 1760.

DOLMER, Joseph   Served in Capt. Peck's Co. in 1761.

DOUBLEDAY, Benjamin of Providence   Volunteered on alarm
of Aug. 1757.

DOVE, Joseph   Enlisted at Newport as a seaman in 1762.

DOWLAS, Michael   Served in Capt. Jenckes' Co. in 1757.

DOLLAS,

DOWNEY, Michael   Served in Capt. J. Whiting's Co. in 1757.

DOYLE, Peter   Served in campaign of 1759.

DRAKE, Joshua   Served in campaign of 1762.

DRANE, William   Served on Privateer George of Newport in
DRAIN,   1758.

DRAPER, Simeon of West Greenwich   Marched as Captain on
alarm of Aug. 1757.

Simeon of Exeter   Marched as Captain on alarm of Aug.
1757.

DRING, Richard   Served in Major Peck's Co. in 1762.

DRISCO, James   Served in Capt. Jenckes' Co. in 1757.

DRISKILL, Philip   Served in Capt. Brown's Co. in 1758 and
1759, and in Capt. Russell's Co. in 1760, and at
Havana in 1762.

DRUMMER, John   Served on Privateer George of Newport in
1758.

DUETT, Israel   Served on Privateer George of Newport in
1758.

DUNBAR, Archibald   Served in campaigns of 1761 and 1762.

    Robert   Served on Privateer George of Newport in 1757,
    and served as Master on same vessel in 1758.

DUNCAN, Daniel   Served on Privateer George of Newport in
1757, and as Captain's Quartermaster of same vessel
in 1758.

    James of Newport   Commander of Privateer Defiance in
    1762.

DUNHAM, Benjamin   Appointed 1st Lieutenant of Capt. Belcher's Co. in 1756.

    Benjamin of Newport   Marched on alarm of Aug. 1757.

    John   Served in Capt. Belcher's Co. in 1756, and in Capt.
    J. Whiting's Co. in 1757.

    Paul   Served in Capt. J. Whiting's Co. in 1757.

DUNLOP, James   Enlisted in H. M. regular army in 1762.

DUNN, Felix   Served in Col. Harris' Regt. in 1760.

    Joseph   Served in Capt. J. Whiting's Co. in 1757.

    William   Enlisted at Newport for campaign of 1762.

DUNSCOMB, John   2nd Lieutenant on Privateer General Johnson in 1757.

DUNTON, Ebenezer of Newport   Marched on alarm of Aug.
1757.

DURFEE, Benjamin   Served in Capt. J. Whiting's Co. in 1757,
and enlisted at Newport for campaign of 1762.

DWYER, Edward   Enlisted in H. M. regular army Jan. 8, 1763.

    John   Served on Privateer George of Newport in 1758.

DYE, Daniel   Served in Col. Babcock's Co. in 1758.

DYER, Abijah   Served in Capt. Kimball's Co. in 1761.

DYER

Edward of North Kingstown   Commander of Privateer Dove of Newport in 1762.

James of East Greenwich   Served in Capt. Fry's Co. in 1756.

Oliver   Served in Col. Harris' Regt. in 1760.

Samuel   Served in Col. Harris' Regt. in 1760.

Samuel, Jr.   Served in Col. Harris' Regt. in 1760.

Samuel of Cranston   Served as hostler on alarm of Aug. 1757.

ESTEN, see ASTEN.

EAKIN, James   Served in Capt. J. Whiting's Co. in 1757.

EARLE, Benjamin   Served in Capt. J. Whiting's Co. in 1757.

EAST, Caleb of Exeter (Indian)   Served in Capt. Greene's Co. in 1757.

Christopher   Served at Fort Stanwix in 1761, and in Capt. Fry's Co. at Havana in 1762.

Edward   Served as gunner on Privateer George of Newport in 1758.

Edward   Served on Privateer George of Newport in 1758.

James of East Greenwich   Served in Capt. Wall's Co. in 1757, and in campaign of 1758.

Joseph   Served in Capt. Greene's Co. in 1757.

EASTON, Henry   Served in campaign of 1761.

Jack   Served on Privateer George of Newport in 1758.

Job of Newport   Served on Privateer George of Newport in 1757, 1st Lieutenant on same vessel in 1758, became Commander of same vessel in 1758, and Commander of Privateer Diana of Newport in 1761 and 1762.

John   Commander of Privateer Africa of Newport in 1756, and 1762 (Sh).

Nicholas   Member of councils of war in 1762.

Peleg of Newport   Commander of Privateer Rabbit of Newport in 1758.

Richard   Member of council of war 11 March 1757.

Simeon   Enlisted at Newport for campaign of 1762.

William   Served on Privateer George of Newport in 1757.

EBER, John, alias PLACE, Eber, q. v.

EDDY, Barnard of Providence Volunteered on alarm of Aug.
1757.

Benjamin Served in Col. Hopkins' Regt. in 1756, as 1st
Lieutenant of Capt. Jenckes' Co. in 1758, and as Captain of 9th Co. in 1759.

Caleb Served in campaign of 1759.

Eliphalet Served in Capt. Kimball's Co. in 1761.

John Served in campaign of 1762.

Joseph Served in campaigns of 1760 and 1762.

Lewis Served in Lt. Col. Angell's Co. in 1756, in Capt.
Jenckes' Co. in 1758, and as drummer in campaign
of 1759.

EDWARDS, John Served in Capt. Jenckes' Co. in 1757.

Joseph of Newport Marched on alarm of Aug. 1757.

Pain Served in Capt. Russell's Co. at Havana in 1762.

Peleg Served in Capt. Russell's Co. in 1760, and in campaign of 1762.

William Served in campaign of 1760.

EGGLESTON, Hezekiah Served on Privateer George of Newport in 1757.

Joseph Served in campaign of 1762.

ELDRED, ELDRIDGE. Also see ALDRICH.

Anthony Served in campaign of 1758.

Benjamin Served on Privateer Defiance of Newport in
1756.

Casey Served in Col. Rose's Regt. in 1762.

Daniel Enlisted at Newport for campaign of 1762.

Henry of Exeter Served in Capt. Greene's Co. in 1757.

Holden of S. Kingstown Marched on alarm of Aug.
1757.

Job Served in campaign of 1762.

John Served in campaigns of 1758 and 1761.

Sylvester of Exeter Served in Capt. Greene's Co. in 1757.

William Appointed 2nd Lieutenant of Capt. Rose's Co.
in 1760, and 1st Lieutenant of Lt. Col. Rose's Co. in
1761.

ELLIOT, Robert of Newport Commander of Privateer Success of Newport in 1757 (Sh), and Commander of Privateer Katherine of Newport in 1758.

ELLISON, James Clerk on Privateer Blackbird in 1762.

William Enlisted at Newport as a seaman in 1762.

EMERSON, William Served in Capt. Jenckes' Co. in 1757.

ENGLAND, Philip Served on Privateer Defiance of Newport in 1756.

ENGLISH, George Enlisted at Newport for campaign of 1762.

William Enlisted at Newport as a seaman in 1762.

ENOS,

EANOSS, Ichabod Served in Capt. Russell's Co. in 1760.

Jesse Served in Capt. Russell's Co. in 1760.

EPHRAIM, Toby of Exeter Marched on alarm of Aug. 1757.

ESTERBROOK, Nathaniel Served in Major Peck's Co. in 1762.

Thomas of Warren Marched on alarm of Aug. 1757.

ESTLICK, John Enlisted in H. M. regular army 10 Jan. 1763.

Samuel of Warren Served in Lt. Col. Angell's Co. in 1756, marched on alarm of Aug. 1757, and enlisted in H. M. regular army 4 Jan. 1763.

EVANS, Charles Enlisted at Newport as a seaman in 1762.

EWIN, John of Newport Marched on alarm of Aug. 1757.

EXCEEN, Benjamin Enlisted at Newport for campaign of 1762.

Jonathan Served in Capt. Belcher's Co. in 1756, and in Capt. J. Whiting's Co. in 1757.

EYRES, John Enlisted at Newport for campaign of 1762, and in H. M. regular army 1 Dec. 1762.

FAIRBANKS, Jeremiah Served as cooper on Privateer George of Newport in 1758.

Jonathan Served in Capt. Jenckes' Co. in 1758, and in campaign of 1759.

FAIRBROTHER, Lovell Served in Capt. Kimball's Co. in 1761.

FAIRFIELD, W. Served in campaign of 1762.

FAIRMAN, Jonathan Served in campaign of 1761.

FARRELL, Peter L. Served on Privateer George of Newport in 1758.

FAULKNER, Nicholas of Little Compton   Marched on alarm of
      Aug. 1757.
FEFERANVON, James   Enlisted at Newport as a seaman in
      1762.
FELIX, Malkiah   Served in Capt. J. Whiting's Co. in 1757.
   Thomas   Served in Capt. Jenckes' Co. in 1758.
FENNER, Arthur, Jr., of Cranston   Served in Capt. Jenckes'
      Co. in 1757, and 1758; Ensign in Capt. Burkett's Co.
      in 1759 and so appointed in 1760, but did not serve;
      2nd Lieutenant in Capt. Kimball's Co. in 1761.
   Jeremiah   Served as Ensign in Capt. Peck's Co. in 1760.
   John of Providence   Marched as Lieutenant on alarm of
      Aug. 1757.
   Stephen   Served in Col. Harris' Regt. in 1760, and in
      campaign of 1761.
FENNING, Nathaniel   Served in Capt. Belcher's Co. in 1756.
FERGUSON, John   Served in Capt. J. Whiting's Co. in 1757.
FIELD, Anthony of Smithfield   Marched on alarm of Aug.
      1757.
FINCH, Henry of Smithfield   Marched on alarm of Aug. 1757.
FINKES, William   Served in campaign of 1760.
FISH, Caleb of Warwick   Marched on alarm of Aug. 1757.
   Isaac of North Kingstown   Served in Capt. Greene's Co.
      in 1757, and in Capt. E. Whiting's Co. in 1758.
   Jonathan of Portsmouth   Marched on alarm of Aug. 1757.
FISHER, Peter   Enlisted at Newport as a seaman in 1762.
   Richard of North Kingstown   Served in Capt. Greene's
      Co. in 1757, and in Col. Rose's Regt. in 1762.
FISK, Jonathan of Cranston   Marched on alarm of Aug. 1757.
   Joshua of Newport   Marched on alarm of Aug. 1757.
   Josiah   Served in Capt. Jenckes' Co. in 1756.
FITCH, Theophilus   Served in Capt. E. Whiting's Co. in 1759.
FLANAGAN, Patrick   Served at Fort George, R. I., in 1758,
      and enlisted at Newport for campaign of 1762.
FLOOD, John   Enlisted in H. M. regular army 4 Jan. 1763.
FLY, Edward   Served in Col. Babcock's Co. in 1758.
FLYNN, William   Served in Capt. Russell's Co. in 1760.
FLYNG,

FOLDS, William Augustus   Served in Lt. Col. Hargill's Co. at Havana in 1762.

FOLLETT, Joseph of Providence   Marched on alarm of Aug. 1757, and served as a Sergeant in 1761.

FONDERCLOIN, Henderick   Enlisted at Newport for campaign of 1762.

FONES, Daniel of North Kingstown   Commander of Privateer Defiance of Newport in 1756 and 1757. and of Privateer Success of Newport in 1760.

    John   Served in Capt. Fry's Co. in 1760, served in campaign of 1761, and in winter service under Col. Whiting in 1761-62.

    John (son of James)   Enlisted in Col. Rose's Regt. in 1762.

    John (son of John)   Served in 1763.

    Samuel   Served in Col. Rose's Regt. in 1762.

FOOTE, Garret   Enlisted in H. M. regular army in 1762.

FORD, Amos   Served in campaign of 1762.

    William   Served on Privateer Defiance of Newport in 1756.

    William   Served in Capt. Kimball's Co. in 1761.

FOREST, Anthony   Served on Privateer Defiance of Newport in 1756.

FORTIN, Thomas   Served in Capt. Fry's Co. at Havana in 1762.

FOSTER, Caleb   Served in Capt. Greene's Co. in 1757, and in campaign of 1762.

    John   Served as Ensign in Major Burkett's Co. in 1760.

    Jonathan of Hopkinton   Marched on alarm of Aug. 1757.

    Jonathan   Served in campaign of 1762.

    Josiah   Served in Capt. Potter's Co. in 1756, and in Col. Harris' Regt. in 1760.

FOWLER, James   Served in Capt. Rose's Co. in 1758.

    Simeon   Served in Col. Babcock's Co. in 1758 and 1759.

FRANAM, Jonathan   Served in Capt. Kimball's Co. in 1761.

FRANCIS, Abraham   Captain of 4th Co. in 1755.

    Nathan   Served on Privateer Defiance of Newport in 1756.

FRANKS, Amos   Served in Col. Babcock's Co. in 1758 and 1759.
FRANCK,

> James of Providence   Marched on alarm of Aug. 1757.
> Prentice   Served in Col. Babcock's Co. in 1758 and 1759.
> Philip   Served in Lt. Col. Angell's Co. in 1756.
> Rufus   Served in Capt. J. Whiting's Co. in 1757, in Capt. Jenckes' Co. in 1758, in campaign of 1759, in Col. Harris' Regt. in 1760, at Fort Stanwix in 1761, and in campaign of 1762.
> Samuel   Served in Col. Harris' Co. in 1756, and in Col. Harris' Regt. in 1760.

FRANKLIN, Moses   Served in Col. Harris' Regt. in 1760.
FRAZER, Hugh   Enlisted in H. M. regular army in 1762.
FRAZIER,

> Isaac of N. Kingstown   Served in Capt. Greene's Co. in 1757.
> John   Served in Col. Rose's Regt. in 1762.
> John   Enlisted at Newport as a seaman in 1762.
> Thomas of South Kingstown   Marched on alarm of Aug. 1757.
> Thomas   Served in Capt. Hopkins' Co. in 1760 and died at Cold Spring 14 Jan. 1761.
> Thomas   Served in Col. Rose's Regt. in 1762.

FREEBODY, Samuel   Member of councils of war in 1756 and 1762.
FREEMAN, Jedediah of Rehoboth   Served in Col. Hopkins' Regt. in 1756, and in Major Peck's Co. in 1762.

> John   Served in Major Peck's Co. in 1762.
> Nathan of Smithfield   Served in Capt. Jenckes' Co. in 1756, marched on alarm of Aug. 1757, and served in campaign of 1759.
> Samuel   Served in Capt. Peck's Co. in 1761.

FRENCH, Abner   Enlisted in H. M. regular army in 1762.
FRIEND, Gabriel of Warwick   Marched on alarm of Aug. 1757, and served in Capt. Hawkins' Co. in 1762.
FROST, Amos   Served in Capt. Jenckes' Co. in 1757.

> Simon of Smithfield   Marched on alarm of Aug. 1757, and served in campaign of 1759.

FRY, Absalom   Enlisted at Newport for campaign of 1762.

James of South Kingstown   Marched on alarm of Aug. 1757.

Oliver of East Greenwich   Served in Lt. Col. Angell's Co. in 1756, marched on alarm of Aug. 1757, and served in Capt. Fry's Co. at Havana in 1762.

Thomas, Jr.   Captain in Col. Harris' Regt. in 1756; served in campaign of 1757, Captain in Col. Babcock's Regt. in 1759, Captain in Col. Harris' Regt. in 1760, Captain-Lieutenant of Col. Whiting's Co. in 1761, special detached command in June 1761, Captain of 5th Co. at Havana in 1762.

Thomas, 3rd   Served in Capt. Fry's Co. at Havana in 1762.

FULLER, Caleb   Served in Capt. Potter's Co. in 1756.

David   Served in Col. Hopkins' Regt. in 1756.

Ezekiel   Served in Capt. Jenckes' Co. in 1758.

Ichabod   Served in Capt. Jenckes' Co. in 1756.

Joseph   Served in Lt. Col. Angell's Co. in 1756.

(———)   Served in campaign of 1759.

FURBAR, James   Served on Privateer Defiance of Newport in 1756.

GAESARD, John   Served in Capt. Wall's Co. in 1757.

GALLUP, Ben Adam   Served at Fort Stanwix in 1761, and in Lt. Col. Hargill's Co. at Havana in 1762.

Richard of W. Greenwich   Served in Capt. Wall's Co. in 1757.

Richard   Served in Capt. J. Whiting's Co. in 1757.

Richard   Served in campaign of 1760, and at Fort Stanwix in 1761.

Samuel   Served in Lt. Col. Hargill's Co. at Havana in 1762.

GALLOWAY, James of Cumberland   Marched on alarm of Aug. 1757.

John   Served in campaign of 1758.

GAMMON, Ezekiel   Drafted on alarm of Aug. 1757.

GARDNER,
GARDINER, Benjamin   Served in Col. Rose's Regt. in 1762.
> Caleb, Jr., of Newport   Marched as Lieutenant on alarm of Aug. 1757; member of council of war 28 Apr. 1760.
>
> Daniel   Served in campaign of 1762.
>
> George, Jr.   Served in campaign of 1755, appointed Captain in 1756, and again in 1757, but was superseded in Feb. 1757 by Ebenezer Whiting.
>
> Henry   Served in Col. Rose's Regt. in 1762.
>
> John   Deputy Governor from Sept. 1756 to 1763, member of committee of war in 1756, 1757, 1759 and 1760, member of councils of war in 1756, 1757, 1758, 1759, 1760, 1761, and 1762.
>
> John of Newport   Marched as hostler on alarm of Aug. 1757.
>
> Joseph of Newport   Commander of Privateer Prussian Hero in 1755, 1756, and 1759.
>
> Joshua   Served in Capt. Russell's Co. in 1760.
>
> Nicholas of Exeter   Member of committee of war in 1759 and 1760.
>
> Robert   Served on Privateer Blackbird in 1762.
>
> Sanford of Newport   Marched on alarm of Aug. 1757.
>
> Silas of Warwick   Marched as Capt. on alarm of Aug. 1757.
>
> William, Jr.   Appointed 1st Lieutenant of Capt. Richmond's Co. in Oct. 1756.
>
> William Thurston   Deputy Commissary of Col. Harris' Regt. in 1756.

GARRAT, Daniel   Served in Capt. J. Whiting's Co. in 1757.
GARZIA, John of Newport   Marched on alarm of Aug. 1757.
GAVAYS, Richard   Served in campaign of 1760.
GAVETT, William   Served as Ensign in Col. Babcock's Co. in 1758, and as Lieutenant in campaign of 1759.
GAZETTE, John of East Greenwich   Served in Capt. Daniel
GARZITTE,   Wall's Co. in 1757.
GORZET,
GEORGE, John   Served in Capt. Fry's Co. in 1762.

GEORGE

Joshua of North Kingstown (mulatto)   Served in Capt. Greene's Co. in 1757, in Lt. Col. Potter's Co. in 1758, and in Col. Rose's Regt. in 1762.

Nicholas   Served on Privateer George of Newport in 1758, and on H. M. S. Pembroke in 1759.

GEVIN, James   Served on Privateer George of Newport in 1757.

GIBBONS, George   Served in Col. Babcock's Co. in 1758.

John   Enlisted at Newport for campagin of 1762.

GIBBS, Abel   Served in Lt. Col. Angell's Co. in 1756, and as Ensign in Capt. Wall's Co. in 1757.

Alexander   Served on Privateer Defiance of Newport in 1756.

Josiah, Jr., of Coventry   Marched on alarm of Aug. 1757.

GIFFORD, Stephen, Jr., of Tiverton   Marched on alarm of Aug. 1757.

(An Indian slave belonging to William Gifford of Tiverton)   Served in campaign of 1756.

GIGGER, Nicholas   Served in Capt. J. Whiting's Co. in 1757.

GILBERT, Phineas   Served on Privateer George of Newport in 1758.

GILLIS, Alexander   Enlisted at Newport for campaign of 1762.

GINNEDO, Lewis   Served in Capt. J. Whiting's Co. in 1757.

GLADDING, Charles   Served in Capt. E. Whiting's Co. in 1757.

Joseph, Jr.   Served in Capt. Belcher's Co. in 1756.

Solomon of Newport   Marched on alarm of Aug. 1757.

GODDARD, Beriah   Served as ship-carpenter at Oswego in 1756, captured by the French 14 Aug. 1756.

Thomas   Served as ship-carpenter at Oswego in 1756, captured by the French 14 Aug. 1756.

GODFREY, Cuff (colored)   Served on Privateer George of Newport in 1757.

Samuel   Served on Privateer Defiance of Newport in 1756.

GOFF, Comfort   Served in Capt. Potter's Co. in 1756.

GOLDTHWAIT, Stephen of Smithfield   Marched on alarm of Aug. 1757.

GOODBIT, John   Served in Col. Rose's Regt. in 1762.
GOODBID,
GOODSELL, Levi   Served in Campaign of 1762.
GOODSPEED, Nathaniel   Served in campaigns of 1760 and 1762.
GOODWILL, John of Hopkinton   Marched on alarm of Aug.
    1757.
GORDON, John   Served as Ensign of Lt. Col. Whiting's Co. in
    1760.
    William   Served in campaign of 1756.
GORHAM, Jabez of Providence   Marched on alarm of Aug.
    1757.
GORTON, Israel, Jr., of Cranston   Marched as Captain on alarm
    of Aug. 1757.
    Joseph   Served at Fort George, R. I., in 1758.
    Othniel of Warwick   Marched on alarm of Aug. 1757.
GOULD, John   Served in Capt. J. Whiting's Co. in 1757.
    Nathaniel of Cumberland   Marched on alarm of Aug.
    1757.
    Prince   Served in Col. Harris' Regt. in 1756, in Capt. J.
    Whiting's Co. in 1757, in Capt. Jenckes' Co. in 1758,
    in campaign of 1759, and in Capt. Hawkins' Co.
    in 1762.
    Prince   Served on Privateer George of Newport in 1758.
GOWING, Timothy of Smithfield   Marched on alarm of Aug.
GOWN,   1757.
GRAFTON, William   Served on Privateer George of Newport in
    1757.
GRAHAM, Alexander   Served in Major Peck's Co. in 1762.
    Richard   Enlisted at Newport for campaign of 1762.
    Robert   Served in Capt. Russell's Co. in 1760.
GRANT, Charles   Enlisted at Newport for campaign of 1762.
    Morris   Served in Capt. J. Whiting's Co. in 1757.
GRAY, Daniel   Served as armorer on Privateer George of New-
        port in 1757.
    Edward of Little Compton   Served as Lieutenant in Capt.
        Babcock's Co. in 1755, and marched as Lieutenant on
        alarm of Aug. 1757.

GRAY

Joseph   Served on Privateer Defiance of Newport in 1756.

Robert   Enlisted at Newport as a seaman in 1762.

GREATRICKS, Sylvanus   Served in campaign of 1761.

GREATREX,

GREENE, Abel   Served in Col. Harris' Regt. in 1760, and in Lt. Col. Hargill's Co. at Havana in 1762.

Amos, Jr., of Charlestown   Marched on alarm of Aug. 1757.

Benjamin of W. Greenwich   Served in Capt. Fry's Co. in 1756, in Capt. Jenckes' Co. in 1758 and in campaign of 1759.

Daniel   Served in Col. Rose's Regt. in 1762.

Edward   Served in campaign of 1761, and in Capt. Fry's Co. in 1762.

Elias   Served in Capt. Fry's Co. at Havana in 1762.

Henry of Cranston   Served in Col. Hopkin's Regt. in 1756, and marched on alarm of Aug. 1757.

Isaac of Coventry   Marched on alarm of Aug. 1757.

James of Coventry (Lieutenant)   Marched on alarm of Aug. 1757.

Jeremiah   Served as Captain of 4th Co. in Col. Angell's Regt. in 1757.

Jeremiah   Served in Capt. Wall's Co. in 1757.

Jeremiah of West Greenwich   Served in Capt. Fry's Co. in 1756.

Job   Served in Col. Rose's Regt. in 1762.

John of North Kingstown   Marched as Ensign on alarm of Aug. 1757.

John of Coventry (son of James)   Marched on alarm of Aug. 1757.

John   Served in Col. Babcock's Co. in 1759.

John   Served in Capt. Peck's Co. in 1761.

Josias   Served in Capt. E. Whiting's Co. in 1759.

Lewis   Served in campaign of 1761, and in Capt. Fry's Co. at Havana in 1762.

Peleg   Served in Capt. Fry's Co. at Havana in 1762.

Philip   Served in Col. Harris' Regt. in 1760.

GREENE

Reuben   Served on Privateer George of Newport in 1757.

Robert   Served in Col. Harris' Regt. in 1760.

Samuel   Served in Col. Harris' Regt. in 1756.

Thomas   Member of committee of war in 1758, 1759 and 1760.

Thomas of Warwick   Marched as Lieutenant on alarm of Aug. 1757.

Thomas of Warwick (Captain)   Marched as hostler on alarm of Aug. 1757.

Thomas   Served in Capt. Peck's Co. in 1761.

Usual   Served in Col. Harris's Regt. in 1760.

William   Governor in 1757 and 1758, commissioner to wait upon the Earl of Loudon in 1758.

William of Newport   Volunteered and marched on alarm of Aug. 1757, served in Capt. Brown's Co. in 1759, and in campaign of 1760.

GREENMAN, Edward of Charlestown   Marched on alarm of Aug. 1757, and served in campaign of 1762.

Ephraim   Served in Capt. J. Whiting's Co. in 1758.

Negro   Served in campaign of 1762.   Probably identical with

Pomp (i. e., Pompey?)   Served in Capt. Russell's Co. in 1762, and died at Havana 6 Sept. 1762.

Silas of Charlestown   Marched on alarm of Aug. 1757.

William of South Kingstown   Marched on alarm of Aug. 1757.

(GRINMAN, —?—)   Boatswain on Privateer Duke of Marlborough in 1758.

GREENWOOD, John, Jr.   Sergeant in Capt. Peck's Co. in 1761 and 1762.

Nathaniel   Sergeant in Capt. Peck's Co. in 1761 and 1762.

GREGORY, Henry   1st Lieutenant on Privateer Duke of Marlborough in 1758.

GRIEVE, Archibald   Served in Capt. Fry's Co. at Havana in 1762.

GRIFFITH, George   Served in campaign of 1762.

GRINALD, Isaac   Served at Fort Stanwix in 1761, and in Lt. Col. Hargill's Co. at Havana in 1762.

GRINNELL, Malachi   Served on Privateer George of Newport in 1757.

Matthew of East Greenwich   Marched on alarm of Aug. 1757.

Stephen   Served in Capt. Russell's Co. in 1760.

Zebedee of Newport   Commander of Privateer Unity of Newport in 1760, and 1762 (Sh).

GROMOCK, Peter of East Greenwich   Served in Capt. Wall's Co. in 1757.

GROVER, Amasa   Served in campaign of 1760.

Eleazer   Served in campaigns of 1758 and 1759.

Penuel   Served in campaign of 1760.

Silas   Served in campaign of 1760.

GUIN, Agnis   Boatswain on Privateer General Johnson in 1757.

GULLY, Stephen   Served in Col. Harris's Regt. in 1756.

GURNSEY, Ezekiel   Served in Col. Harris' Regt. in 1760, and in Capt. Kimball's Co. in 1761.

GWIN, James   Served in campaign of 1757.

GYLES, Bartholomew   Enlisted in H. M. regular army in 1762.

Jacob   Served as a seaman in campaign of 1762.

HACKER, Caleb   Appointed Ensign of Capt. Whiting's Co. in 1755, but refused to serve.   Appointed Adjutant of Col. Hopkins' Regt. in 1756; commissioned Adjutant in May 1757 and served as Adjutant on alarm of Aug. 1757.   Succeeded Potter as Captain of the 9th Co. in 1758, but left his command in Aug. 1758.

George   Served on Privateer George of Newport in 1757.

HACKES, Jonathan   Served in Capt. Rose's Co. in 1758, and in Col. Babcock's Co. in 1759.

HADSAIL, Jonathan   Served in campaign of 1762.

HAINIS, John   Served in Capt. Potter's Co. in 1756.

HALL, Benjamin (son of Nathaniel)   Appointed Lieutenant of Capt. Whiting's Co. in 1755.

HALL

Benjamin Served in Capt. Peck's Co. in 1761.

Clarke of Newport Marched on alarm of Aug. 1757.

George Served in Capt. Wall's Co. in 1757.

Isaac of Newport Marched on alarm of Aug. 1757.

James Served in campaign of 1761, in winter service of 1761-62, and enlisted in H. M. regular army in 1762.

(———, son of Thomas) Served in campaign of 1762.

John Served in campaign of 1762.

Joseph Served in Capt. J. Whiting's Co. in 1758, in Capt. E. Whiting's Co. in 1759, and in Capt. Russell's Co. in 1760.

Joshua Enlisted in H. M. regular army in 1762.

Robin Served in campaign of 1760.

Stephen Served in Capt. E. Whiting's Co. in 1757, and in Col. Babcock's Co. in 1759.

Sylvester Served in Capt. Rose's Co. in 1758, and in campaign of 1762.

Timothy Served in Capt. Russell's Co. in 1760

Tucker Served in Capt. Russell's Co. in 1762 and died at Havana 19 Sept. 1762.

Valentine Served in campaign of 1762.

William of Newport Marched on alarm of Aug. 1757.

HALLETT, Daniel Served at Fort George, R. I. in 1762.

HALLOWAY, Joseph Commissary and Sutler of Col. Babcock's Regt. in 1759.

Thomas Served as seaman at Oswego in 1756 and was taken prisoner by the French.

HAM, Weymouth Served in Capt. Jenckes' Co. in 1758, and as Sergeant in campaign of 1759.

HAMBLETON, Benedict of East Greenwich Marched in Capt.

HAMILTON, Sheffield's Co. on alarm of Aug. 1757, and served in Col. Rose's Regt. in 1762.

John Served in Capt. Jenckes' Co. in 1758, and in Major Peck's Co. in 1762.

Patrick of Newport Marched on alarm of Aug. 1757.

HAMBLIN, Elisha Served in campaign of 1759.

John Enlisted at Newport for campaign of 1762.

HAMBLIN

Nathaniel   Enlisted at Newport for campaign of 1762.

HAMILTON, see HAMBLETON.

HAMMER, Charles of Westerly   Marched on alarm of Aug. 1757.

>   Daniel   Served in Capt. E. Whiting's Co. in 1758.

>   James   Served in Capt. Russell's Co. in 1760, and in 1762; and died at Havana 26 Aug. 1762.

HAMMETT, Malachi   Served in Capt. Fry's Co. at Havana in 1762.

HAMMOND, Amos   Appointed Capt. of 6th Co. in Col. Harris' Regt. in Aug. 1755, and Captain of 10th Co. in Feb. 1756, but was discharged 1 Sept. 1756.

>   John   Served in Major Peck's Co. at Fort Stanwix in 1762.

>   John   Served on Privateer George of Newport in 1757 and 1758.

>   Thomas of Cranston   Marched on alarm of Aug. 1757.

>   Thomas   Served in Capt. Belcher's Co. in 1756.

>   William, Jr., of Cranston   Marched on alarm of Aug. 1757.

HANES, see HAYNES.

HARDEN, John   Carpenter on Privateer Roby in 1759.

HARDING, Joseph   Second Mate on Privateer George of Newport in 1758.

>   Joseph   Served in campaign of 1760.

HARDIE,

HARDY, John   Enlisted at Newport as seaman in 1762.

>   William   Served in campaign of 1761, and winter service of 1761-62.

HARGILL, Christopher   Lieutenant in Capt. Bosworth's Co. in 1755, and 1756; appointed 1st Lieutenant in Capt. Gardner's Co. in 1757, but was superseded on March 19, 1757.   Appointed Captain in 1759, and 1760, Major of Col. Whiting's Regt. in 1761, and Lieutenant Colonel of Col. Rose's Regt. in 1762, being in command of the detachment of that regiment which served at the capture of Havana.

HARKNESS, George   Served in Capt. Belcher's Co. in 1756, and enlisted at Newport for campaign of 1762.

HARRINGTON, see HERRENDEN.

HARRIS, Andrew of Cranston   Marched on alarm of Aug. 1757.

Charles   Served in campaign of 1761.

Christopher   Colonel of Rhode Island Regiment in campaigns of 1755, 1756 and 1760.

Christopher   Served in campaigns of 1758 and 1759.

George   Enlisted at Newport and served as A. B. seaman on H. M. S. Pembroke in 1759. Died in 1760.

George   Enlisted at Newport as a seaman in 1762.

James of Cranston   Marched on alarm of Aug. 1757.

John   Served in Col. Harris' Regt. in 1756.

Nathaniel of Providence   Marched on alarm of Aug. 1757.

Primus   Served in Capt. J. Whiting's Co. in 1757.

Samuel   Served in campaign of 1760.

Zachariah   Served on Privateer Defiance of Newport in 1756.

HARRISON, Peter (Captain)   Appointed on committee to prepare a plan of the harbor of Newport and a profile of Fort George in 1755.

HART, Anthony   Served on Privateer George of Newport in 1758.

Joseph of Portsmouth   Marched on alarm of Aug. 1757.

Peleg   Served in Col. Babcock's Co. in 1759 and 1760.

Robert   Served as a seaman at Oswego in 1756 and was taken prisoner by the French. Later he served on a privateer under Capt. Brown.

Smiton of Tiverton   Marched on alarm of Aug. 1757.

HARVEY, Edward of Charlestown   Marched on alarm of Aug.
HARVIE,   1757, and served in Capt. Brown's Co. in 1759.

James   Served in Capt. J. Whiting's Co. in 1758, and in Capt. E. Whiting's Co. in 1759.

John   Served in campaign of 1761.

Joseph   Served in Capt. Brown's Co. in 1759, in Capt. Russell's Co. in 1760, and in campaign of 1762.

HASTINGS, Daniel   Served in Capt. Russell's Co. in 1760.

James   Gunner at Fort George, R. I., in 1755 and 1756.

Jonathan   Served in Capt. J. Whiting's Co. in 1758.

HATHAWAY, Caleb of Warwick Marched on alarm of Aug. 1757.

Jeremiah Served in campaign of 1758.

HATHORN, William Enlisted at Newport as a seaman in 1762.

HASSARD, see HAZARD.

HAVENS, Cornelius Served in Capt. Jenckes' Co. in 1756, and
HEAVENS, in campaign of 1759.

Silas of West Greenwich Served in Col. Hopkins' Regt. in 1756, in Capt. Wall's Co. in 1757, enlisted at Newport for campaign of 1762, and enlisted in H. M. regular army in Nov. 1762.

Simon Served in campaign of 1759.

HAWKINS, Abraham of Providence Served in Capt. Jenckes' Co. in 1756, marched on alarm of Aug. 1757, served in campaign of 1760, 2nd Lieutenant in Capt. Peck's Co. in 1761, and Captain of 4th Co. in 1762.

Daniel of Providence Marched on alarm of Aug. 1757.

Hazabiah Drummer in Capt. Hawkins' Co. in 1762.

Jeremiah Master on Privateer Roby in 1759.

Jeremiah Served in campaign of 1761.

Job of Providence Marched on alarm of Aug. 1757.

John of Providence Marched on alarm of Aug. 1757.

HAWKS, John of Smithfield Served in Capt. Jenckes' Co. in
HAWKE, 1757 and in Capt. Russell's Co. at Havana in 1762.

Uriah of Smithfield Served in Lt. Col. Angell's Co. in 1756, in Capt. Jenckes' Co. in 1757, in campaigns of 1758 and 1759, in Col. Harris' Regt. in 1760, in campaign of 1761, and in Lt. Col. Hargill's Co. in 1762.

HAYNES, John Served on Privateer Defiance of Newport in
HANES, 1756.

John Enlisted in H. M. regular army 7 Jan. 1762.

HAZARD, Harry of Richmond (Indian) Marched on alarm of
HASSARD, Aug. 1757, served in Capt. J. Whiting's Co. in 1758, in Capt. E. Whiting's Co. in 1759, in Capt. Russell's Co. in 1760 and in Capt. Russell's Co. at Havana in 1762.

Joseph Member of committee of war in 1760.

HEALY, Ezra of Providence   Marched on alarm of Aug. 1757.
    Ithamar   Served in campaign of 1755, and in Major Peck's
        Co. in 1762.
    John   Served in Capt. Peck's Co. in 1761.
    Joseph   Served in Capt. Peck's Co. in 1761, and in Major
        Peck's Co. in 1762.
    Nathaniel   Served in Capt. Jenckes' Co. in 1758.
    William, Jr.   Served in campaign of 1761, and in Major
        Peck's Co. in 1762.
HEARN, Samuel   2nd Lieutenant in Capt. Babcock's Co. in
        1756, and 2nd Lieutenant in Capt. Greene's Co. in
        1757.
HEATHER, Francis   Enlisted at Newport as a seaman in 1762.
HEFFERMAN, William of Richmond   Marched on alarm of
HEFFERNAN,   Aug. 1757.
    Jeremiah of Newport   Volunteered and marched as En-
        sign on alarm of Aug. 1757.
HELME, Oliver   Appointed Commissary of Col. Harris' Regt.
        in 1760.
    William   Enlisted at Newport for campaign of 1762.
HELTON, see HILTON.
HENMAN, James   Served in campaign of 1762.
    John   Served as Sergeant in Capt. Russell's Co. in 1762
        at Havana.
HENRY, John of Westerly   Marched on alarm of Aug. 1757.
HERREN, Newman   Served as Corporal in Capt. Russell's Co.
        at Havana in 1762.
    Robert   Served in Capt. Russell's Co. in 1760.
HERRENDEN, Ananias of Smithfield   Served in Capt. Jenckes'
HARRINGTON,   Co. in 1757.
    Arthur   Served in Col. Harris's Co. in 1760.
    Baraciah   Served in Capt. Jenckes' Co. in 1758.
    Benjamin   Served in Capt. Greene's Co. in 1757, and in
        campaign of 1761.
    David   Served in Capt. Jenckes' Co. in 1756.
    Elisha   Served in campaign of 1760, and in Capt. Haw-
        kins' Co. in 1762.

HARRINGTON

Ezekiah   Served in campaign of 1759, and in Capt. Hawkins' Co. in 1762.

Hezekiah of Smithfield   Marched on alarm of Aug. 1757.

Israel of Smithfield   Served in Capt. Jenckes' Co. in 1757.

James   Served in campaign of 1759.

Jonathan   Served in Capt. Jenckes' Co. in 1756, and 1757, in campaign of 1758, and in Capt. Hawkins' Co. in 1762.

Newman   Served in Capt. Brown's Co. in 1759.

Obadiah   Served in Capt. Jenckes' Co. in 1758, and in campaigns of 1759 and 1762.

Othniel of Gloucester   Marched on alarm of Aug. 1757, and served in Col. Harris' Regt. in 1760.

Rufus   Served in Col. Harris' Regt. in 1760, in Capt. Kimball's Co. in 1761, and in Capt. Hawkins' Co. in 1762.

Stephen of Gloucester   Marched on alarm of Aug. 1757, and served in campaign of 1759.

Thomas of Smithfield   Served in Col. Harris' Regt. in 1756, in Capt. Jenckes' Co. in 1757, in campaigns of 1758, 1759 and 1761, and in Capt. Kimball's Co. in 1762.

William   2nd Lieutenant in Capt. Tew's Co. in 1762.

William   Served in campaign of 1759, in Capt. Kimball's Co. in 1761, in Capt. Hawkins' Co. in 1762, and enlisted in H. M. regular army in Oct. 1762.

HERRY, Andrew   Served in Capt. Russell's Co. in 1760.

Joseph   Served in Capt. Russell's Co. in 1760.

HEWES, John   Enlisted in H. M. regular army in 1762.

HEWETT, Joseph .   Served in Capt. E. Whiting's Co. in 1757, and 1758, and in Col. Rose's Regt. in 1762.

Reuben   Served in Col. Babcock's Co. in 1758 and 1759.

Silas   Served in Capt. E. Whiting's Co. in 1758 and 1759.

Simeon   Served in Capt. E. Whiting's Co. in 1758 and 1759.

HICKS,

HIX, Barney   Served in Capt. Jenckes' Co. in 1758.

HICKS

> Benjamin of Newport Commander of Privateer Conformation of Newport in 1758, and of Privateer Conformator in 1762 (Sh).
>
> David Enlisted at Newport for campaign of 1762.
>
> Jacob Enlisted at Newport for campaign of 1762.
>
> John Served on Privateer Defiance of Newport in 1756.
>
> Joseph Servèd in campaign of 1759.
>
> Robert Served in campaign of 1758, and in Capt. Fry's Co. at Havana in 1762.
>
> William Served at Fort Stanwix during winter of 1761-62.

HILL, Caleb Served in campaign of 1758, and in Capt. Tew's Co. in 1762.

> David Served in Capt. Jenckes' Co. in 1757.
>
> Jonathan Served in Capt. Fry's Co. in 1761, and in Capt. Tew's Co. in 1762.
>
> Joseph Served at Fort George, R. I., from 1756 to 1760.
>
> Samuel Served in campaigns of 1758 and 1762.
>
> Thomas Enlisted at Newport for campaign of 1762.
>
> Tom, alias Potter, q. v.

HILTON, Israel of Providence Served in Capt. Jenckes' Co. in 1756, and marched on alarm of Aug. 1757.

HINDALL, John Served in Capt. Kimball's Co. in 1761.

HINES,

HIND, Philemon Served in campaigns of 1758 and 1759.

> William Served in Capt. Tew's Co. in 1762.

HIRKMAN, John Served on Privateer George of Newport in 1758.

HISCOX, Simeon Served in Capt. Brown's Co. in 1759.

> Thomas Served in campaign of 1760.

HITT, Joseph of North Kingstown Marched on alarm of Aug. 1757.

HIX see HICKS.

HOAR, Edward Doctor on Privateer Blackbird in 1762.

> Hezekiah Served in campaign of 1762.
>
> John Enlisted at Newport for campaign of 1762.
>
> William Served in campaign of 1762.

HODGE, William of Jamestown   Marched on alarm of Aug. 1757.

HODGKINS, Ebenezer   Served in Col. Babcock's Co. in 1759.

HOGAN, Edmund   Served at Fort George, R. I., in 1762.

HOGG, Abraham of Smithfield   Served in Col. Harris' Regt. in 1756, marched on alarm of Aug. 1757, and served in campaigns of 1758 and 1760.

HOLDEN, Robert   Served on Privateer George of Newport in 1757.

HOLDREDGE, Daniel   Served in Col. Babcock's Co. in 1758 and 1759.

HOLLOWELL,

HOLLOWAY, Jonathan of South Kingstown   Marched on alarm

HOLLEY,   of Aug. 1757.

    John   Served in Col. Rose's Regt. in 1762.

HOLMES, Isaac   Served in Capt. E. Whiting's Co. in 1757.

HONYMAN, James   Member of councils of war in 1756, 1757, 1758, 1759, 1760 and 1761.   Appointed to wait upon the Earl of Loudon in Jan. 1757.

HOPER, Joseph   Served on Privateer Defiance of Newport in 1756.

HOPKINS, Benjamin   Served in campaign of 1758, and in Capt. Russell's Co. at Havana in 1762.

    Beriah   Ensign in Capt. Tew's Co. in 1762, and in charge of 2nd detachment, which went to Albany.

    Christopher of Providence   Commander of Privateer William in 1756, and of Privateer Prince George in 1757.

    George of Providence   Served in Col. Harris' Regt. in 1756, volunteered on alarm of Aug. 1757, and served on Privateer Providence in 1757 and 1758.

    Esek of Providence   Commander of a privateer in 1757.

    Henry   Served at Fort George, R. I., in 1756 and 1757, served in campaign of 1760, and in Lt. Col. Hargill's Co. in 1762.

    Isaac   Captain of Privateer (Providence?) in 1757.

    Joseph   Served at Fort George, R. I., in 1756.

    Lawton   Served in Capt. Tew's Co. in 1762.

HOPKINS

Robert of Exeter   Lieutenant of Capt. Bradford's Co. in 1755.

Robert   Lieutenant of Capt. Hopkins' Co. in 1755.

Robert   Lieutenant of Capt. Potter's Co. in 1758.

Robert   Enlisted for campaign of 1760 in Capt. Hopkins' Co.

Rufus   Commissary of Col. Harris' Regt. in 1756.

St. Jago   Served on Privateer Blackbird in 1762.

Stephen of Providence   Governor from May 1755 to May 1757, and from March 1758 to May 1762; member of committee of war in 1755, 1756 and 1757; commissioner to meet with commissioners of other Colonies in 1755, Colonel of 2nd Regiment in 1756, volunteered on alarm of Aug. 1757.

Thomas   Served at Fort George, R. I., in 1757.

Tibbitts   1st Lieutenant of Lt. Col. Wall's Co. in 1759, 1st Lieutenant and later Captain-Lieutenant of Col. Harris' Co. in 1760, and Captain of 6th Co. in 1761.

HORSEWELL, Josiah   Served in Capt. J. Whiting's Co. in 1757.

Luke of Little Compton   Marched on alarm of Aug. 1757.

HORTON, Ephraim   Served in campaign of 1761, and in Major Peck's Co. in 1762.

Job   Served in campaign of 1761, and in Major Peck's Co. in 1762.

HOTH, Richard, Jr., of Portsmouth   Marched on alarm of Aug. 1757.

Thomas of Portsmouth   Marched on alarm of Aug. 1757.

HOUGHTON, Nicholas   1st Lieutenant on Privateer General Johnson in 1757.

HOUSE, Christopher   Enlisted at Newport as A. B. seaman and served on H. M. S. Pembroke in 1759.

HOWARD, Benjamin of Warwick   Served in Capt. Potter's Co. in 1756, and in Capt. Wall's Co. in 1757.

Boutwill   Served on Privateer George of Newport in 1757.

Daniel of Gloucester   Marched on alarm of Aug. 1757.

Ebenezer   Served in Capt. Jenckes' Co. in 1756, and in campaigns of 1758, 1759 and 1761.

HOWARD

Henry   Served in Capt. E. Whiting's Co. in 1757, and in Capt. Brown's Co. in 1759.

Isaac   Served in Col. Harris' Regt. in 1760.

John of Cumberland   Marched on alarm of Aug. 1757, and served in campaign of 1762.

Robert   Served on Privateer George of Newport in 1757.

Samuel   Served in Capt. Jenckes' Co. in 1757.

Thomas   Served in Capt. Jenckes' Co. in 1758, and in campaign of 1759.

William   Served as boy on Privateer George of Newport in 1758.

HOWE, Estes of Newport   1st Lieutenant of Privateer Defiance of Newport in 1756, and Commander of Privateer Duke of Marlborough of Newport in 1758.

HOWELL, Thomas   Served in Capt. Belcher's Co. in 1756.

William   Served in Capt. Jenckes' Co. in 1757.

HOXSIE, Joseph   Served in Capt. Belcher's Co. in 1756.

HOYLE, John   Served in campaign of 1761.

HOYT, Jonathan   Served in Capt. Jenckes' Co. in 1757.

HUBBARD, John   Served on Privateer George of Newport in 1757.

John   Served as boy on Privateer George of Newport in 1757.

HUDSON, Daniel   Served in campaigns of 1758, 1759, 1760 and 1761.

Henry   Served in campaign of 1759.

Reuben of Warren   Served in Capt. Peck's Co. in 1758 and 1759.

Thomas   Served in Capt. Greene's Co. in 1757.

Thomas of Newport   Marched on alarm of Aug. 1757.

HULL, Joseph (colored)   Served on Privateer George of Newport in 1757.

Samuel   Served in Capt. J. Whiting's Co. in 1758.

HUMPHREYS, Abijah   Enlisted in H. M. regular army in 1762.

HUNT, Benjamin   Served in campaign of 1757.

Ebenezer   Served in Capt. Fry's Co. in 1762.

Ezekiel   Served in Col. Harris' Regt. in 1760.

HUNT

Job   Served in Capt. E. Whiting's Co. in 1757, and in campaign of 1758, being wounded at Ticonderoga.

John of Newport   Voluntered and marched on alarm of Aug. 1757.

Samuel   Served in Col. Harris' Regt. in 1756 and 1760.

HUNTER, James   Served in Col. Harris' Regt. in 1756, and in Capt. Jenckes' Co. in 1758.

William   Surgeon in Col. Harris' Regt. in 1755, and in campaigns of 1756, 1757 and 1758.

HUTCHINSON, John   Served in campaign of 1760.

HUTCHISON, Joseph   Enlisted at Newport as a seaman in 1762.

HUTTEN, Alexander   Enlisted at Newport for campaign of 1762.

IDE, John of Smithfield   Marched on alarm of Aug. 1757, served in Capt. Jenckes' Co. in 1758, and as Sergeant in campaign of 1759.

INGRAHAM, Hezekiah   Served in Capt. E. Whiting's Co. in 1758 and 1759.

John   Served on Privateer George of Newport in 1758.

Timothy of Newport   Marched as Ensign on alarm of Aug. 1757, and was member of councils of war in 1762.

(Jeremiah Ingraham's apprentice)   Marched on alarm of Aug. 1757.

INMAN, Abraham Served in Capt. Jenckes' Co. in 1757.

Elisha of Scituate   Served in Capt. Jenckes' Co. in 1757, in Capt. Rose's Co. in 1758, and in Col. Rose's Regt. in 1762.

John   Served in Capt. Jenckes' Co. in 1757.

Joseph of Smithfield   Marched on alarm of Aug. 1757.

Michael   Served in campaign of 1761.

IRESON, Ichabod (Indian)   Served on Privateer Providence in 1759.

Joseph of Newport   Marched on alarm of Aug. 1757.

IRISH, George of Newport   Marched on alarm of Aug. 1757.

IRONS, Samuel Served in campaign of 1762.

William Served in campaign of 1762.

ISAACS, Michael Served in campaign of 1755.

JACKETESS, Caleb (Indian) Served on Privateer George of Newport in 1757.

JACKOTIS, John Served in campaign of 1755.

JACQUAYS, John Served in Capt. Russell's Co. in 1760, and in Col. Rose's Regt. in 1762.

Nathan Served in Capt. Greene's Co. in 1757, and in Capt. Rose's Co. in 1758.

Samuel of N. Kingstown Marched on alarm of Aug. 1757, served in Capt. Rose's Co. in 1758, and in Col. Rose's Regt. in 1762.

JACKSON, Fryas Served on Privateer George of Newport in 1758.

George Member of committee of war in 1762.

John Served in campaigns of 1758 and 1760, in Capt. Kimball's Co. in 1761, and in campaign of 1762.

Joseph Served in campaign of 1759.

Stephen Served in campaign of 1759.

William Served on Privateer George of Newport in 1757.

JACOBS, Cornelius Served in campaign of 1760, and in Capt. Peck's Co. in 1761.

Silas Served in Capt. E. Whiting's Co. in 1757.

JAMES, John Served in Capt. Russell's Co. in 1760.

John of Newport Commander of Privateer Amazon of Newport in 1756 and 1760.

Samuel Served on Privateer Defiance of Newport in 1756.

William of Newport Marched on alarm of Aug. 1757.

JAYES, Richard of Newport Volunteered and marched on alarm of Aug. 1757.

JEFFREYS, Caleb Served at Fort George, R. I., in 1762.

Jethro Served in campaign of 1755.

JELERO, Philip Served in campaign of 1760.

JENCKES, Amos Served in Capt. Hawkins' Co. in 1762.

Daniel Member of committee of war from 1755 to 1760.

JENCKES

    Daniel of Cumberland Marched on alarm of Aug. 1757.

    Ebenezer Lieutenant of Capt. Richmond's Co. in 1755, Lieutenant of Capt. Whiting's Co. in 1755-6, Captain in 1756, 1757, 1758 and 1759. Died in 1759.

    John Served in Capt. Jenckes' Co. in 1756.

    Joseph Served in Capt. Kimball's Co. in 1761, and in campaign of 1762.

JENKINS, Palmer Served in campaign of 1761.

    Thomas Served in Col. Hopkins' Regt. in 1756, and as 1st Lieutenant of Capt. Fry's Co. in 1759.

    Zephaniah Served on Privateer George of Newport in 1758.

JENNINGS, James Served in Lt. Col. Angell's Co. in 1756.

    James Served on Privateer George of Newport in 1758.

    James of Bristol Marched on alarm of Aug. 1757.

    Jeremiah Served in Lt. Col. Angell's Co. in 1756.

    Peter of S. Kingstown Marched on alarm of Aug. 1757, and served in Capt. Rose's Co. in 1758.

JEPSON, John Member of committee of war in 1761 and 1762.

JILLSON, Jonathan of Cumberland Marched on alarm of Aug. 1757.

JOB, Cornelius Served in Capt. E. Whiting's Co. in 1757.

JOHNSON, Asa Served in Capt. Jenckes' Co. in 1758, and in campaign of 1759.

    David Enlisted at Newport for campaign of 1762.

    Francis Served in Capt. Peck's Co. in 1761.

    George (Indian) Served on Privateer George of Newport in 1757.

    James Served in campaign of 1755.

    James (Indian) Served on Privateer George of Newport in 1757.

    John Served as Coxswain on Privateer George of Newport in 1758, and served on H. M. S. Pembroke in 1759 and 1760.

    John Enlisted in H. M. regular army in 1762.

    Nathaniel Served in campaign of 1762.

JOHNSON

    Samuel of Newport Commander of Privateer Nancy in 1761, and of Privateer Pompey of Newport in 1762.

    William Enlisted in H. M. regular army in 1762.

JOHNSTON, Augustus 1st Lieutenant of Lt. Col. Wickham's Co. in 1756.

    Thomas Enlisted at Newport as a seaman in 1762.

JOLES,

JOLLS, John Served as Corporal in Major Peck's Co. in 1762.

    Robert Served in Capt. Wall's Co. in 1757.

    Robert Gunner on Privateer Roby in 1759.

JONES, Benjamin Served as Corporal in Capt. Whiting's Co. at Fort William Henry during winter of 1755-56.

    Benjamin of Exeter Marched on alarm of Aug. 1757.

    Benjamin Served in Col. Rose's Co. in 1762.

    Ebenezer of Cumberland Served in Col. Harris' Regt. in 1756, marched on alarm of Aug. 1757, served in campaigns of 1758 and 1760.

    Elijah of Cumberland Marched on alarm of Aug. 1757.

    Henry Served in Capt. Jenckes' Co. in 1758.

    Henry Served in campaign of 1760.

    Immanuel of Exeter Served in Capt. Greene's Co. in 1757, and in campaign of 1758.

    John of Warren Marched on alarm of Aug. 1757.

    John of Newport Marched on alarm of Aug. 1757.

    John of Smithfield Served in Col. Harris' Co. in 1756, in Capt. Jenckes' Co. in 1757 and 1758, and in campaigns of 1759 and 1762.

    Joshua Served in Major Burkett's Co. in 1760, and in campaign of 1762.

    Peter Served in Capt. Kimball's Co. in 1761.

JORDAN, Daniel Served on Privateer George of Newport in 1758.

    Ebenezer Served in Capt. Kimball's Co. in 1761.

    John Served in Capt. Kimball's Co. in 1761, and in Major Peck's Co. in 1762.

JOSIAH, of Newport (an Indian) Marched on alarm of Aug. 1757.

Joy, Peter of Cranston   Marched on alarm of Aug. 1757.

Joyce, John   Served in Lt. Col. Angell's Co. in 1756, and in Capt. Fry's Co. at Havana in 1762.

    Richard of Newport   Marched on alarm of Aug. 1757.

Joyel, John   Enlisted in H. M. regular army in 1762.

Jupiter, James   Served in Capt. Jenckes' Co. in 1757, and in campaign of 1758.

Justin, John   Served in Capt. Rose's Regt. in 1762.

Kay, Ezekiel   Served on Privateer Defiance of Newport in 1756.

Kay, see Keyes.

Keech, Benjamin, Jr., of Gloucester   Marched on alarm of Aug. 1757.

    Joseph of Gloucester   Marched on alarm of Aug. 1757.

    Joel   Served in Col. Harris' Regt. in 1760.

    Zephaniah of Smithfield   Marched on alarm of Aug. 1757.

Keen, Isaiah of Newport   Marched on alarm of Aug. 1757.

Keith, Stephen of Smithfield   Marched on alarm of Aug. 1757.

Kelley, Benjamin   Served as Sergeant in Capt. E. Whiting's Co. in 1759.

    Charles   Served in Lt. Col. Angell's Co. in 1756.

    Daniel   Served in Capt. Peck's Co. in 1761, and in Major Peck's Co. in 1762.

    John of Warren   Marched on alarm of Aug. 1757.

    Michael   Enlisted in H. M. regular army in 1762.

    Wing of Smithfield   Marched on alarm of Aug. 1757.

Kellom, John   Served in Col. Hopkins' Regt. in 1756.

Kenney, Lovett   Served in Major Burkett's Co. in 1760.

Kentley, James   Served in Col. Rose's Regt. in 1762.

Ketchup, James   Served in campaigns of 1761 and 1762.

Kettle, Elias of Newport   Marched on alarm of Aug. 1757, and served in campaign of 1758.

    Mansir   Served at Fort George, R. I., in 1756.

    Thomas   Served at Fort George, R. I., in 1757, in Col. Harris' Regt. in 1760, at Fort Stanwix in 1761, and in Lt. Col. Hargill's Co. at Havana in 1762.

KEYES, Daniel   Served in Capt. Brown's Co. in 1759.

Solomon of Cumberland   Marched on alarm of Aug. 1757, and served in campaign of 1758.

William of Warwick   Served as Sergeant in Capt. Wall's Co. in 1757.

KEYES, see KAY.

KILBURN, John of Newport   Volunteered and marched on alarm of Aug. 1757.

KILLEY, see KELLEY.

KILTON, Samuel   Served in Col. Harris' Regt. in 1756, and in Capt. Jenckes' Co. in 1757.

KIMBALL, Asa   Served in Lt. Col. Angell's Co. in 1756, in Capt. Jenckes' Co. in 1757, as Ensign in Capt. Eddy's Co. in 1759, 2nd Lieutenant in Major Burkett's Co. in 1760, Captain of 4th Co. in 1761, 2nd Lieutenant of Capt. Hawkins' Co. in 1762, and Adjutant of Col. Rose's Regt. in 1762.

John   Served in Capt. Jenckes' Co. in 1757, and in campaign of 1758.

Moses   Served in Col. Babcock's Co. in 1758.

Philemon   Served in campaigns of 1758, 1759 and 1760, in Capt. Kimball's Co. in 1761, and Sergeant in campaign of 1762.

KING, Anthony   Served in Capt. J. Whiting's Co. in 1757, and in Capt. Russell's Co. in 1760.

Benjamin of Tiverton   Marched on alarm of Aug. 1757, and served in campaign of 1761.

Clement   Served in Col. Harris' Regt. in 1760.

John of S. Kingstown   Marched on alarm of Aug. 1757.

Obadiah of Cranston   Marched as Ensign on alarm of Aug. 1757.

Thomas of Newport   Marched on alarm of Aug. 1757.

Thomas   Served in Capt. Hopkins' Co. in 1760 and died at Amherst.

KINNICUT, Amos of Providence   Volunteered on alarm of Aug. 1757.

Joseph of Providence   Commander of Privateer Victory in 1762.

KINYON, Benjamin of Charlestown   Marched on alarm of
    Aug. 1757, and served in Capt. Russell's Co. in 1760.
    Daniel   Served in campaign of 1762.
    George of Newport   Marched on alarm of Aug. 1757.
    Thomas, Jr., of Charlestown   Marched on alarm of Aug.
    1757.
KIRBY, Edward   Enlisted at Newport for campaign of 1762.
KNAPP, Abiel   Served in campaign of 1760, in Capt. Peck's
    Co. in 1761, and in Major Peck's Co. in 1762.
    Elijah of Newport   Served in Capt. Cole's Co. in 1755,
    volunteered and marched on alarm of Aug. 1757, and
    served as Sergeant in campaign of 1760.
    John   Served in Capt. Potter's Co. in 1756, and in Capt.
    Wall's Co. in 1757.
KNIGHT, Benjamin   Served in Capt. J. Whiting's Co. in 1757.
KNOWLTON, John   Enlisted in H. M. regular army in 1762.
KNOWLES, Edward of Providence   Marched on alarm of Aug.
    1757.
KYE, see KEYES.

LACY, Neptane   Served in Capt. Belcher's Co. in 1756.
LADD, Jeremiah   Served in Col. Harris' Regt. in 1760.
    Samuel   Served in Capt. Jenckes' Co. in 1758, and in cam-
    paign of 1759.
    William of Newport   Commander of Privateer Lydia of
    Newport in 1760.
    William of Newport   Volunteered and marched on alarm
    of Aug. 1757.
LADEE, Nicholas   Served as drummer in Capt. Peck's Co. in
LEDIES,   1761, and in Major Peck's Co. in 1762.
LUDEE,
LAKE, Edward   Served in Capt. J. Whiting's Co. in 1757.
    Ephraim   Served in Capt. Greene's Co. in 1757, and in
    Capt. Brown's Co. in 1759.
    Jeremiah   Served in Capt. Brown's Co. in 1759.
    Joseph   Served in Capt. J. Whiting's Co. in 1757.
    William   Served on Privateer Defiance of Newport in
    1756.

LAMB, John   Served in Capt. Belcher's Co. in 1756, and in Capt. J. Whiting's Co. in 1757.

Thomas   Enlisted in H. M. regular army in 1762.

LANCE, John   Commander of Privateer Maggott of Newport in 1757, 1758 and 1760.

LANE, Ephraim   Served in campaign of 1759.

LANGWORTHY, Goodson   Served on Privateer George of Newport in 1757.

Southcote   Served as armorer on Privateer George of Newport in 1758.

LANPHERE, Abel   Served in Capt. E. Whiting's Co. in 1757, and in Col. Babcock's Co. in 1758 and 1759.

Asa   Served in Capt. Brown's Co. in 1758 and 1759.

Elisha   Served in Capt. Russell's Co. at Havana in 1762. Died Sept. 3, 1762.

J.   Served in campaign of 1762.

John   Served in Capt. E. Whiting's Co. in 1757, and in Col. Babcock's Co. in 1759.

Joshua   Served in Capt. Brown's Co. in 1758 and 1759, and in campaign of 1762.

Nathaniel   Served in Capt. Russell's Co. at Havana in 1762.

Stephen   Served in campaign of 1762.

LAPHAM, Benjamin   Served in campaign of 1757.

LAPTHORNE, William   Served in campaign of 1759.

LARKHAM, Launcelot   Served in Col. Rose's Regt. in 1762.

LARKIN, Daniel   Served as Corporal in Capt. Russell's Co. at Havana in 1762.

Joshua   Served in Capt. Greene's Co. in 1757.

Nicholas of Richmond   Marched as Captain on alarm of Aug. 1757.

Stephen   Served in campaign of 1761.

LATHART, Henry   Served on Privateer Blackbird in 1762.

LATHOM, William of Cranston   Marched on alarm of Aug. 1757.

LAW, Benjamin   Served in Capt. Peck's Co. in 1761.

Samuel   Enlisted at Newport for campaign of 1762.

LAWLESS, William Served in Capt. Belcher's Co. in 1756, and in Capt. Wall's Co. in 1757.

LAWRENCE, Jonathan Served in Capt. Belcher's Co. in 1756, and in Capt. Wall's Co. in 1757.

Joseph of Providence Volunteered on alarm of Aug. 1757.

Justus of Newport Marched on alarm of Aug. 1757.

William (Indian) Served on Privateer Providence in 1759.

LAWTON, Robert Member of councils of war in 1757 and 1761.

Thomas Served in Capt. Peck's Co. in 1761, and in Major Peck's Co. in 1762.

LEACH, James 2nd Surgeon in Col. Harris' Regt. in 1755, and served in Col. Babcock's Regt. in 1758.

James Served on Privateer George of Newport in 1757.

LEE, Jonathan of East Greenwich Marched on alarm of Aug. 1757.

Jonathan of West Greenwich Served in Capt. Fry's Co. in 1756.

John Served in campaign of 1758.

Peter Served in Capt. Potter's Co. in 1756.

Robert Served in campaign of 1755.

Robert (Irishman) Served in Lt. Col. Hargill's Co. in 1762.

LEONARD, Robert Served in Col. Harris' Regt. in 1760.

LESBROOK, Charles Served in Capt. Jenckes' Co. in 1757.

LESLEY, Lawrence of Newport Marched on alarm of Aug. 1757.

LETSON, Jeremiah of Coventry Marched on alarm of Aug. 1757.

Mitchell Served in Lt. Col. Angell's Co. in 1756.

LEWIS, Arnold Served in Col. Harris' Regt. in 1760.

Ebenezer Served in Capt. Wall's Co. in 1757, in campaign of 1758, as Corporal in campaign of 1759, and in Col. Harris' Regt. in 1760.

Enoch of Richmond Served in Capt. Greene's Co. in 1757.

James Served in Capt. Belcher's Co. in 1756, and in Capt. J. Whiting's Co. in 1757.

Jesse Served in campaign of 1762.

LEWIS

Joel (colored)   Served in Col. Harris' Co. in 1760, and in Capt. Hawkins' Co. in 1762.

Jonathan of Hopkinton   Marched on alarm of Aug. 1757.

Nathaniel   Served in campaign of 1762.

Oliver   Served in Capt. Brown's Co. in 1758 and 1759, and as drummer in Capt. Russell's Co. at Havana in 1762.

Peter   Served in Capt. J. Whiting's Co. in 1757.

Samuel   Served in Capt. Brown's Co. in 1758 and 1759.

Thomas   Served in Capt. Russell's Co. in 1760.

Waite   Served in Col. Babcock's Co. in 1758.

William   Served in Capt. Brown's Co. in 1758 and 1759.

Zebulon   Served in Capt. Greene's Co. in 1757, and in Capt. Brown's Co. in 1758.

(An Indian boy)   Served in campaign of 1762 and 1763.

LILLESBURY, George   Served on Privateer George of Newport in 1758.

LILLIBRIDGE, David   Served in Capt. Russell's Co. in 1760, and in Col. Rose's Regt. in 1762.

Prince   Served on Privateer George of Newport in 1757.

LINDSEY, Christopher of Newport   Marched on alarm of Aug. 1757.

John   Enlisted in H. M. regular army in 1762.

LINSCOMB, John   Lieutenant in Col. Harris' Regt. in 1755, and 1st Lieutenant in Capt. Gardner's Co. in 1756.

Samuel   Served in Capt. Wall's Co. in 1757.

LITTLE, Charles   Served in campaign of 1761.

Fobes, Jr., of Little Compton   Marched on alarm of Aug. 1757.

Nicholas of Newport   Marched on alarm of Aug. 1757.

Samuel of Smithfield   Marched on alarm of Aug. 1757.

Samuel   Commander of Privateer General Johnson in 1757.

LITTLEFIELD, Edmund   Served in Capt. Greene's Co. in 1757.

Nathaniel of South Kingstown   Served in Capt. Greene's Co. in 1757.

LOCK, Timothy   Served in Capt. Russell's Co. in 1760.

Thomas   Served in Lt. Col. Angell's Co. in 1756.

LOCKWOOD, Abraham   Served in campaign of 1760.

(Amos Lockwood's boy)   Served in Capt. Potter's Co. in 1756.

LODGE, Abraham   Served in Lt. Col. Hargill's Co. at Havana in 1762.

LOMBERS, Joshua   Served on Privateer George of Newport in 1758.

LORING, Thomas   Served in Lt. Col. Angell's Co. in 1756, and as Corporal in Capt. Walls' Co. in 1757.

Thomas   Served on Privateer George of Newport in 1758.

LOSCELLS, William   Enlisted at Newport for campaign of 1762.
LASCELLS,

LOUD, Benjamin   Served on Privateer George of Newport in 1757.

LOVE, John   Served in Capt. Fry's Co. at Havana in 1762.

Jonathan   Served in campaign of 1759.

Josiah   Served in Capt. J. Whiting's Co. in 1757, and enlisted at Newport for campaign of 1762.

Robert   Served in Capt. Wall's Co. in 1757.

William of Coventry   Marched on alarm of Aug. 1757.

LOVELL, John   Served in Capt. Jenckes' Co. in 1757 and 1758, and in campaign of 1760.

Nathaniel   Enlisted in H. M. regular army in 1762.

Samuel   Served on Privateer George of Newport in 1758.

LOW, Benjamin   Served in campaign of 1759, in Major Burkett's Co. in 1760, in Capt. Peck's Co. in 1761, and as Corporal in Capt. Hawkins' Co. in 1762.

LURDJUBEE, James of Smithfield   Served in Capt. Jenckes' Co. in 1757.

LUTHER, Peres   Served in Capt. Jenckes' Co. in 1758, and in campaign of 1759.

Sylvester of Newport   Marched on alarm of Aug. 1757.

LYNCH, James   Served on Privateer George of Newport in 1757.

LYNDON, Josiah   Appointed member of special court martial in Dec. 1758, and served as member of councils of war in 1756, 1757 and 1758.

LYONS, John   Served in Col. Harris' Regt. in 1760.

Thomas of East Greenwich   Served in Capt. Fry's Co. in 1756, and marched on alarm of Aug. 1757.

William of Newport (colored)   Marched on alarm of Aug. 1757.

MACARBY, Elect   Served on Privateer Defiance of Newport in 1756.

McCARTHY, Benjamin   Served in Capt. J. Whiting's Co. in 1757.

Edward   Enlisted at Newport for campaign of 1762.

John   Served in Capt. J. Whiting's Co. in 1757.

Owen   Served on Privateer George of Newport in 1758.

William   Served in Col. Rose's Regt. in 1762.

See CARTY.

McCLOUD, Roderick of Newport   Commander of Privateer Prince Ferdinand of Newport in 1757 (Sh), and of Privateer Lord Howe in 1758.

McDANIEL, Martin   Served as seaman at Oswego in 1756 and was taken prisoner.

Peter   Armorer's Mate on Privateer George of Newport in 1757.

McDONALD, Alexander   Enlisted at Newport for campaign of 1762.

Canet   Served in campaign of 1758.

James   Enlisted at Newport for campaign of 1762.

John   Served in campaign of 1758.

McGIVAR, Thomas   Served on Privateer George of Newport in 1757 and 1758.

MACHOLY, Alexander   Served in Capt. Belcher's Co. in 1756.

McINTIRE, Rufus, Jr.   Served in campaign of 1756, in Capt. Jenckes' Co. in 1758, and in campaign of 1759.

McINTOSH, Daniel   Enlisted at Newport for campaign of 1762.

MACKALOM, John   Served at Fort George, R. I., in 1762.

MACKAY, James   Served in campaign of 1756.

See MICAY.

McMULLEN, John   Surgeon on Privateer Roby in 1759.

McNeal,

McNeil, Henry Enlisted at Newport for campaign of 1762.
Neal Served in campaign of 1759.

Mackquease, Jacob Served in Capt. J. Whiting's Co. in 1757.

Mahane, Charles Served in Capt. J. Whiting's Co. in 1757.

Malbone, Boston Served on Privateer George of Newport in 1758.

Caesar Served on Privateer George of Newport in 1758.

Francis Commander of Privateer Othello of Newport in 1756 and 1758 (Sh).

Godfrey, Jr., of Newport Member of councils of war in 1756 and 1757, appointed Colonel of R. I. Regt. in March 1758, but was superseded by Babcock in May 1758.

Jack of Newport Marched on alarm of Aug. 1757.

Manchester, George Served in Capt. J. Whiting's Co. in 1757.

Gideon of Providence Volunteered on alarm of Aug. 1757.

Isaac of Tiverton Marched as Captain on alarm of Aug. 1757.

John Served in Capt. J. Whiting's Co. in 1757.

John of Portsmouth Ensign of Capt. Hargill's Co. in 1759, and appointed Ensign of Lt. Col. Whiting's Co. in 1760, but did not serve.

Joseph Served on Privateer George of Newport in 1758.

Matthew of Cranston Marched as hostler on alarm of Aug. 1757.

William of Tiverton Marched as hostler on alarm of Aug. 1757, and served in Capt. Tew's Co. in 1762.

Mann, Oliver of Smithfield Marched on alarm of Aug. 1757.

Manson, James Served as seaman at Oswego in 1756 and was taken prisoner.

Manton, Gideon Served in Major Burkett's Co. in 1760.

Manwhom, George Served in Capt. Brown's Co. in 1758 and 1759.

William of Newport Marched on alarm of Aug. 1757.

Marden, Nathan Served on Privateer George of Newport in 1758.

MARGARET, William of South Kingstown   Served in Capt. Greene's Co. in 1757.

MARSH, Daniel   Served in campaign of 1758.

John   Served as ordinary seaman on H. M. S. Pembroke in 1759 and 1760.

John, Jr., of South Kingstown   Marched on alarm of Aug. 1757, served in Capt. Rose's Co. in 1758, and in Capt. Brown's Co. in 1759.

Rowland   Served in Capt. Greene's Co. in 1757, and in Capt. Rose's Co. in 1758.

MARSHALL, John of Charlestown   Marched on alarm of Aug. 1757.

Thomas   Served in Col. Rose's Regt. in 1762.

MARTIN, Gideon   Served in Col. Harris' Regt. in 1760.

Henry   Served in Capt. Kimball's Co. in 1761, and in Capt. Hawkins' Co. in 1762.

Simon   Served in campaign of 1758.

William   Served in campaign of 1761.

MARTINDALE, Sion of Newport   Volunteered and marched as 1st Lieutenant on alarm of Aug. 1757, and served as 1st Lieutenant on Privateer Roby in 1759.

MATTHEWS, Abraham   Served in Capt. Russell's Co. in 1760.

Henry   Served in Capt. J. Whiting's Co. in 1758.

Jeremiah   Served in Major Peck's Co. in 1762.

MATHEWSON, Abraham of Providence   Marched on alarm of Aug. 1757.

Clement   Served in Capt. Wall's Co. in 1757.

George   Served in Col. Harris' Regt. in 1760.

Isaac   Served in Col. Rose's Regt. in 1762.

John   Served in Capt. Jenckes' Co. in 1758, and in campaign of 1760.

John, Jr.   Served in Capt. Jenckes' Co. in 1758.

Joseph of East Greenwich   Marched on alarm of Aug. 1757.

Thomas of West Greenwich   Served in Capt. Fry's Co. in 1756, in Capt. Wall's Co. in 1757, and in campaign of 1761.

Uriah   Served in Capt. Fry's Co. in 1762.

MATHEWSON

Zachariah   Served in Capt. Jenckes' Co. in 1757, transferred to Capt. Wall's Co. in 1757, served in Capt. Jenckes' Co. in 1758, and in campaigns of 1759 and 1760.

MATTIS, William   Served in Lt. Col. Angell's Co. in 1756.

MAXON, Daniel   Served in Col. Babcock's Co. in 1759.

Joel   Served in Capt. Russell's Co. at Havana in 1762 and died 5 Sept. 1762.

Jonathan of Newport   Marched on alarm of Aug. 1757. and served in Capt. Russell's Co. in 1760.

MAXWELL, James   Enlisted at Newport for campaign of 1762.

William   Served in Col. Harris' Regt. in 1756.

MAY, Ebenezer   Served in campaigns of 1758 and 1759.

Samuel of Providence   Marched on alarm of Aug. 1757.

MAYHEW, Adonijah of Newport   Marched on alarm of Aug. 1757.

MAYLEM, John   Enlisted at Newport for campaign of 1762.

MEACH, Elkanah   Served in Capt. Brown's Co. in 1759.

John   Served in Col. Babcock's Co. in 1758 and 1759.

MEGG, Stephen of Little Compton   Marched on alarm of Aug. 1757.

Stephen   Served in Capt. J. Whiting's Co. in 1757.

MENEY, John Daniel   Enlisted in H. M. regular army in 1762.

MERITHEW, Samuel   Served in Capt. Jenckes' Co. in 1757, in Col. Harris' Regt. in 1760, and in Capt. Hawkins' Co. in 1762.

MERRY, David   Served in campaign of 1758.

METCALF, Nathaniel   Member of Council of War in 1762.

William of Providence   Commander of Privateer Game Cock in 1756 (Sm), and 1759, of Privateer Goldfinch of Newport in 1760, and of Privateer Blackbird in 1762.

MEW, George of Warwick (Mulatto)   Served in Capt. Potter's Co. in 1756, in Capt. J. Whiting's Co. in 1757, and was taken prisoner at the capture of Fort William Henry.

George   Served in Capt. Fry's Co. at Havana in 1762.

MEW

John   Served at Fort Stanwix in 1761, and in Capt. Fry's
Co. at Havana in 1762.

MICAY, John   Enlisted at Newport for campaign of 1762.
McKAY,

MICHINER, Abel of Newport   Commander of Privateer Success of Newport in 1760.

MIDDLETON, William of Newport   Marched on alarm of Aug.
1757, and served in Col. Babcock's Co. in 1758 and
1759.

MILFORD, William   Enlisted in H. M. regular army in 1762.

MILLARD, Jonathan   Served in campaign of 1760, and as
Ensign in Capt. Hawkins' Co. in 1762.

Nelmes   Served in Col. Babcock's Co. in 1758.

MILLEMAN, Bryant   Served in Capt. Greene's Co. in 1757,
and in Capt. Rose's Co. in 1758.

John of S. Kingstown   Marched on alarm of Aug. 1757.

MILLER, George   Served in Col. Harris' Regt. in 1760.

MINGO, Joseph   Served in Capt. Peck's Co. in 1761.

MINOR, ——— (son of Simeon)   Served in campaign of 1762.

MITCHELL, Anthony   Served in Capt. J. Whiting's Co. in
1757.

Daniel   Served in campaign of 1762.

Elisha   Served in Capt. Jenckes' Co. in 1757, in Capt.
Rose's Co. in 1758, in campaign of 1759, in Col. Harris' Regt. in 1760, and in Capt. Hawkins' Co. in 1762.

Ephraim   Served in Capt. Greene's Co. in 1757.

Ezekiel   Served in campaign of 1762.

Hezekiah   Served in Col. Rose's Regt. in 1762.

Josiah   Served in Capt. Fry's Co. at Havana in 1762.

Obadiah   Served in Col. Harris' Co. in 1756.

Richard   Served in Capt. Greene's Co. in 1757.

Thomas   Ensign in Capt. Brown's Co. in 1760.

Zebedee   Served in Col. Hopkins' Regt. in 1756.

MITHORN, James   Served in Capt. Rose's Co. in 1758.

MOFFATT, John   Served in campaign of 1758.

MONCKCOME, Samuel   Served in Capt. J. Whiting's Co. in
1757.

Money, Levi   Served in Col. Rose's Regt. in 1762.

Montaigne, Dennis   Served in campaign of 1758.

Moon, Peleg of Exeter   Marched on alarm of Aug. 1757, and served in campaign of 1758.

Moore, Christopher   Served in campaigns of 1758 and 1759, and in Capt. Peck's Co. in 1761.

William   Served in Capt. E. Whiting's Co. in 1758, and in Col. Harris' Regt. in 1760.

See More.

Moorhead, James   Served on Privateer Defiance of Newport in 1756.

More, Alexander   Enlisted in H. M. regular army in 1762.

Thomas   Enlisted in H. M. regular army in 1762.

Morgan, Francis   Served in Capt. Belcher's Co. in 1756.

John   Enlisted for campaign of 1762.

Roswell   Served in Col. Babcock's Co. in 1758.

Morin, Walter   Served in Lt. Col. Angell's Co. in 1756.

Morris, Owen of Newport   Commander of Privateer Rising Sun in 1759.

Phineas of Newport   Volunteered and marched on alarm of Aug. 1757.

William   Served in Capt. Belcher's Co. in 1756.

Morrison, of Newport   Marched on alarm of Aug. 1757.

Morse, Joseph   Served in Capt. Belcher's Co. in 1756, in Capt. J. Whiting's Co. in 1757, and enlisted at Newport for campaign of 1762.

Valentine of Coventry   Marched as Captain on alarm of Aug. 1757, and served as First Lieutenant of Capt. Tew's Co. in 1758.

William of Scituate   Served in campaign of 1762, and in Capt. Cornell's Co. at Fort Stanwix in 1762.

Moses, Isaac   Served in Capt. J. Whiting's Co. in 1757.

Moshier, Ephraim   Served in Capt. E. Whiting's Co. in 1759.

Philip of Newport   Marched on alarm of Aug. 1757.

Mott, Benjamin   Served in Capt. Greene's Co. in 1757, and in Capt. Russell's Co. in 1760.

Caleb of W. Greenwich   Served in Capt. Wall's Co. in 1757.

MOTT

Gershom   Served in campaign of 1762.

James   Served in campaign of 1758.

Samuel   Served as sawer-in-the-pit at Oswego in 1756 and was taken prisoner.

MOWRY, Jacob   Served in Capt. Jenckes' Co. in 1756, and in the campaign of 1760.

James of Smithfield   Served in Capt. Jenckes' Co. in 1757 and 1758, and in campaigns of 1759 and 1762.

Philip   Served on Privateer George of Newport in 1758.

Thomas   Served in Capt. Jenckes' Co. in 1757, and in campaign of 1759.

Zephaniah   Served in campaign of 1760.

MUCKAMOGG, Josiah   Served in campaign of 1762.

MUETT, Josiah   Served in Capt. Peck's Co. in 1761, and in Major Peck's Co. in 1762.

MUKLE, Isaac   Served in Capt. Russell's Co. in 1760.

MUMFORD, Jeremiah   Served on Privateer Defiance of Newport in 1756.

Peter   Marched as Captain on alarm of Aug. 1757, and served as Member of Council of War in 1762.

Peter of Newport   Marched as Cornet and Quarter Master on alarm of Aug. 1757.

Thomas of S. Kingstown   Marched on alarm of Aug. 1757.

Richard   Served on a Privateer under Capt. John Davis between 1755 and 1758.

William   Captain of Fort George, R. I., in 1756, 1758, 1759, 1760; member of Councils of War in 1756, 1757 and 1758.

MUNRO, George   Served as caulker and sawer-in-the-pit at Oswego in 1756, and was taken prisoner.

John   Enlisted in H. M. regular army in 1762.

Joseph   Served on Privateer George of Newport in 1758.

Nathaniel of Newport   Marched on alarm of Aug. 1757.

Thomas   Surgeon's Mate in Col. Babcock's Co. in 1759.

William   Served in Col. Babcock's Co. in 1759.

MURPHY, Edward   Served in campaign of 1758, and as A. B. seaman on H. M. S. Pembroke in 1759.

NASH, Jonathan   Served in Col. Babcock's Co. in 1758 and
1759, in Capt. Russell's Co. in 1760, and in campaign
of 1762.

Nathan   Served in Capt. Russell's Co. at Havana in 1762.

NEGRO, Benjamin of Bristol   Marched on alarm of Aug. 1757,
and served in Capt. Peck's Co. in 1761.

Benjamin   Served in Capt. Wall's Co. in 1757.

Benjamin   Served on Privateer George of Newport in
1758.

Francisco   Served in Col. Harris' Co. in 1756, and in
Capt. Jenckes' Co. in 1757.

Port   Served in Col. Babcock's Co. in 1758 and 1759.

NEGROMAN, See NEGRO.

NEGUS, Job of Tiverton   Marched on alarm of Aug. 1757.

NELSON, Andrew   Served as A. B. seaman on H. M. S. Pembroke in 1759 and 1760.

William   Served as ship-carpenter and seaman at Oswego
in 1756, and taken prisoner by the French.

NESSECOMPT, William   Served in Capt. Greene's Co. in 1757,
NESSIAIMP,   in Capt. J. Whiting's Co. in 1758, and in
Capt. E. Whiting's Co. in 1759.

NEWALL, Thomas   Served on Privateer Defiance in 1756.

NEWBERRY, Jeremiah   Served in Capt. Russell's Co. at Havana
in 1762.

NEWBURY, James   Enlisted at Newport for campaign of 1762.

NICHOLS, Abraham   Served in Capt. J. Whiting's Co. in 1757.

Andrew   Served in Capt. Brown's Co. in 1759.

Benjamin   Served as sawer-aloft at Oswego in 1756 and
taken prisoner to France, where he died.

Benjamin   Served in campaign of 1758.

Caleb   Served in Capt. Jenckes' Co. in 1758, and in Capt.
Russell's Co. in 1760.

Christopher   Served as Surgeon's Mate in Col. Angell's
Regt. in 1757.

David of Richmond   Marched on alarm of Aug. 1757, and
in campaign of 1758.

George of Newport   Commander of Privateer Nancy of
Warren in 1762.

NICHOLS

Henry   Served at Fort George, R. I., in 1756.

Jack   Enlisted at Newport for campaign of 1762.

James   Served in campaign of 1758.

John of E. Greenwich   Served in Capt. Greene's Co. in 1757, and in Col. Harris' Regt. in 1760.

Jonathan   Served as Commissary in 1755, and as member of Committee of War in 1755 and 1756.

Joseph of E. Greenwich   Marched as hostler on alarm of Aug. 1757.

Robert   Served at Fort George, R. I., in 1756, in Capt. Fry's Co. in 1760 and 1761, and in Lt. Col. Hargill's Co. in 1762.

Samuel   Served as Lieutenant of Capt. Cole's Co. in 1755.

Stephen   Served in Capt. Jenckes' Co. in 1758.

Thomas   Served at Fort George, R. I., in 1757, and in Lt. Col. Hargill's Co. at Havana in 1762.

William   Served as Ensign in Capt. Bosworth's Co. in 1755.

William   Served in campaign of 1761.

NICKES, Isaac of E. Greenwich   Served in Capt. Wall's Co. in 1757, in campaign of 1761, and in Capt. Fry's Co. in 1762.

NICKLESS, John   Served on Privateer George of Newport in 1757.

NILES, Caesar   Served in Capt. E. Whiting's Co. in 1757.

Caleb   Served in Col. Babcock's Co. in 1758 and 1759, in Capt. Russell's Co. in 1760, and in Capt. Russell's Co. at Havana in 1762.

James   Served in Capt. Greene's Co. in 1757, in campaign of 1758, in Capt. Brown's Co. in 1759, and in Capt. Russell's Co. in 1760.

Jeremiah of South Kingstown   Marched on alarm of Aug. 1757.

John   Served in Capt. Russell's Co. in 1760, and enlisted at Newport and served in campaign of 1762.

(John of W. Greenwich?)   Captain in 1757, 1758 and 1759.

NILES

Peter   Served in Capt. Greene's Co. in 1757, and in Capt.
J. Whiting's Co. in 1758.

Samuel   Served in Capt. Greene's Co. in 1757.

Timothy   Served in Capt. J. Whiting's Co. in 1757.

NINIGRET, Charles   Served in campaign of 1762 and died.

NOBLE, Mark   Second Lieutenant of Lt. Col. Angell's Co. in
1756, and Second Lieutenant of Capt. Jenckes' Co. in
1757.

NOCAKE, James   Served in Capt. Russell's Co. in 1760.

NORRIS, John of Newport   Marched on alarm of Aug. 1757.

NORTHUP, Stephen, Jr., of N. Kingstown   Marched on alarm
of Aug. 1757.

NOWLIAN, Morgan   Served in Capt. Belcher's Co. in 1756.

NORTON, Peter of E. Greenwich   Served in Lt. Col. Angell's
Co. in 1756, in Capt. Wall's Co. in 1757, in campaign
of 1760, in Capt. Kimball's Co. in 1761, and in campaign of 1762.

NUTTER, Richard   Served on Privateer George of Newport
in 1758.•

NYLES, see NILES.

O'BRYANT, Timothy   Served in Capt. Wall's Co. in 1757.

OLNEY, Benjamin of Providence   Volunteered on alarm of
Aug. 1757.

Coggeshall   Served in Col. Harris' Regt. in 1760.

Ezra   Served in campaign of 1758.

Isaac   Second Lieutenant of Col. Hopkins' Co. in 1756.

Jabez of Smithfield   Marched on alarm of Aug. 1757.

James   Served in Capt. Jenckes' Co. in 1758, and in campaign of 1762.

Jeremiah   Served in Capt. Potter's Co. in 1756 and died.

John   Served in Capt. J. Whiting's Co. in 1757, in campaign of 1758, and as Corporal in campaign of 1769.

Jonathan of Providence   Marched as hostler on alarm of
Aug. 1757.

Nathaniel of Providence   Volunteered on alarm of Aug.
1757.

OLNEY

    Nedebiah   Served in Major Burkett's Co. in 1760, and in Capt. Kimball's Co. in 1761.

    Thomas of Warwick   Marched on alarm of Aug. 1757.

    Thomas of Providence   Marched as Captain on alarm of Aug. 1757.

    William of Providence   Served in Col. Harris' Co. in 1756, and marched on alarm of Aug. 1757.

O'NEIL, Beriah   Enlisted in H. M. regular army in 1762.

    William   Served on Privateer Defiance of Newport in 1756.

ONION, John   Served in Capt. J. Whiting's Co. in 1757.

ONMONOCK, Joseph   Served in Capt. J. Whiting's Co. in 1757.

ORANGE, James   Enlisted at Newport for campaign of 1762.

ORCHARD, Samuel   Enlisted at Newport for campaign of 1762.

ORMSBEE, Ebenezer of Warren   Marched on alarm of Aug. 1757, and served in campaign of 1760.

OSBORNE, Edward   Served in Capt. J. Whiting's Co. in 1757.

    Samuel   Served in campaign of 1758.

OTIS, Jonathan   Member of Councils of War in 1757, 1758 and 1759.

OWEN, Joseph of Providence   Commander of Privateer Robie of Warren in 1757, and of Privateer Industry in 1758.

PAGE, James of Gloucester   Marched on alarm of Aug. 1757.

    Joseph   Served in Capt. Potter's Co. in 1756, in Capt. Jenckes' Co. in 1757, in Col. Harris' Regt. in 1760, and in campaign of 1762.

    Stephen   Served in campaign of 1762.

    William   Served in campaign of 1759.

PAINE, Lawrence   Served in Capt. Belcher's Co. in 1756.

PALLOU, Antonio   Served as A. B. Seaman on H. M. S. Pem-
PELOU,   broke in 1759 and 1760.

PALMER, Israel   Served in Capt. E. Whiting's Co. in 1757.

    Joseph   Served in Capt. Wall's Co. in 1757, and in Capt. Peck's Co. in 1761.

    Lawton   Served in campaign of 1762.

PALMER

Moses Second Lieutenant of Capt. Babcock's Co. in 1758, and Captain in 1759.

PALMETER, Andrew Served in Capt. Brown's Co. in 1758.

Benajah Served in Capt. Brown's Co. in 1759.

Jesse Served in Capt. Brown's Co. in 1759, and in campaign of 1760.

John Served as Sergeant in Capt. Russell's Co. at Havana in 1762.

Silas Served in Capt. Brown's Co. in 1759.

PARK, Benjamin of Westerly Served in campaign of 1756, and marched as an officer on alarm of Aug. 1757.

Joseph, Jr., of Westerly Served in campaign of 1756, and marched as an officer on alarm of Aug. 1757.

Thomas Served in campaign of 1756, marched as an officer on alarm of Aug. 1757, appointed Second Lieutenant of Capt. Potter's Co. in 1758, but was transferred to Col. Babcock's Co.

PARKER, Jacob Served in campaign of 1762.

John of Gloucester Served in Capt. Jenckes' Co. in 1756 and 1757.

Joseph Served in Capt. Hawkins' Co. in 1762.

Peter Served in campaign of 1758.

PARR, Moses Served in Capt. Greene's Co. in 1757.

Thomas Served in Capt. Greene's Co. in 1757, and in Capt. Rose's Co. in 1760.

PARRY, John Served on Privateer George of Newport in 1757.

PARTLOW, John Served in Capt. Greene's Co. in 1757.

PATTERSON, John of Bristol Marched on alarm of Aug. 1757.

Joseph Served in Capt. Peck's Co. in 1761.

Robert Served on Privateer George of Newport in 1757.

PAUGONUTT, John (Indian) Served in campaign of 1760.

PAULL, Joshua Served on Privateer George of Newport in 1757 and 1758.

PEABODY, Ephraim of Providence Marched on alarm of Aug. 1757.

PEACHMAN, Peter Served in Capt. Russell's Co. at Havana in 1762, and died 21 Aug. 1762.

PEALMAN, Andrew   Enlisted at Newport for campaign of
    1762.
PEARCE, Benoni of Providence   Volunteered on alarm of Aug.
    1757.
    Ephraim   Served in Capt. Peck's Co. in 1761.
    James   Ensign of Capt. Hargill's Co. in 1760.
    James   Served in Capt. Kimball's Co. in 1761, and in
        campaign of 1762.
    Michael of Warwick   Marched on alarm of Aug. 1757.
    See PEIRCE.
PECK, Ichabod of Cumberland   Marched as Captain on alarm
    of Aug. 1757.
    Israel   Ensign of Capt. Gardner's (E. Whiting's) Co. in
        1757, Lieutenant in campaign of 1758, 1st Lieutenant
        of Capt. Palmer's Co. in 1759, 1st Lieutenant of Capt.
        Tew's Co. in 1760, appointed Ensign of Col. Whit-
        ing's Co. in 1761, advanced to Lieutenant and trans-
        ferred as Lieutenant to Capt. Peck's Co. in 1761,
        and 1st Lieutenant of Major Peck's Co. in 1762.
    Nathaniel of Warren   Ensign of Capt. Richmond's Co. in
        1755, 2nd Lieutenant of Capt. Richmond's Co. in
        1756, 1st Lieutenant of Capt. Wall's Co. in 1757,
        Captain in campaigns of 1758, 1759, 1760 and 1761,
        and Major of Col. Rose's Regt. in 1762.
PECKHAM, Caleb, Jr., of Newport   Marched on alarm of Aug.
    1757.
    Peleg   Served in campaign of 1762.
    Philip of Newport   Marched on alarm of Aug. 1757.
    ———— (son of Isaac of Westerly)   Served in campaign
        of 1760.
PEIRCE, Benjamin of Warwick   Marched on alarm of Aug.
    1757.
    Reuben of E. Greenwich.   Served in Capt. Fry's Co. in
        1756, and in Capt. Wall's Co. in 1757.
    Samuel of Warwick   Marched on alarm of Aug. 1757, and
        served in campaign of 1759.
    See PEARCE and PURSE.
PENDER, Peleg   Served in Capt. J. Whiting's Co. in 1757.

PENDLETON, Abel 'Served in Capt. E. Whiting's Co. in 1757.
James Served in campaign of 1762.
Stephen Served in Capt. E. Whiting's Co. in 1758.
PENDOCK, Benoni Enlisted in H. M. regular army in 1762.
PENNY, Benjamin of Charlestown (Indian) Served in Capt.
Greene's Co. in 1757.
Daniel Served in Capt. Greene's Co. in 1757.
PERRIGO, Robert Served as Sergeant in Capt. Hawkins' Co.
in 1762.
PERRY, Abraham Served in Capt. Russell's Co. in 1760.
Daniel Served in Capt. Brown's Co. in 1759, in Capt.
Russell's Co. in 1760, and in Capt. Russell's Co. at
Havana in 1762.
John of Newport Marched on alarm of Aug. 1757,
served in Capt. J. Whiting's Co. in 1758, and in Capt.
E. Whiting's Co. in 1759.
Simeon Served in Capt. Potter's Co. in 1756.
Zephaniah Served in Major Peck's Co. in 1762.
See PARRY.
PETERS, Abraham Enlisted in H. M. regular army in 1762.
Daniel Served in Capt. Jenckes' Co. in 1757, in campaign
of 1759, and in Capt. Hawkins' Co. in 1762.
Joseph Served in Capt. E. Whiting's Co. in 1757.
Mark Served in Capt. Kimball's Co. in 1761.
Solomon Served in Capt. E. Whiting's Co. in 1757.
William Served in Capt. Hawkins' Co. in 1762.
PETERSON, Joseph Served as ship-carpenter at Oswego in
1756, and was taken prisoner by the French.
Lemuel Served in campaign of 1762.
PETTY, Benjamin Served in campaign of 1762.
James Served in Capt. Rose's Co. in 1758.
PEW, William of Jamestown Marched on alarm of Aug. 1757.
PHENIX, Solomon of New York Commander of Privateer
Sampson of New York. Recommissioned at Newport
in 1759.
PHETTEPLACE, Resolved of Gloucester Served in Capt.
Jenckes' Co. in 1756 and 1757, in campaigns of 1758,
1759 and 1760, and as Sergeant in 1762.

III

PHILLIPS, Andrew of East Greenwich   Marched on alarm of Aug. 1757.

Charles   Served in Capt. Greene's Co. in 1757, in Capt. Brown's Co. in 1758 and 1759, and in campaign of 1762.

Elisha   Served on Privateer Defiance of Newport in 1756.

Frederick   1st Lieutenant on Privateer Blackbird in 1762.

Gideon   Served in Capt. J. Whiting's Co. in 1757.

Hanley of N. Kingstown (Colored)   Marched on alarm of Aug. 1757.

Israel   Served in Capt. J. Whiting's Co. in 1757.

James of Gloucester   Marched on alarm of Aug. 1757.

Jeremiah of Smithfield   Marched on alarm of Aug. 1757, and served in Col. Harris' Regt. in 1760.

Jeremiah   Served on Privateer George of Newport in 1757.

John of Portsmouth   Marched on alarm of Aug. 1757, and served in campaign of 1762.

Joseph   Served on Privateer George of Newport in 1757 and 1758.

Joshua   Enlisted at Newport and served in campaign of 1762.

Michael   Commander of Privateer Defiance of Newport in 1757.

Michael   Served in campaign of 1761.

Peter   Served as sutler in campaign of 1762.

Rowland   Served at Fort George, R. I., in 1757.

Samuel of Exeter   Served in Capt. Wall's Co. in 1757.

William of Gloucester   Marched on alarm of Aug. 1757.

William   Served in Capt. J. Whiting's Co. in 1757, and enlisted at Newport for campaign of 1762.

Zebedee   Served in Col. Harris' Regt. in 1760.

PIKE, Joseph   Served as sawer-in-the-pit at Oswego in 1756, and was taken prisoner by the French.

Joseph   Served as Steward on Privateer George of Newport in 1758.

PINCH, John   Served in Capt. Greene's Co. in 1757.

PINNEGAR, William   Commander of Privateer Rising Sun of Newport in 1759 and 1762.

PITMAN, Gilbert   Served in Capt. Belcher's Co. in 1756.

PITTS, James   Served on Privateer Defiance of Newport in 1756.

John of Bristol   Marched on alarm of Aug. 1757.

PLACE, Anthony of Gloucester   Marched on alarm of Aug. 1757, and served in campaign of 1758.

Eber; alias John Eber of N. Kingstown (Indian)   Marched on alarm of Aug. 1757.

George   Served in campaign of 1758.

Jesse   Served in Col. Harris' Co. in 1756.

John   Served in Capt. Kimball's Co. in 1761, and enlisted in 1762.

Joseph   Served in Capt. Rose's Co. in 1758.

Stephen   Served in Capt. Rose's Co. in 1758, and in campaign of 1762.

PLUMMER, Ebenezer   Served in Capt. Jenckes' Co. in 1757.

Richard   Served in Capt. Angell's Co. in 1755.

Samuel of Smithfield   Served in Capt. Jenckes' Co. in 1757, and in campaigns of 1760 and 1762.

POMP, Daniel   Served in Capt. Brown's Co. in 1759.

GREENMAN, see GREENMAN, Pomp.

Simon   Served in Capt. Russell's Co. at Havana in 1762, and died Sept. 5, 1762.

POOLE, Edmund   Served in Capt. E. Whiting's Co. in 1757.

POOLER, George of Charlestown   Marched on alarm of Aug. 1757, served in Capt. Rose's Co. in 1758, and in Capt. Brown's Co. in 1759.

Zaccheus of Hopkinton   Marched on alarm of Aug. 1757, and served in Col. Babcock's Co. in 1759.

POOR, David   Served on Privateer George of Newport in 1758.

William   Served in Capt. Rose's Co. in 1758.

POPPLE, John   Served in campaign of 1762.

Stephen   Served in Col. Rose's Regt. in 1762.

PORTER, Nathan   Served in campaign of 1762.

Timothy   Served in Capt. Greene's Co. in 1757.

POTHEAGUE, Joshua   Served in Capt. E. Whiting's Co. in 1759.

Peter   Served in Capt. E. Whiting's Co. in 1759.

Stephen   Served in Capt. Russell's Co. at Havana in 1762, and died 28 Aug. 1762.

William   Served in Capt. E. Whiting's Co. in 1757.

POTTER, Abel of Coventry   Marched on alarm of Aug. 1757, and served in Capt. Hawkins' Co. in 1762.

Caleb of Cranston   Marched on alarm of Aug. 1757.

Christopher   Served in Capt. Rose's Co. in 1758, and in campaign of 1762.

Ebenezer of Hopkinton   Served in Capt. Russell's Co. at Havana in 1762.

Fisher   Served in campaign of 1761.

Gideon of Cranston   Served in Lt. Col. Angell's Co. in 1756, and was killed.

Gideon   Served in Capt. Wall's Co. in 1757.

Ichabod   Served in Capt. Rose's Co. in 1758.

Israel   Boatswain on Privateer Blackbird in 1762.

James of Newport   Commander of Privateer Prince Frederick of Newport in 1757, and of Privateer Wolf of Newport in 1760 and 1761.

John, Jr.   Captain of 9th Co. in Col. Harris' Regt. in 1755, Captain in 1756, 1757 and 1758; appointed Lieutenant Colonel in May 1758.

Joseph   Served in Capt. Russell's Co. in 1760.

Joseph of Warwick   Ensign of Capt. Francis' Co. in 1755.

Josiah of Cranston   Marched on alarm of Aug. 1757.

Joshua of Exeter   Served in Capt. Greene's Co. in 1757.

Nathaniel   Served in campaign of 1758, in Col. Babcock's Co. in 1759, in campaign of 1760, and as Sergeant in Capt. Russell's Co. at Havana in 1762.

Robert   Member of Committee of War in 1757, 1758, 1759, 1761 and 1762; and Member of Court Martial in 1758.

Stephen of Coventry   Marched as Major on alarm of Aug. 1757.

Thomas, Jr.   Member of Committee of War in 1762.

POTTER

Tom, alias Tom Hill (Indian)   Served in campaign of
1755.

William   Served in Capt. Jenckes' Co. in 1757, in Capt.
Rose's Co. in 1758, and in campaign of 1760.

POTTS, John   Served as A. B. seaman on H. M. S. Pembroke
in 1759 and 1760.

POWERS, Benjamin   Served in Capt. J. Whiting's Co. in 1757.

John of Providence   Volunteered on alarm of Aug. 1757.

John, Jr.   Appointed 1st Lieutenant of Capt. Windsor's
Co. in Sept. 1756.

Morris   Served in Col. Harris' Regt. in 1760.

Nicholas   Served in campaign of 1759.

PRESTON, Benjamin   Served in campaign of 1759.

PRISTON,

William   Served in Capt. Belcher's Co. in 1756.

PRICE, Isaac   Served in Capt. Jenckes' Co. in 1758, and in
campaign of 1759.

Israel   Served in Capt. Wall's Co. in 1757.

John   Served on Privateer George of Newport in 1757.

Joseph of Newport   Volunteered and marched on alarm
of Aug. 1757.

Samuel   Served in campaign of 1758.

PRIEST, Darius   Served in campaign of 1760.

PRINCE, Pero,   Served in Capt. Jenckes' Co. in 1757.

Peter   Served in Capt. Jenckes' Co. in 1757.

PRITCHARD, John   Enlisted at Newport for campaign of 1762.

PRIOR, William   Ensign of Capt. Kimball's Co. in 1761, and
2nd Lieutenant of Lt. Col. Hargill's Co. in 1762.

PROCTOR, Samuel   Served in Capt. J. Whiting's Co. in 1757.

PROUD, William   Served in Col. Harris' Regt. in 1760.

PUCKEY, Samuel   Served in Capt. Greene's Co. in 1757.

PUGH, Henry   Enlisted in H. M. regular army in 1762.

PULLEN,

PULLING, Nicholas   Served in Col. Harris' Regt. in 1760.

William   2nd Lieutenant of Capt. Palmer's Co. in 1759,
1st Lieutenant of Capt. Brown's Co. in 1760, and 1st
Lieutenant of Capt. Kimball's Co. in 1761.

PULLEN

William, Jr. Served in campaign of 1760.

PURCHESS, William Enlisted at Newport for campaign of 1762.

PURSE, Francis Served on Privateer George of Newport in 1757.

PYNE, Jonathan Enlisted in H. M. regular army in 1762.

QUAGANAH, John Served in Capt. Brown's Co. in 1759.

QUAM, Edward Served in Capt. E. Whiting's Co. in 1757.

Joshua Served in Major Peck's Co. in 1762.

QUENNELL, Robin Served in Col. Babcock's Co. in 1759, and in Capt. Russell's Co. in 1760.

QUOM, Samuel Served in Capt. Peck's Co. in 1761.

QUON, John Served in Capt. J. Whiting's Co. in 1757.

QUINCE, Samuel Served in Capt. E. Whiting's Co. in 1757.

RAINER, Thomas of Middletown Marched on alarm of Aug. 1757.

RALPH, John Served in Capt. Fry's Co. at Havana in 1762.

RAMSDELL, Abner Enlisted at Newport for campaign of 1762.

RAMSEY, James of New York Commander of Privateer Diamond of Newport in 1762.

RANDALL, David Served in campaign of 1762.

Edward Served in Capt. J. Whiting's Co. in 1757.

Ichabod Served as Corporal in Capt. Russell's Co. at Havana in 1762, and died 4 Sept. 1762.

John of Providence Volunteered on alarm of Aug. 1757.

John of Providence Commander of Privateer Black Snake in 1758 and 1759, and was captured by the enemy January 6, 1759.

William Served in Capt. Brown's Co. in 1759.

RATHBONE, Roger Served in Col. Rose's Regt. in 1762.

Thomas, 3rd 2nd Lieutenant of Capt. Coggeshall's Co. in 1756.

Thomas of N. Kingstown Served in Capt. Greene's Co. in 1757.

William Served in Col. Rose's Regt. in 1762.

RAWSON, Pirn   Served in Col. Harris' Regt. in 1760.

READ, Benjamin   Served on Privateer George of Newport in
REED,   1757.

>Benjamin of Cranston   Marched on alarm of Aug. 1757.

>Daniel   Enlisted at Newport for campaign of 1762.

>David   Served in Col. Rose's Regt. in 1762.

>Joseph   Served in Capt. E. Whiting's Co. in 1757, in
Capt. Rose's Co. in 1758, and in Col. Rose's Regt. in
1762.

>Joseph (Colored)   Served in Capt. Rose's Co. in 1760.

>Joseph of S. Kingstown   Marched on alarm of Aug. 1757.

>Simeon   Served as carpenter at Oswego in 1756, and was
taken prisoner.

>Thomas   Served in Capt. Hawkins' Co. in 1762.

>William of Newport   Served at Fort George, R. I., in
1755 and 1756, Captain of Fort George in 1761 and
1762, Member of Councils of War in 1762.

REMINGTON, Peleg of Warwick   Served in Capt. Wall's Co.
in 1757.

>Ruel of Warwick   Served in Capt. Wall's Co. in 1757.

>Thomas   Served on Privateer George of Newport in
1758.

RENHOLT, Kenulle   Enlisted at Newport and served as A. B.
seaman on H. M. S. Pembroke in 1759 and 1760.

RENIFF, John   Served in Capt. Jenckes' Co. in 1758, and in
campaign of 1759.

REOCH, Charles   Enlisted at Newport as a seaman in 1762.

REPLEY, David   Served in campaign of 1761.

>John   Served in campaign of 1761.

REYNOLDS, Benjamin of Newport   Marched on alarm of Aug.
1757.

>Clement   Served in Col. Rose's Regt. in 1762.

>Ebenezer   Served in Capt. Brown's Co. in 1758.

>Elias   Served in Capt. Brown's Co. in 1758 and 1759.

>Elisha   Member of Court Martial in 1758.

>George of W. Greenwich   Served in Col. Hopkins Regt.
in 1756, and in Capt. Wall's Co. in 1757.

REYNOLDS

Grindal 1st Lieutenant of Capt. Potter's Co. in 1756, and marched as Captain on alarm of Aug. 1757.

Grindal of Bristol Marched as Ensign on alarm of Aug. 1757.

James Served in campaign of 1758.

John Served in campaign of 1759.

John, Jr. Served in campaign of 1757.

Oliver 2nd Lieutenant of Capt. Rose's Co. in 1758, and served in Col. Rose's Regt. in 1762.

Peter Served in Capt. Peck's Co. in 1761, and in Major Peck's Co. in 1762.

Robert Served in campaign of 1762.

Shibnah alias Cyperin of E. Greenwich Served in Capt. Wall's Co. in 1757.

Thomas Served in Col. Harris' Regt. in 1760.

(husband of Ruth) Served in campaign of 1762.

RHODES, Peleg Served in Col. Harris' Regt. in 1760.

RICE, Nathan Member of Committee of War in 1758, 1759 and 1760.

Nathan Ensign in Capt. Peck's Co. in 1759.

Thomas of W. Greenwich Served in Capt. Wall's Co. in 1757.

RICHARDS, William of Newport Commander of Privateer Trumpeter of Newport in 1756 and 1757 (Sh.).

RICHARDSON, Isaac of Gloucester Served in Col. Harris' Co. in 1756, and marched on alarm of Aug. 1757.

James Served in Capt. E. Whiting's Co. in 1758, as Ensign and Quarter Master in campaign of 1759, and in Lt. Col. Hargill's Regt. at Havana in 1762.

RICHMOND, Barzillai of Providence Captain of 11th Co. of Col. Harris' Regt. in 1755, Captain in 1756, volunteered on alarm of Aug. 1757, and served at Ticonderoga in the campaign of 1758.

Eliakim of Gloucester Marched as Ensign on alarm of Aug. 1757.

Ephraim of Little Compton Marched on alarm of Aug. 1757.

Richmond

Seth of Gloucester   Marched on alarm of Aug. 1757.

Sylvester of Little Compton   Marched on alarm of Aug. 1757.

William, Jr., of Little Compton   Lieutenant of Capt. Potter's Co. in 1755, 1st Lieutenant of Lt. Col. Champlin's Co. in Feb. 1756, Captain of 5th Co. in Col. Hopkins' Regt. in Oct. 1756, marched on alarm of Aug. 1757, and served as 1st Lieutenant of Col. Babcock's Co. in 1758.

Rider, John   Gunner's Mate on Privateer George of Newport in 1758.

Joseph   Gunner's Mate on Privateer Defiance of Newport in 1756.

Right, Samuel of Exeter   Marched as Captain on alarm of
Weight,   Aug. 1757.

Rightson, Charles of Newport   Marched on alarm of Aug.
Wrightson,   1757.

Ripley, see Repley.

Ritto, Peter   Served on Privateer Providence in 1758, and made Prize Master in April 1758.

Rivers, Joseph   Commander of Privateer Abercrombie of
Rivas,   Newport in 1757 and 1758.

Robin, Isaac (Indian)   Served in Col. Rose's Regt. in 1761.
      [Error either for Lt. Col. or 1762.]
Robins,

Robbins, Benoni   Served in Lt. Col. Hargill's Co. in 1762.

Daniel   Served in campaign of 1759, and in Capt. Russell's Co. at Havana in 1762, and died 27 Aug. 1762.

Moses   Served in campaign of 1762.

Peter   Served in Capt. J. Whiting's Co. in 1757.

Roberts, Elias of Newport   Marched on alarm of Aug. 1757.

John   Served in Capt. Fry's Co. at Havana in 1762.

Peter of Cranston   Served in Capt. Potter's Co. in 1756, marched on alarm of Aug. 1757, served in Col. Harris' Regt. in 1760, at Fort Stanwix in 1761, and in Capt. Fry's Co. at Havana in 1762.

Peter, Jr.   Served in Capt. Potter's Co. in 1757.

ROBERTS

Thomas   Served in Capt. Wall's Co. in 1757.

William of Cranston   Served in Capt. Potter's Co. in 1756, marched on alarm of Aug. 1757, and served in campaigns of 1759 and 1760.

William   Marched on alarm of Aug. 1757.

ROBINSON, Gain   Served as Sergeant in Capt. Peck's Co. in 1761.

George   Served in campaign of 1762.

Hugh   Served on Privateer George of Newport in 1758.

Isaac   Served in Major Burkett's Co. in 1760, and in campaign of 1762.

James   Served in campaign of 1759.

Jeremiah   Served in Capt. Kimball's Co. in 1761.

Joseph   Served in Capt. Russell's Co. in 1760.

Mark of Newport   Volunteered and marched on alarm of Aug. 1757, and served in Capt. Rose's Co. in 1758.

Obadiah   Served in campaign of 1760.

Samuel   Served in Col. Harris' Regt. in 1760.

Solomon   Served in campaign of 1760.

William   Enlisted in H. M. regular army in 1762.

ROCK, Joseph   Enlisted in H. M. regular army in 1762.

ROCKWELL, Joseph   Served in Capt. Babcock's Co. in 1755.

RODMAN, Abiathar of Richmond (Indian)   Marched on alarm of Aug. 1757, and served in Capt. Rose's Co. in 1758.

Oliver   Served in Capt. Rose's Co. in 1758.

Thomas   Doctor on Privateer Defiance of Newport in 1756, and Surgeon of R. I. Regiment in 1759 and 1760.

Thomas of Newport   Commander of Privateer Dolphin in 1762.

ROFFEY, Solomon   2nd Lieutenant of Capt. Peck's Co. in 1759 and 1760.

ROGERS, Benjamin   Served in Col. Harris' Regt. in 1760, and in Capt. Tew's Co. in 1762.

Caleb   Served in Col. Harris' Regt. in 1760.

James of Newport   Member of Council of War in 1759.

Jeremiah   Served in Col. Harris' Regt. in 1760.

ROGERS

Jonathan   Served in Capt. J. Whiting's Co. in 1757.

Joshua   Served in Capt. Russell's Co. in 1760.

Joseph   Enlisted in H. M. regular army in 1762.

Josias   2nd Lieutenant of Capt. Belcher's Co. in 1756.

Thomas   Served in Capt. Greene's Co. in 1757, and in Col. Rose's Regt. in 1762.

William   Member of councils of war in 1756, 1757 and 1758.

ROOD, Thomas   Served in campaign of 1762.

ROSE, Samuel   2nd Lieutenant of Capt. Hammond's Co. in 1756, Lieutenant of Capt. E. Whiting's Co. in 1757, Captain in 1758, 1759 and 1760, Lieutenant Colonel in 1761, and Colonel of R. I. Regiment in 1762.

Thomas   Ensign of Capt. Peck's Co. in 1758 and advanced to 2nd Lieutenant, 1st Lieutenant of Capt. Peck's Co. in 1759, 1760 and 1761, 2nd Lieutenant of Col. Rose's Co. in 1762, served and died at Havana in 1762.

ROSS, Alexander   Served in Col. Harris' Co. in 1756, in Capt. Wall's Co. in 1757, and in campaign of 1762.

Andrew   Enlisted in H. M. regular army in 1762.

Benjamin   Served in campaign of 1762.

James   Enlisted at Newport for campaign of 1762.

Robin   Served in Capt. E. Whiting's Co. in 1757.

Thomas   Served in Capt. Brown's Co. in 1759.

Thomas, Jr.   Served in Capt. Russell's Co. at Havana in 1762 and died 22 Dec. 1762.

William of Newport   Served in Lt. Col. Angell's Co. in 1756, marched on alarm of Aug. 1757, and served in Col. Babcock's Co. in 1758.

ROSSE, John   Commander of Privateer King of Prussia of Newport in 1757.

ROWLAND, James   Sergeant in Capt. Peck's Co. in 1761, and in Major Peck's Co. in 1762.

Lewis   Served in Capt. Peck's Co. in 1761.

ROWSE, Benjamin   Served in Capt. Wall's Co. in 1757, and in
ROUSE,   Col. Harris' Regt. in 1760.

James of E. Greenwich   Marched on alarm of Aug. 1757.

Rouse
John of Warwick Served in Capt. Wall's Co. in 1757.
Jonathan Served at Fort Stanwix in 1761, and in Capt. Fry's Co. in 1762.
Roy, Caleb of Coventry Served in Capt. Wall's Co. in 1757.
Richard Served in Capt. Wall's Co. in 1757.
William Served in Lt. Col. Angell's Co. in 1756.
Ruddy, James Served as A. B. seaman on H. M. S. Pembroke
Readay, in 1759 and 1760.
Ruggles, Thomas Doctor on Privateer George of Newport in 1758.
Rumreill, Ebenezer of Newport Marched as Captain-Lieutenant on alarm of Aug. 1757, and served as member of councils of war in 1757, 1758 and 1759.
Russell, Daniel Member of councils of war in 1757.
David Served in Col. Harris' Regt. in 1760.
Giles Ensign of Capt. Hopkins' Co. in 1755, 1st Lieutenant of Capt. Babcock's Co. in 1756, Adjutant in 1756, 1st Lieutenant of Capt. Greene's Co. in 1757, 1st Lieutenant of Capt. J. Whiting's Co. in 1758, Adjutant in 1758, wounded at Ticonderoga July 8, 1758, 1st Lieutenant of Capt. Brown's Co. in 1759, Adjutant in 1759, Captain July 10, 1759, Captain in 1760, 1761 and 1762, served at Havana in 1762.
John Served in Capt. J. Whiting's Co. in 1757, and in Capt. Jenckes' Co. in 1758.
Rust, Benjamin of Newport Marched on alarm of Aug. 1757.
Ryan, Michael of Newport Commander of Privateer Harlequin of Newport in 1762.

Sabin, Elijah Served in Capt. E. Whiting's Co. in 1757.
Henry of Newport Marched on alarm of Aug. 1757.
Sachem, Thomas Served in Capt. Russell's Co. in 1760.
Sake, Ephraim Served in campaign of 1760.
Salisbury, Aaron of Cranston Served in campaigns of 1756, 1757 and 1758 and was wounded.
Abraham Served in Capt. Jenckes' Co. in 1758, in campaigns of 1759 and 1760, and in Capt. Kimball's Co. in 1761.

SALISBURY

Barnard   Served in Capt. Wall's Co. in 1757.

Edward   Served in Col. Harris' Co. in 1756.

George of Warren   Marched on alarm of Aug. 1757.

John   Served in Capt. E. Whiting's Co. in 1757, and in Major Peck's Co. in 1762.

Jonathan   Served in Capt. Potter's Co. in 1756.

SAMBO, Caesar of Warwick   Served in Lieut. Col. Angell's Co. in 1756, and in Capt. Wall's Co. in 1757.

James   Served in Lt. Col. Angell's Co. in 1756, and in Capt. Jenckes' Co. in 1757.

SAMPSON, John   Enlisted in H. M. regular army in 1762.

SANFORD, Benjamin of Newport   Marched on alarm of Aug. 1757.

John   Served in Capt. J. Whiting's Co. in 1757.

Joshua of N. Kingstown   Marched on alarm of Aug. 1757.

SANSON, William   Served as A. B. seaman on H. M. S. Pembroke in 1759.

SATTERLY, Amos   Served in campaigns of 1761 and 1762.

Gideon   Served in Col. Babcock's Co. in 1758 and 1759, and in Capt. Russell's Co. at Havana in 1762.

SAUNDERS, David   Served in Col. Babcock's Co. in 1758 and
SANDERS,   1759.

Ezekiel of Newport   Marched on alarm of Aug. 1757.

Hezekiah   Served in Capt. E. Whiting's Co. in 1757, in Capt. Brown's Co. in 1758, appointed Ensign of Capt. Russell's Co. in 1760, 2nd Lieutenant of Capt. Hopkins' Co. in 1761, and 1st Lieutenant of Capt. Russell's Co. at Havana in 1762.

Jacob   Served in Major Peck's Co. in 1762.

John   Served in campaign of 1759.

Noah   Served in campaigns of 1758 and 1759.

Peleg of N. Kingstown   Marched on alarm of Aug. 1757.

Samuel   Served in Lt. Col. Angell's Co. in 1756, Ensign of Capt. Jenckes' Co. in 1757, 2nd Lieutenant of Capt. Hacker's Co. in 1758, and 1st Lieutenant of Capt. Eddy's Co. in 1759.

SANDERS

Samuel   Served in Col. Babcock's Co. in 1758 and in Capt. Russell's Co. in 1760.

Thomas   Served in Capt. J. Whiting's Co. in 1757.

Waite   Served in Col. Babcock's Co. in 1759, and in campaign of 1761.

SAVAGE, Samuel   Served in Col. Harris' Co. in 1756.

SAWNIS, John of Exeter (Indian)   Served in Capt. Greene's
SAWNAS,   Co. in 1757, and in campaign of 1758.

SAYLES, David of Smithfield   Marched on alarm of Aug. 1757.

Joseph of Smithfield   Marched on alarm of Aug. 1757.

SCADDER, Josiah   Served on Privateer George of Newport in 1758.

SCOTT, Alexander   Enlisted at Newport as a seaman in 1762.

Charles   Served in Capt. Jenckes' Co. in 1756.

David   Served in Capt. Jenckes' Co. in 1756, and as Sergeant in campaign of 1759.

Francis of Newport   Marched on alarm of Aug. 1757.

Jeremiah   Served in campaign of 1760.

Sylvanus of Smithfield   Marched on alarm of Aug. 1757, and served in campaign of 1758.

SCRANTON, Daniel   Served in Capt. Fry's Co. at Havana in 1762.

John   Enlisted at Newport for campaign of 1762.

Samuel of Cranston   Marched on alarm of Aug. 1757.

Stephen   Served in Lt. Col. Angell's Co. in 1756.

Stukeley   Served in Capt. Fry's Co. at Havana in 1762.

SCUDDER, Josiah   Served as A. B. seaman on H. M. S. Pembroke in 1759.   See SCADDER.

SEABURY, Ichabod of Tiverton   Marched on alarm of Aug. 1757.

SEAMANS, Gilbert of Providence   Marched on alarm of Aug. 1757.

Isaac   Served in campaign of 1756.

John   Served in Lt. Col. Angell's Co. in 1756.

SEARLE, James of Newport   Marched on alarm of Aug. 1757.

James of Little Compton   Marched on alarm of Aug. 1757.

SEARLE

Nathaniel of Little Compton   Marched on alarm of Aug. 1757.

Richard   Served as an officer in campaign of 1758.

Richard, Jr., of Cranston   Marched on alarm of Aug. 1757.

SEARS, James   Served in campaign of 1762.

Remington   Served in Capt. Brown's Co. in 1759.

SEAVY, Joseph   Served in Capt. J. Whiting's Co. in 1757.

SEWALL, Joseph   Served in Capt. Jenckes' Co. in 1756.

SEYMOUR, John   Served in campaign of 1758.

SHADDOCK, Anthony   Served in Capt. J. Whiting's Co. in 1758.

SHAITE, Henry   Served at Fort George, R. I., in 1756.

SHAW, Benamuel   Served in Capt. E. Whiting's Co. in 1757.

Comfort   Served in campaign of 1762.

Daniel   Served on Privateer Blackbird in 1762.

Jeremiah, Jr., of Little Compton   Marched on alarm of Aug. 1757, 1st Lieutenant of Lt. Col. Whiting's Co. in Feb. 1760, and Captain in Dec. 1760.

John of Newport   Marched on alarm of Aug. 1757.

Joseph, son of Thomas of Voluntown   Served in Capt. Fry's Co. in 1760, and in Lt. Col. Hargill's Co. at Havana in 1762.

Peter   Served in Major Burkett's Co. in 1760.

Thomas of Little Compton   Marched on alarm of Aug. 1757.

SHAWN, Caleb   Served in Capt. J. Whiting's Co. in 1757 and
SHON,   in Capt. E. Whiting's Co. in 1758 and 1759.

SHAY, Patrick   Enlisted at Newport for campaign of 1762, and in H. M. regular army in Dec. 1762.

SHEFFIELD, Amos of Newport   Marched on alarm ot Aug. 1757.

Caleb of E. Greenwich   Marched as Captain on alarm of Aug. 1757.

Ichabod   Served in Col. Babcock's Co. in 1758.

James   Captain of Fort George, R. I., in 1755 and 1756.

Joseph   Served in Col. Rose's Regt. in 1762.

Nathan of S. Kingstown   Marched on alarm of Aug. 1757.

SHEFFIELD

Thomas   Served in Major Burkett's Co. in 1760.

William of Newport   Drafted on alarm of Aug. 1757.

SHEHAN, William   Sergeant and Quarter Master in campaign of 1756, Lieutenant and Quarter Master in 1757, and 1st Lieutenant of Major Whiting's Co. in 1759.

SHELDON, Caleb   Served in Capt. Rose's Co. in 1758.

Ezekiel   Served in Capt. Rose's Co. in 1758.

George of N. Kingstown   Served in Capt. Greene's Co. in 1757.

Joseph   Served on committee to build sloop of war in 1757.

Nathaniel   Served in Capt. Peck's Co. in 1761.

Stephen   Served in campaign of 1758.

SHELLEY John of Portsmouth   Marched on alarm of Aug. 1757.

SHEPARD, Daniel   Served in Capt. Jenckes' Co. in 1757.

John   Served as boat-builder at Oswego in 1756 and was taken prisoner.

John of Newport   Marched on alarm of Aug. 1757.

Joseph   Served as seaman at Oswego in 1756 and was taken prisoner.

SHERBURN, Benjamin of Newport   Member of councils of war in 1757, 1758, 1760, 1761 and 1762.

SHERMAN, Benjamin of Exeter   Served in Capt. Greene's Co. in 1757, and in Capt. Brown's Co. in 1758.

Benoni of N. Kingstown   Marched on alarm of Aug. 1757.

Eleazer   Served at Fort George, R. I., in 1756, and in campaign of 1759.

George   2nd Lieutenant of Capt. Potter's Co. in 1756, 2nd Lieutenant of Capt. J. Whiting's Co. in 1757, 2nd Lieutenant of Capt. Jenckes' Co. in 1758.

George   Served in Col. Rose's Regt. in 1762.

Henry   2nd Lieutenant of Major Champlin's Co. in 1756.

Ichabod of Exeter   Marched on alarm of Aug. 1757.

John   Served at Fort Stanwix in 1761.

Jonathan of Newport   Volunteered and marched on alarm of Aug. 1757.

Joshua   Served in campaign of 1762.

SHERMAN

Levi Served on Privateer George of Newport in 1757, and as Prize Master on Privateer George of Newport in 1758.

Philemon Enlisted at Newport for campaign of 1762.

Samuel Served in Lt. Col. Angell's Co. in 1756.

SHERRINGTON, William Served in campaign of 1762.

SKESUCK, Daniel Served in campaign of 1760.

Jona Served in Capt. E. Whiting's Co. in 1759 and in Col. Rose's Regt. in 1762.

Levi Served in Capt. Russell's Co. at Havana in 1762 and died 13 Oct. 1762.

Moses Served in Capt. J. Whiting's Co. in 1757, and in Capt. E. Whiting's Co. in 1759.

William Served in Capt. E. Whiting's Co. in 1757.

SHIELDS, William Enlisted in H. M. regular army in 1762.

SHIPPEE, David Served at Fort George, R. I., in 1756.

Jonathan Served in Capt. Jenckes' Co. in 1757.

William Served in campaign of 1759, in Major Burkett's Co. in 1760, in Capt. Kimball's Co. in 1761, and Sergeant in campaign of 1762.

SHREIVE, John Served on Privateer George of Newport in
SHREFE, 1757.

Constant Served in Capt. J. Whiting's Co. in 1757.

SIMMONS, Aaron of Little Compton Marched on alarm of
SIMON, Aug. 1757.
SIMONS,

Cornelius of Little Compton Marched on alarm of Aug. 1757.

James Served in Capt. Brown's Co. in 1759, in Capt. Russell's Co. in 1760, and in Capt. Russell's Co. at Havana in 1762.

John of Newport Marched on alarm of Aug. 1757, served in Capt. Brown's Co. in 1759, and in Capt. Russell's Co. in 1760. Cf. SIMS.

Simon Served in Major Peck's Co. in 1762.

Stephen Served in Capt. Russell's Co. in 1760.

SIMS, John of Newport (alias Simmons)   Marched on alarm
SIMES,   of Aug. 1757.
  John   Enlisted in H. M. regular army in 1762.
  John   Served on Privateer Defiance of Newport in 1756,
    on Privateer George of Newport in 1758, and as A. B.
    seaman on H. M. S. Pembroke in 1759 and 1760.
  William of Newport   Marched on alarm of Aug. 1757,
    and served in Capt. E. Whiting's Co. in 1758 and
    1759.
SINGLETON, Robert   Enlisted at Newport for campaign of
    1762.
SISCO, Ebenezer of Warwick   Marched on alarm of Aug. 1757.
THISCO,   and served in Col. Harris' Regt. in 1760.
  Eleazer of Cranston   Marched on alarm of Aug. 1757.
SISSON, Nathan   Served in Col. Babcock's Co. in 1759, and as
    Sergeant in Capt. Russell's Co. at Havana in 1762.
  Samson   Served in Lt. Col. Angell's Co. in 1756, and in
    Capt. Jenckes' Co. in 1757.
  William   Enlisted at Newport for campaign of 1762.
SKILLIAN, John   Served in Lt. Col. Angell's Co. in 1756, in
    Capt. Jenckes' Co. in 1758, as Corporal in 1759, at
    Fort Stanwix in 1761, and in Lt. Col. Hargill's Co. in
    1762.
SLACK, Benajah   Served in Capt. Brown's Co. in 1758.
SLEW, Philip   Enlisted in H. M. regular army in February
    1763.
SLOCUM, Ebenezer of Warwick   Marched on alarm of Aug.
    1757.
  Jeremiah   Served in campaign of 1760.
  John of N. Kingstown   Served in campaign of 1756.
  Peleg   Served in Capt. Jenckes' Co. in 1758, Ensign of
    Capt. Palmer's Co. in 1759, Ensign of Col. Harris'
    Co. in 1760, appointed 2nd Lieutenant of Capt. Rus-
    sell's Co. in March 1761, but served as Ensign of
    Capt. Kimball's Co. in April and May 1761.
  Thomas of Warwick   Served in Capt. Wall's Co. in 1757.
SMITH, Abraham   Member of committee of war in 1758, 1759
    and 1760

SMITH

Abram   Served in Capt. Jenckes' Co. in 1758, and in campaign of 1759.

Benjamin   Served on Privateer Providence in 1757, and was killed Dec. 21, 1757, off Porte Plate.

Benjamin of Smithfield   Marched on alarm of Aug. 1757.

Benjamin   Served as A. B. seaman on H. M. S. Pembroke in 1759 and 1760.

Daniel   Served in campaign of 1760.

Edmund   Served in Capt. Russell's Co. at Havana in 1762, and died Aug. 26, 1762.

Edward of Providence   Volunteered on alarm of Aug. 1757, and served as 1st Lieutenant in Capt. Hacker's Co. in 1758.

Enoch   Served in Capt. Jenckes' Co. in 1756, in campaigns of 1760 and 1762.

Fones   Served in Col. Rose's Regt. in 1762.

Gehu   Served in Major Burkett's Co. in 1760.

George   Enlisted in H. M. regular army in 1762.

Hazael   Served in campaign of 1762.

Ichabod   Served in Capt. Belcher's Co. in 1756, and on Privateer George of Newport in 1757.

Israel   Served as A. B. seaman on H. M. S. Pembroke in 1759 and 1760.

Jahleel   Served in campaign of 1761 and 1762.

James   Served at Fort George, R. I., in 1758 and 1759, and in Capt. Kimball's Co. in 1761.

James, Jr.   Served as drummer in Capt. Peck's Co. in 1761.

James   Linguist on Privateer Blackbird in 1762.

Jeremiah of Providence   Marched on alarm of Aug. 1757.

John   Served as A. B. seaman on H. M. S. Pembroke in 1759 and 1760.

Jonathan   Served in campaign of 1762.

Joseph   Served in campaigns of 1758 and 1760, and in Capt. Hawkins' Co. in 1762.

Nathan   Served on Privateer Defiance of Newport in 1756.

SMITH

Nathaniel   Served on Privateer George of Newport in 1758.

Nathaniel   Served in campaign of 1760.

Nedebiah   Served in Capt. Jenckes' Co. in 1756, and in campaigns of 1758 and 1759.

Nehemiah   Served in campaigns of 1757 and 1762.

Newcomb   Carpenter on Privateer Blackbird in 1762.

Peter   Served in Capt. Kimball's Co. in 1761.

Philip   Served in Capt. Belcher's Co. in 1756, in Capt. Jenckes' Co. in 1757, in campaign of 1758, and in Capt. Hawkins' Co. in 1762.

Richard   Served in Capt. Jenckes' Co. in 1758, Sergeant in campaign of 1759, in Col. Harris' Regt. in 1760, in campaign of 1762, and enlisted in H. M. regular army in 1762.

Richard, Jr.   Ensign of Capt. Jenckes' Co. in 1758, and advanced to Lieutenant before June 5, 1758. Perhaps the Lieut. Smith who was wounded at Ticonderoga.

Robert of Gloucester   Served in Capt. Jenckes' Co. in 1757.

Robert   Served in Capt. Wall's Co. in 1757.

Samuel of Smithfield   Marched on alarm of Aug. 1757, and served in Capt. Russell's Co. in 1760.

Simon of Providence   Commander of Privateer Roby of Warren in 1758.

Solomon of Smithfield   Served in Capt. Jenckes' Co. in 1757 and 1758, in campaign of 1759, and in Major Burkett's Co. in 1760.

Stephen, Jr.   Served in Capt. Jenckes' Co. in 1757, and in campaigns of 1761 and 1762.

Thomas   Served in Col. Babcock's Co. in 1759, in Capt. Russell's Co. in 1760, and in Col. Rose's Regt. in 1762.

William   Served on Privateer Defiance of Newport in 1756.

William   Served in Col. Harris' Co. in 1756, and in Capt. J. Whiting's Co. in 1758. Wounded and extolled for bravery.

SMITH

William Served in Capt. Brown's Co. in 1759, in Major
Burkett's Co. in 1760, in Col. Rose's Regt. in 1762,
and enlisted in H. M. regular army in 1762.

William of Providence Volunteered on alarm of Aug.
1757.

William of S. Kingstown Marched on alarm of Aug.
1757.

SNOW, Benjamin Served at Fort George, R. I., in 1759.

Daniel of Providence Marched on alarm of Aug. 1757.

SOCHOSO, Jesse Served in campaign of 1761.

Obot Served in campaign of 1761.

SOCK, Anthony Served in Capt. J. Whiting's Co. in 1758, and
SOCKS, in Capt. E. Whiting's Co. in 1759.

John Served in campaign of 1755.

SOCKOMONO, Joseph Served at Fort Stanwix during winter
of 1761-62.

SOLOMON, Simon Served at Fort Stanwix during winter of
1761-62.

SOMOG, John (Indian) Served in Capt. Whiting's Co. in 1760
and died at Crown Point.

SOUTHWORTH, Isaac of Little Compton Marched on alarm of
Aug. 1757.

SOUZEZUY, Samson of E. Greenwich Served in Capt. Jenckes'
Co. in 1757.

SOWERS, Daniel Served in Capt. Russell's Co. at Havana in
1762, and died 28 Sept. 1762.

SOWLE, Henry of Newport Member of council of war in 1761.

SPARKS, Samuel Served in Capt. Jenckes' Co. in 1757.

SPAULDING, Ephraim Served in campaign of 1761.

Joseph of Smithfield Marched on alarm of Aug. 1757.

SPEARS, Elkanah 2nd Lieutenant of Col. Harris' Co. in 1756,
SPEERE, and 1st Lieutenant of Capt. Potter's (Jenckes')
Co. in 1757. Died 12 July 1757.

Jonathan Served in Capt. Jenckes' Co. in 1757, in cam-
paign of 1758, as 1st Lieutenant of Capt. Burkett's
Co. in 1759 and 1760, and 1st Lieutenant of Major
Hargill's Co. in 1761.

SPEERE
    Joseph   Served in campaign of 1761.

SPENCER, Benjamin   Served in Capt. Fry's Co. in 1762.
    Caleb   Enlisted at Newport for campaign of 1762.
    Griffin   Served in Capt. Fry's Co. at Havana in 1762.
    James   Served in Lt. Col. Angell's Co. in 1756.
    John   Served in Lt. Col. Angell's Co. in 1756, in Capt.
        Wall's Co. in 1757, in Capt. Jenckes' Co. in 1758, and
        in Capt. Fry's Co. in 1762.
    Joshua   Served in Capt. Fry's Co. at Havana in 1762.
    Nathan   Served as 2nd Lieutenant in Capt. Lathom
        Clark's Co. in 1756, and in Col. Harris' Regt. in 1760.
    Theophilus   Served in campaign of 1758.
    William   Served in campaign of 1757.

SPINK, Eldred   Served in Col. Rose's Regt. in 1762.
    Josiah   Served in Capt. Fry's Co. in 1762.

SPOONER, Charles of Newport   Member of council of war in
    1761.

SPRAGUE, Daniel of Smithfield   Marched on alarm of Aug.
    1757.
    Daniel of Providence.   Marched on alarm of Aug. 1757.
    Daniel   Served in Capt. Jenckes' Co. in 1758, and in cam-
        paign of 1759.
    Enoch of Smithfield   Marched on alarm of Aug. 1757.
    Ezekiel of Newport   Marched on alarm of Aug. 1757, and
        served on Privateer George of Newport in 1758.
    Jedediah   Served in Capt. Jenckes' Co. in 1758, and as
        Sergeant in campaign of 1759.
    Jesse of Providence   Marched on alarm of Aug. 1757.
    John   Served in campaigns of 1758, 1759 and 1760.
    Joseph   Served in Col. Harris' Co. in 1756.

SPRINGER, Lawrence of Tiverton   Marched on alarm of Aug.
    1757.
    William   Served in Capt. J. Whiting's Co. in 1757.

SPYWOOD, Benjamin of Warwick   Served in Capt. Wall's Co.
    in 1757.
    Jeremiah   Served in Capt. Potter's Co. in 1756.

SPYWOOD

Nehemiah of Warwick   Served in Capt. Wall's Co. in 1757.

Samuel of Warwick   Served in Capt. Wall's Co. in 1757, and in campaigns of 1760 and 1761.

Thomas (Indian)   Served in campaign of 1760, and in Capt. Kimball's Co. in 1761.

William of Warwick   Marched on alarm of Aug. 1757.

STACK, Thomas   Served on Privateer Defiance of Newport in 1756.

STAFFORD, David   Served in Capt. Brown's Co. in 1759, and enlisted at Newport for campaign of 1762.

John   Served on Privateer Defiance of Newport in 1756.

Michael   Served in campaign of 1759.

Stukeley   Served in Capt. Jenckes' Co. in 1757, Ensign of Lt. Col. Wall's Co. in 1759, and Ensign of Capt. Fry's Co. in 1760.

Thomas   Served in campaign of 1759.

Uriah   Served in Capt. Jenckes' Co. in 1758, and in campaign of 1759.

STANLEY, Samuel   Served as A. B. seaman on H. M. S. Pembroke in 1759 and 1760.

STANTON, Azariah   Served in Capt. Rose's Co. in 1758, and as Lieutenant in campaign of 1759.

Benjamin   Served in Col. Rose's Regt. in 1762.

Joseph, Jr.   2nd Lieutenant of Col. Babcock's Co. in 1759.

Samuel   Served in campaign of 1762.

Sock   Served in Capt. J. Whiting's Co. in 1758.

STAPLES, David   Served in Lt. Col. Angell's Co. in 1756, and in Capt. Jenckes' Co. in 1758.

Joshua   Served in Lt. Col. Angell's Co. in 1756, and in Capt. Jenckes' Co. in 1757.

William of Smithfield   Marched on alarm of Aug. 1757.

STARK, Matthias of S. Kingstown   Served in Capt. Greene's Co. in 1757, and in Capt. Rose's Co. in 1758.

STARKWEATHER, Ephraim   Chaplain of Col. Harris' Regt. in 1756.

STATES, Peter   Ensign of Capt. Rose's Co. in January, 1759.

STEERE, Samuel   Served in Lt. Col. Angell's Co. in 1756.

STELLE, Isaac   Member of councils of war in 1756 and 1757.

STENSON, William of Gloucester   Served in Capt. Jenckes' Co.
STINSON,   in 1757.

STERRY, Robert   Appointed Lieutenant in February 1755, and
 Captain of Second Co. in March 1755, but apparently
 was superseded by Samuel Angell. Served as
 Armorer of Col. Harris' Regt. in 1756.

(———, son of Robert)   Served as Assistant Armorer in
 Col. Harris' Regt. in 1756.

STEVENS, Caesar   Served on Privateer George of Newport in
STRIVENS,   1758.

 George   Served in Capt. Hawkins' Co. in 1762.

 Harrison   Enlisted in H. M. regular army in 1762.

 Henry   Served in Capt. Jenckes' Co. in 1758, and in campaigns of 1759 and 1762.

 John   Served in Capt. Jenckes' Co. in 1758, and in campaigns of 1759, 1760 and 1762.

 John   Served in Col. Rose's Regt. in 1762.

 Samuel   Served in Major Burkett's Co. in 1760.

 Simeon   Served in Col. Harris' Co. in 1756, in Capt.
 Jenckes' Co. in 1757, in Col. Harris' Regt. in 1760,
 and as Ensign of Major Peck's Co. in 1762.

STEWARD, William   Served in campaign of 1762.

STILL, Joseph   Served in Capt. J. Whiting's Co. in 1757.

STODDARD, Joshua of Newport   Commander of Privateer
 Three Brothers of Newport in 1760 and 1761.

 Ned (colored)   Served on Privateer George of Newport
 in 1758.

STONE, Ezra   Served in campaign of 1757.

 James   Served in Lt. Col. Angell's Co. in 1756.

 John   Served in Capt. Hawkins' Co. in 1762.

 Nathan of Portsmouth   Marched on alarm of Aug. 1757,
 served in campaigns of 1758, 1759, 1760, and in Capt.
 Kimball's Co. in 1761.

 Sylvester of Scituate   Served in Col. Harris' Regt. in
 1761, in campaign of 1762, and in Capt. Cornell's Co.
 at Fort Stanwix in 1762.

STONEMAN, John   Enlisted at Newport for campaign of 1762.

> Samuel   Served in Capt. J. Whiting's Co. in 1757, 2nd Lieutenant in Capt. J. Whiting's Co. in 1758, 1st Lieutenant in Capt. Hargill's Co. in 1759 and 1760, Adjutant in 1760, 2nd Lieutenant of Major Hargill's Co. in 1761, and Adjutant in 1761.

STRANGE, Sylvanus   Served in Capt. Belcher's Co. in 1756.

STRAIGHT, Daniel   Served in campaign of 1761, and in Capt. Fry's Co. at Havana in 1762.

> Henry of W. Greenwich   Served in Capt. Wall's Co. in 1757.

> John   Served in campaign of 1761.

> Jonathan   Served in campaign of 1759.

> Samuel   Served in Capt. Tew's Co. in 1762.

> Thomas of Coventry   Marched an alarm of Aug. 1757, and served in campaigns of 1758 and 1759.

> William of Exeter   Served in Capt. Wall's Co. in 1757, and in Col. Rose's Regt. in 1762.

STREETER, Ebenezer   Served in Capt. Jenckes' Co. in 1757.

> Isaiah of Cumberland   Marched on alarm of Aug. 1757.

> Josiah   Served in Col. Harris' Co. in 1756.

STRINGER, John   Served in Capt. Hawkins' Co. in 1762, and enlisted in H. M. regular army in November 1762.

STUTSON, Thomas   Served in campaign of 1762.

SULLIVAN, Humphrey   Served on Privateer George of Newport in 1758.

> William   Served in campaign of 1759.

SUMMERS, Philip   Served in Capt. Belcher's Co. in 1756.

SUNDERLAND, Joseph of N. Kingstown   Marched on alarm of Aug. 1757, served in campaign of 1758, and enlisted in H. M. regular army in 1762.

SUTOX, John   Served in campaign of 1762.

SWAN, George   Served in Capt. E. Whiting's Co. in 1757.

> Jesse   Served in Capt. E. Whiting's Co. in 1757.

SWEET, Albro   Served at Fort Stanwix in 1761.

> Amos of E. Greenwich   Served in Capt. Wall's Co. in 1757.

SWEET

Benedict   Served in Col. Harris' Regt. in 1760, and in Lt. Col. Hargill's Co. at Havana in 1762.

Caleb of Coventry   Served in Lt. Col. Angell's Co. in 1756, in Capt. Wall's Co. in 1757, at Fort Stanwix in 1761, and in Capt. Fry's Co. at Havana in 1762.

Caleb, Jr.   Served at Fort Stanwix in 1761, and in Capt. Fry's Co. at Havana in 1762.

Francis   Served in Capt. Jenckes' Co. in 1758, and in campaign of 1759.

Griffin   Served in campaign of 1758, at Fort Stanwix in 1761, and in Capt. Fry's Co. at Havana in 1762.

Henry   Served in Lt. Col. Hargill's Co. at Havana in 1762.

Job   Served in Lt. Col. Hargill's Co. at Havana in 1762.

John of N. Kingstown   Marched on alarm of Aug. 1757, and served in campaign of 1762.

Jonathan   Served in Capt. Jenckes' Co. in 1758, in Col. Harris' Regt. in 1760, in Capt. Kimball's Co. in 1761, and as Sergeant in Capt. Fry's Co. at Havana in 1762.

Jonathan   Served in campaign of 1762.

Matthew   Served in campaign of 1762.

Nathaniel   Served in Capt. E. Whiting's Co. in 1757, and in Col. Rose's Regt. in 1762.

Philip   Served at Fort George, R. I., in 1758, at Fort Stanwix in 1761, and in Capt. Fry's Co. in 1762.

Richard of N. Kingstown   Served in Capt. Greene's Co. in 1757, and in campaign of 1758.

Samuel of Newport   Commander of Privateer New Concert of Newport in 1756 and 1758, and Commander of Privateer Diana of Newport in 1759 and 1760.

Samuel   Served in Col. Harris' Regt. in 1760.

Samuel, Jr., of Exeter   Marched on alarm of Aug. 1757.

Stephen   Served in Capt. Rose's Co. in 1758, in Capt. Tew's Co. in 1762, in Capt. Cornell's Co. during winter of 1762-63 at Fort Stanwix, and was transferred into H. M. regular army at Fort Ontario on June 13, 1763, and served there until 1765.

William   Served in Lt. Col. Hargill's Co. in 1762.

SWEETING, Nathaniel of Providence   Commander of Privateer
    Black Snake in 1756 and 1757.
SWINBURN, Thomas, Jr., of Newport   Marched on alarm of
    Aug. 1757, and served as Ensign of Major Whiting's
    Co. in 1759.
SYLVESTER, Christopher   Served on Privateer George of New-
    port in 1758.

TABER, Daniel   Served in Capt. J. Whiting's Co. in 1757.
    John of Portsmouth   Marched on alarm of Aug. 1757.
    Record of S. Kingstown   Marched on alarm of Aug. 1757,
        served in Capt. Rose's Co. in 1758, and as Ensign in
        Capt. Rose's Co. in 1759 and 1760.
TALBEE, see TALBY.
TALBOT, William   Enlisted at Newport as a seaman in Aug.
    1762.
TALBURY, Caesar   Served in Capt. Fry's Co. at Havana in
    1762.
TALBY, Edward   2nd Lieutenant of Capt. Bosworth's Co. in
    1756, 2nd Lieutenant of Capt. Wall's Co. in 1757,
    2nd Lieutenant of Capt. Peck's Co. in 1758, and 1st
    Lieutenant of Col. Babcock's Co. in 1759.
TALFEAR, Charles   Served in campaigns of 1757 and 1758.
TALKER, James, perhaps same as
TALLMAN, James   Served in Capt. J. Whiting's Co. in 1757.
    John of Portsmouth   Marched on alarm of Aug. 1757.
    Stephen of Tiverton   Marched on alarm of Aug. 1757.
TANNER, George   Served in Capt. Greene's Co. in 1757, in
    Capt. Russell's Co. in 1760, and in Col. Rose's Regt.
    in 1762.
    John   Served in campaign of 1762.
    Palmer   Served in Capt. Jenckes' Co. in 1757 and 1758,
        Corporal in campaign of 1759, and Sergeant in cam-
        paign of 1762.
TANNING, Nathan   Served on Privateer George of Newport
    in 1757.
TARBOX, John   Served as ship-carpenter at Oswego in 1756
    and was taken prisoner by the French.

TARBOX

Peter   Served in Col. Harris' Regt. in 1760, and in Capt. Fry's Co. at Havana in 1762.

Samuel   Served as Sergeant in Capt. Clarke's Co. in 1756, and in Capt. Fry's Co. at Havana in 1762.

Spink   Served in Col. Harris' Regt. in 1760, and in Capt. Tew's Co. in 1762.

TATE, Robert Enlisted in H. M. regular army in 1762.

TAYRE, Benjamin of Newport 2nd Lieutenant in Lt. Col. Wick-
TAYER,   ham's Co. in 1756, and marched on alarm of Aug. 1757.

TAYLOR, John of South Kingstown   1st Lieutenant of Major Champlin's Co. in 1756.

John of Newport   Marched on alarm of Aug. 1757, and enlisted at Newport as a seaman in 1762.

John   Served in Capt. Jenckes' Co. in 1757 and in Capt. Hawkins' Co. in 1762.

William   Served in campaign of 1762.

TEAGUE, Jesse of E. Greenwich   Marched on alarm of Aug. 1757.

TEFFT, see TIFFT.

TENNANT, Daniel   Served on Privateer George of Newport in 1758.

Havens of N. Kingstown   Marched on alarm of Aug. 1757.

TEW, Henry, Jr., of Middletown   Marched on alarm of Aug. 1757.

James, Jr.   Ensign of Capt. Potter's Co. in 1755, 2nd Lieu-tenant of Capt. Gardner's Co. in Feb. 1756, 1st Lieu-tenant of Capt. Gardner's Co. Sept. 1, 1756, 1st Lieu-tenant of Capt. J. Whiting's Co. in 1757, Captain in 1758 and 1759.

Thomas   Served in Capt. Belcher's Co. in 1756, in Capt. J. Whiting's Co. in 1757, Ensign in Capt. Tew's Co. in 1758, 1st Lieutenant in Capt. Tew's Co. in 1759, Captain in 1760 and 1762.

TEWBY, John   Served in Capt. Russell's Co. at Havana in 1762.
TEWKYE,

TEWGOOD, Samuel   Served in Col. Harris' Regt. in 1760.
Simeon   Sergeant in campaign of 1760.

THAYER, George   Served on Privateer Blackbird in 1762.
Simeon   Served in Col. Harris' Co. in 1756.

THOMAS, Benjamin   Enlisted at Newport for campaign of 1762.

Ephraim   Served in Capt. Rose's Co. in 1758, and in campaign of 1760.

George of N. Kingstown   Marched as Captain on alarm of Aug. 1757.

Isaac   Served as Corporal in Capt. Peck's Co. in 1761.

James   Enlisted at Newport for campaign of 1762, and in H. M. regular army Feb. 1, 1763.

John, Jr. of Providence   Volunteered on alarm of Aug. 1757.

John of Exeter   Served in Capt. Wall's Co. in 1757.

John   Served in campaign of 1755.

John   Served in Capt. E. Whiting's Co. in 1757.

John   Served on Privateer George of Newport in 1757.

Samuel   Served in Capt. Russell's Co. in 1760.

THOMPSON, Benjamin of Smithfield   Marched on alarm of Aug. 1757, and served in Lt. Col. Hargill's Co. in 1762.

George of Newport   Volunteered and marched on alarm of Aug. 1757.

John of Newport   Commander of Privateer Sarah in 1761 and in 1762.

John   Served on Privateer George of Newport in 1757.

John   Served in Capt. J. Whiting's Co. in 1757.

Matthew   Served as ship-carpenter at Oswego in 1756 and was captured by the French.

Matthew of Newport   Marched on alarm of Aug. 1757.

Moses   Served at Fort George, R. I., in 1760 and 1761.

William   Enlisted at Newport as a seaman in 1762.

THORN, Isaac   Served in Col. Babcock's Co. in 1758 and 1759, and in Capt. Russell's Co. at Havana in 1762.   Died 1 Nov. 1762.

THORN

William   Served in campaign of 1758, in Col. Harris'
Regt. in 1760, and in Lt. Col. Hargill's Co. in 1762.

THORNTON, Christopher of Providence   Marched on alarm of
Aug. 1757.

Josiah of Providence   Marched as Captain on alarm of
Aug. 1757.

Nehemiah   Served in Capt. Jenckes' Co. in 1756.

Richard of Providence   Served in Capt. Potter's Co. in
1756, and marched on alarm of Aug. 1757.

Samuel   Served in Major Burkett's Co. in 1760, and as
1st Lieutenant of Capt. Fry's Co. in 1762.

Thomas   Served in campaigns of 1758, 1759, 1760 and
1762.

William   Served in Col. Hopkins' Regt. in 1756, and in
campaign of 1760.

THRUSTON, see THURSTON.

THURBER, Barnabas   Served in campaign of 1758.

Ichabod   Served in Major Peck's Co. in 1762.

James of Providence   Volunteered on alarm of Aug.
1757.

Leonard   Served in Major Peck's Co. in 1762.

Samuel of Providence   Marched as Lieutenant on alarm
of Aug. 1757.

Thomas   Served in Major Peck's Co. in 1762.

Timothy   Served in Capt. Jenckes' Co. in 1757.

THURRELL,

THURRILL, George   Served in Capt. Belcher's Co. in 1756.

William   Enlisted at Newport for campaign of 1762.

THURSTON,

THRUSTON, Edward   Served in Col. Babcock's Co. in 1759.

John   Served in Capt. Belcher's Co. in 1756.

Lovett of Newport   Commander of Privateer Charming
Polly and Sally of Newport in 1762.

Vaul   Doctor's Mate on Privateer George of Newport in
1758.

William   Carpenter on Privateer George of Newport in
1757 and 1758.

THRUSTON

William of Hopkinton   Marched on alarm of Aug. 1757.

TIFFT,

TEFFT, David of Cranston   Marched on alarm of Aug. 1757.

Gideon   Served in Capt. Fry's Co. at Havana in 1762.

John   Served in Capt. Russell's Co. in 1760, and as Ensign in Capt. Russell's Co. at Havana in 1762.

Joshua   Enlisted at Newport for campaign of 1762.

TIKEN, Abner   Served in campaign of 1757.

TILLEY, James   Enlisted at Newport for campaign of 1762.

TILLINGHAST, Amos (Colored)   Served on Privateer George of Newport in 1757.

Pardon   Served in Col. Hopkins' Regt. in 1756.

TITUS, Comfort   Served in Capt. Kimball's Co. in 1761, and in Major Peck's Co. in 1762.

John   Served in Major Peck's Co. in 1762.

Sylvanus   Served in Capt. Kimball's Co. in 1761, and in Major Peck's Co. in 1762.

TOBEY,

TOBY, John   Served in Capt. Russell's Co. in 1760.

Samuel   Ensign of Capt. Tew's Co. in 1760.

Stephen   Served as A. B. seaman on H. M. S. Pembroke in 1759.

TOCKCUP, James   Served in Capt. J. Whiting's Co. in 1757,
COUCHUP,   and in Col. Harris' Regt. in 1760.

TODD, Amos   Served in Capt. Russell's Co. at Havana in 1762. Died 15 Sept. 1762.

TOMEY, Lango   Served on Privateer Defiance of Newport in 1756.

TOPHAM, Theodore   Quarter Master on Privateer Defiance of Newport in 1756.

TORREY,

TORY, Nathan   Served as Corporal in Capt. Peck's Co. in 1761.

William   On one of Capt. Wall's muster rolls; doubtless an error for

Wilson   Served in Capt. Wall's Co. in 1757, Sergeant in Capt. Peck's Co. in 1761, and Sergeant in Major Peck's Co. in 1762.

Tosh, James   Served on Privateer George of Newport in 1757.

Tourtellot, Abraham   Served in Capt. Kimball's Co. in 1761, and in campaign of 1762.

Stephen   Served in Col. Harris' Regt. in 1760.

William   Served in campaign of 1762.

Tower, Enoch of Cumberland   Marched on alarm of Aug. 1757.

John of Cumberland   Served in Lt. Col. Angell's Co. in 1756, marched on alarm of Aug. 1757, served in Col. Harris' Regt. in 1760, and in campaign of 1761.

Jonathan   Served in Capt. Jenckes' Co. in 1757 and 1758, and in campaign of 1759.

Joseph of Cranston   Served in Lt. Col. Angell's Co. in 1756, marched on alarm of Aug. 1757, and served in campaign of 1759.

Tracy, Edward   Served in campaign of 1761.

Prince of Providence   Marched on alarm of Aug. 1757.

(———)   Served in campaign of 1755.

Trask, Ebenezer of Smithfield   Marched on alarm of Aug. 1757.

Trim, Robert   Served in Capt. Russell's Co. at Havana in 1762.   Died 18 Oct. 1762.

Tripp, Caleb   Ensign of Capt. Rose's Co. in 1758, 2nd Lieutenant of Capt. Brown's Co. in 1758, and 1st Lieutenant of Capt. Rose's Co. in 1759 and 1760.

Edward   Served in campaign of 1761.

John   Served in Col. Harris' Regt. in 1760, and in Major Peck's Co. in 1762.

Othniel   Appointed Ensign of Capt. Tew's Co. in 1760, but did not serve.

Peleg   Served in Col. Rose's Regt. in 1762.

Thomas   Served in Capt. Russell's Co. in 1760.

William   1st Lieutenant of Capt. Rose's Co. in 1758, and Captain in 1759.

William of Warwick   Marched on alarm of Aug. 1757.

Trowbridge, Benjamin   Served as A. B. seaman on H. M. S. Pembroke in 1759 and 1760.

TRUCK, Benjamin of Bristol   Marched on alarm of Aug. 1757, and served in Capt. Peck's Co. in 1761.

TUCKER, Abner   Served in campaign of 1762.

John   Served in Capt. J. Whiting's Co. in 1757.

Morris   Served in campaign of 1760.

Rhodes   Served in campaign of 1758.

Silas of Smithfield   Served in Capt. Jenckes' Co. in 1757, in campaigns of 1758 and 1759, and in Capt. Kimball's Co. in 1761.

Simeon   Served in Col. Rose's Regt. in 1762.

William   Enlisted in H. M. regular army in 1762.

TUCKHAM, Thomas   Served on Privateer Defiance of Newport in 1756.

TUKIE,

TUKEY, John   Served in Capt. Russell's Co. in 1760.

Joseph   Served in Capt. E. Whiting's Co. in 1757.

TUNISON, Tunis   Served as ordinary seaman on H. M. S. Pembroke in 1759 and 1760.

TUNQUIT, Daniel   Served in campaign of 1755.

TUPPER, Elijah   Served at Fort George, R. I., in 1760.

Seth   Served at Fort George, R. I., in 1757, 1758, 1760, 1761 and 1762, and enlisted at Newport for campaign of 1762.

TURNER, William   Served in campaign of 1759.

TYKING, Daniel   Served in Capt. Russell's Co. in 1760.

Tyask   Served in Col. Babcock's Co. in 1758 and 1759, and in Capt. Russell's Co. in 1760.

See TIKEN.

TYLER, Cornelius   Enlisted in H. M. regular army in 1762.

Ebenezer   Served in Lt. Col. Angell's Co. in 1756, in Capt. Jenckes' Co. in 1757 and 1758, in campaigns of 1759, 1760 and 1761, and in Capt. Fry's Co. in 1762.

Jonathan   Served in Capt. Potter's Co. in 1756, in Capt. Jenckes' Co. in 1758, and in campaign of 1759.

William   Served in Col. Harris' Regt. in 1760.

William   Served on Privateer Blackbird in 1762.

UNDERWOOD, Benjamin of Warwick   Served in Capt. Potter's
Co. in 1756, and in Capt. Wall's Co. in 1757.

James   Served in Capt. Wall's Co. in 1757.

Samuel   Served on Privateer George of Newport in 1757.

Thomas of Newport   Commander of Privateer Industry
of Newport in 1760 and in 1762 (Sh).

UPDIKE, Daniel   Commissioner to meet with those from the
other colonies in 1755.

UPSTELL, Thomas   Served on Privateer Blackbird in 1762.

UTLEY, Jeremiah   Served in Lt. Col. Hargill's Co. at Havana
in 1762.

UTTER, Abraham of Hopkinton   Marched on alarm of Aug.
1757.

Isais (Isaiah)   Served in Col. Babcock's Co. in 1758.

Simeon   Served in Capt. Russell's Co. in 1760, and in Col.
Rose's Regt. in 1762.

VALENTINE, Mark   Commander of Privateer Hawke of Newport in 1757.

VALETT, David   Served in campaign of 1759.

VAUGHN, Benjamin of Newport   Marched on alarm of Aug.
1757.

Daniel, Sen.   Gunner at Fort George, R. I., in 1756, 1757,
1758, 1759, 1760 and 1762.

Daniel, Jr.   Served at Fort George, R. I., in 1760, 1761
and 1762.

Gorton   Served at Fort George, R. I., in 1762.

John of N. Kingstown   Marched on alarm of Aug. 1757.

Jonathan of N. Kingstown   Marched on alarm of Aug.
1757.

Samuel   Served in campaign of 1761.

VENABLES, John   Served on Privateer George of Newport in
1757.

VEZEY, John   Served in campaign of 1762.

VINCENT, Joshua   Served in Capt. Jenckes' Co. in 1757.

William of Gloucester   Served in Col. Harris' Co. in 1756,
and marched on alarm of Aug. 1757.

VOMLIN, Gideon   Served on Privateer George of Newport in
1758.

WADE, Abner   Served in Col. Harris' Regt. in 1760, and in campaign of 1762.

Nathan   Served in Capt. Potter's Co. in 1756.

WAGGS, John   Served in Capt. Russell's Co. at Havana in 1762, and died 23 Aug. 1762.

WAITE, Thomas of Hopkinton   Served in campaign of 1758, and was killed at Ticonderoga.

WALCOTT, John   Served in campaign of 1761.

WALDRON, Daniel of Bristol   Commander of Privateer Phebe in 1760.

WALKER, Daniel of Coventry   Served in Col. Hopkins' Regt. in 1756, and in campaign of 1759.

Elijah   Served in Capt. Jenckes' Co. in 1757, and in campaign of 1759.

Ephraim of Providence   Marched on alarm of Aug. 1757.

James   Enlisted in H. M. regular army in 1762.

John   Served in Capt. J. Whiting's Co. in 1757.

Joseph   Served on Privateer George of Newport in 1758.

Munroe   Served in Capt. Rose's Co. in 1758.

Nathan   Served in Capt. Fry's Co. in 1762.

(———) (Brother of Joseph)   Served in campaign of 1762.

WALL, Daniel   Lieutenant of Capt. Fry's Co. in 1756, Captain of 5th Co. in Col. Angell's Regt. in 1757, Major of Col. Babcock's Regt. in 1758, but resigned in camp. Lt. Colonel of Col. Babcock's Regt. in 1759, but being sick resigned.

William   Served as Mate on Privateer Defiance of Newport in 1756.

WALLACE, Josias   Served on Privateer George of Newport in 1757.

William   Served in campaign of 1756.

WALLING, Cornelius of Smithfield   Marched on alarm of Aug. 1757.

Jeremiah of Smithfield   Marched on alarm of Aug. 1757.

WALMSLEY, James   Enlisted at Newport for campaign of 1762.

WALMSLEY

Thomas   Served in Col. Harris' Regt. in 1760, and in Capt. Hawkins' Co. in 1762.

WALTER, Daniel of Gloucester   Marched on alarm of Aug. 1757.

WAMPY,

WAWPY, Joseph   Served in Capt. J. Whiting's Co. in 1757.

Roger of Richmond   Marched on alarm of Aug. 1757.

WANTON, Benjamin   Commander of Privateer George of Newport in 1757 and 1758, and of Privateer Defiance of Newport in 1759.

James   Drafted in Oct. 1756, but did not serve.

Joseph, Jr., of Newport   Member of Councils of War in 1756, 1757 and 1758, member of Court Martial in 1758, and marched as Lieut. Colonel on alarm of Aug. 1757.

WARD, Jeremiah   Served on Privateer Defiance of Newport in 1756.

Marmaduke   Served in Capt. Belcher's Co. in 1756.

Nehemiah   Served in Col. Harris' Regt. in 1760.

Samuel   Commissioner to wait upon the Earl of Loudon in 1758, Governor in 1762 and 1763, and member of Council of War in 1762.

Samuel   Served in campaign of 1762.

WARDWELL, John   Lieutenant of Capt. Francis' Co. in 1755.

WARE, William of Providence   Marched on alarm of Aug. 1757.

WARNER, Jeremiah   Served in campaign of 1760.

Oliver Ring   Commander of Privateer Dolphin in 1758 and 1761.

William   Served in Col Hopkins' Regt. in 1756.

WARREN, John of Newport   Commander of Privateer Scorpion of Newport in 1758.

Moses   1st Lieutenant of Capt. Coggeshall's Co. in 1756, 2nd Lieutenant of Capt. Greene's Co. in 1757, served in Capt. E. Whiting's Co. in 1758, 2nd Lieutenant of Capt. Rose's Co. in 1759, 1st Lieutenant of Capt. Russell's Co. in 1760, 2nd Lieutenant of Lt. Col.

Rose's Co. in 1761, and 2nd Lieutenant of Major
Peck's Co. in 1762.

WARRY, John   Served in campaigns of 1760 and 1761, and in
winter service of 1761-62.

WASSAMOGG, Thomas   Served in Capt. Jenckes' Co. in 1758,
and in campaign of 1762.

WATERMAN, Christopher of Providence   Commander of Privateer King Hendrick in 1757.

John of Providence   Volunteered on alarm of Aug. 1757.

Joseph of Providence   Marched as hostler on alarm of
Aug. 1757.

Marmaduke   Served in Col. Harris' Regt. in 1760.

Prince of Providence (Colored)   Marched on alarm of
Aug. 1757.

William of Cranston   Marched as Lieutenant on alarm of
Aug. 1757, but styles himself Captain.

WATKINS, Phineas   Served in Col. Harris' Regt. in 1760.

WATSON, Aaron   Served in Capt. J. Whiting's Co. in 1757.

Benedict   Served in Capt. J. Whiting's Co. in 1757, and
in Capt. Brown's Co. in 1759.

Hazard   Served in Lt. Col. Hargill's Co. at Havana in
1762.

John   Enlisted at Newport and served in campaign of
1762.

Levi   Served in Capt. Greene's Co. in 1757, and in campaign of 1762.

Nicholas   Served in Lt. Col. Hargill's Co. at Havana in
1762.

Samuel, Jr., of Exeter   2nd Lieutenant of Capt. Fry's Co.
in 1759, and 1st Lieutenant of Capt. Fry's Co. in 1760.

WAWPY, see WAMPY.

WEATHERBY, Samuel   Served in Col. Harris' Regt. in 1756,
marched on alarm of Aug. 1757, and served as 2nd
Lieutenant in Capt. Tripp's Co. in 1759.

WEATHERHEAD, Daniel   Served in Col. Harris' Regt. in 1756,
and in Capt. Jenckes' Co. in 1757.

John   Served in campaign of 1760.

Levi   Served in Capt. Jenckes' Co. in 1758.

WEAVER, Abiel of E. Greenwich   Served in Capt. Greene's
 Co. in 1757.

 Benedict of N. Kingstown   Served in Capt. Greene's Co.
 in 1757.

 Caleb   Served on Privateer Defiance of Newport in 1756.

 Christopher   Served in Capt. Fry's Co. at Havana in
 1762.

 David of N. Kingstown   Served in Capt. Greene's Co. in
 1757.

 Edward   Served in campaign of 1762.

 Elisha of Warwick   Marched as Ensign on alarm of Aug.
 1757.

 Job   Served in Lt. Col. Hargill's Co. at Havana in 1762.

 John   Served in Capt. Fry's Co. in 1761 and 1762.

 Joseph   Served in Lt. Col. Hargill's Co. at Havana in
 1762.

 Peter of N. Kingstown   Served in Capt. Greene's Co. in
 1757, and in Capt. Fry's Co. in 1762.

 Thomas   Served in Lt. Col. Hargill's Co. at Havana in
 1762.

 William of E. Greenwich   Served in Capt. Greene's Co.
 in 1757, and in campaign of 1759.

WEEDEN, John   Served on Privateer George of Newport in
 1757.

 Jonathan of Newport   Marched on alarm of Aug. 1757.

WEEKS, James   Served in Capt. E. Whiting's Co. in 1759.

 Jethro   Served in Capt. E. Whiting's Co. in 1759.

WEIGHT, Reuben of Exeter   Served in Capt. Greene's Co. in
 1757.

 Thomas   Served in Capt. Rose's Co. in 1758.

 See RIGHT.

WELDON, Peter   Enlisted in H. M. regular army in 1762.

WELLS, George   Served on Privateer Defiance of Newport in
 1756.

 Shadrach   Served in Capt. Hawkins' Co. in 1762.

 Thomas   Served in campaign of 1758.

WELSH, John   Enlisted in H. M. regular army in 1762.

 Morris   Enlisted at Newport for campaign of 1762.

WELSH

William of Charlestown Marched on alarm of Aug. 1757.

WENER, David Served in Capt. Greene's Co. in 1757.

WESCONESS, Thomas Served in campaign of 1762.

WEST, Abner Served in Capt. Belcher's Co. in 1756, as Sergeant in Col. Angell's Regt. in 1757, being advanced to Ensign and then made Quarter Master to the regiment with the rank of 2nd Lieutenant; served in Capt. J. Whiting's Co. in 1757, 2nd Lieutenant in Capt. Tew's Co. in 1758 and 1759 and so appointed in 1760, but did not serve.

Caleb Served in Capt. Wall's Co. in 1757, in campaign of 1761, and in Capt. Fry's Co. at Havana in 1762.

Ebenezer Served in Capt. E. Whiting's Co. in 1757, and in Capt. Brown's Co. in 1759.

James Served in campaign of 1755.

John Served in Capt. E. Whiting's Co. in 1757.

Jonathan Served in Col. Babcock's Co. in 1758 and 1759, and in Capt. Russell's Co. in 1760.

Joseph Enlisted at Newport for campaign of 1762.

Prince Served in Capt. Fry's Co. at Havana in 1762.

William of Bristol Marched on alarm of Aug. 1757.

WESTCOTT, Jeremiah Served in Capt. Potter's Co. in 1756.

Johnson Served in campaign of 1758.

Josiah Served in Lt. Col. Angell's Co. in 1756, in Capt. Jenckes' Co. in 1757, and in campaign of 1759.

Oliver Served in Capt. Jenckes' Co. in 1758, and in campaigns of 1759 and 1760.

Peleg Served in campaign of 1760, in Capt. Kimball's Co. in 1761, and in Capt. Hawkins' Co. in 1762.

William Served in Col. Harris' Regt. in 1760.

Zorobabel of N. Kingstown Marched on alarm of Aug. 1757.

WESTGATE, James Served as Carpenter's Mate on Privateer George of Newport in 1758.

WHALEY, Theophilus Served in Col. Harris' Regt. in 1756.

Joseph of Exeter Served in Capt. Greene's Co. in 1757, and in Capt. Rose's Co. in 1758.

WHEATON, Noah   Served in Major Peck's Co. in 1762.

William of Providence   Marched on alarm of Aug. 1757.

WHEDEN, Samuel   Served in campaign of 1760.

WHEELER, John   Served in campaign of 1755.

WHEELOCK, Simeon   Served in Col. Harris' Regt. in 1760.

WHETFORD, see WHITFORD.

WHIPPLE, Abraham   Commander of a privateer in 1759 and
1760.   Commander of Privateer Gamecock.

Benjamin   Served in Col. Hopkins' Regt. in 1756.

Daniel, Jr., of Cumberland   Marched as Ensign on alarm
of Aug. 1757.

Israel   Served in Capt. Jenckes' Co. in 1757.

John   Served in Capt. Potter's Co. in 1756, in Capt.
Jenckes' Co. in 1757, and in campaigns of 1758, 1759
and 1760.

Jonathan of Gloucester   Marched on alarm of Aug. 1757.

Nathaniel of Cumberland   Marched as Captain on alarm
of Aug. 1757.

Stephen of Providence   Marched on alarm of Aug. 1757.

Stephen of Smithfield   Marched on alarm of Aug. 1757.

WHITAKER, Joseph   Served in Major Peck's Co. in 1762.

Nathaniel   Served in Major Peck's Co. in 1762.

Samuel   Served in Capt. J. Whiting's Co. in 1757.

William   Served in campaign of 1762.   (Also as Whitteson.)

WHITCOMB, Abner   Served in campaign of 1762.

WHITE, Robert   Enlisted in H. M. regular army in 1762.

William   Served in Capt. E. Whiting's Co. in 1757.

WHITFORD, James of Coventry   Marched on alarm of Aug.
1757.

John of N. Kingstown   Served in Capt. Greene's Co. in
1757, and in Lt. Col. Hargill's Co. at Havana in 1762.

Joshua of Hopkinton   Marched on alarm of Aug. 1757.

Nicholas of So. Kingstown   Marched on alarm of Aug.
1757.

Pasco (Pasker)   Served in Capt. Belcher's Co. in 1756, in
Capt. Wall's Co. in 1757, and in Capt. Fry's Co. at
Havana in 1762.

WHITEHORN, George of Newport   Marched on alarm of Aug. 1757.

Peck of South Kingstown   Marched on alarm of Aug. 1757.

WHITEHOUSE, George   Served in Capt. Belcher's Co. in 1756.

WHITING, Amos   Served as Ensign in Capt. J. Whiting's Co. in 1757.

Daniel   Served in Major Peck's Co. in 1762.

Ebenezer   Captain in Col. Harris' Regt. in 1756, Captain of First Co. in 1757, Captain at Fort Edward during winter of 1757-58, Captain of Tenth Co. in 1758, Captain in campaign of 1759, in which campaign Col. Babcock requested his promotion to the office of Major, and he was probably so commissioned.

Henry of Newport   Marched on alarm of Aug. 1757.

John of Newport   Captain of Fifth Co. and ranking officer of Second Detachment in 1755, Adjutant of winter garrison at Fort William Henry in 1755-56, Captain of Third Co. in 1757, Captain of Fourth Co. in 1758, Major of Col. Babcock's Regt. in Feb. 1759, promoted to Lt. Colonel in 1759, Lt. Colonel of Col. Harris' Regt. in 1760, and Colonel of R. I. Regt. in 1761.

WHITMAN, George of N. Kingstown   Marched as Captain on alarm of Aug. 1757.

WHITMORE, Samuel   Served in Col. Harris' Co. in 1756.

WHITTESON, William   See WHITAKER.

WICKES, Joseph   Served in Capt. Fry's Co. at Havana in 1762.

WICKHAM, Benjamin   Lt. Colonel of Col. Hopkins' Regt. in 1756.

WIGNERON, Norbert of Newport   Marched on alarm of Aug. 1757.

WILBUR, Constant of Newport   Marched on alarm of Aug. 1757.

Isaac   2nd Lieutenant in Capt. Gardner's (E. Whiting's) Co. in 1757.

Isaac   Served as A. B. seaman on H. M. S. Pembroke in 1759 and 1760.

WILBUR

Joseph of Newport   Marched on alarm of Aug. 1757.

J.   Served on Privateer George of Newport in 1758.

William of Richmond   Marched on alarm of Aug. 1757, and served in campaign of 1758.

WILCOX, Abraham   Served in Capt. Russell's Co. in 1760, and in Col. Rose's Regt. in 1762.

Daniel of Newport   Served as Mate on Privateer George of Newport in 1758, Commander of Privateer Hornet of Newport in 1760 and 1762, and of Privateer Harlequin of Newport in 1762.

Daniel   Served in Capt. J. Whiting's Co. in 1757.

Derick   Served in campaign of 1762.

George   Served in Capt. Russell's Co. in 1760, and in campaign of 1761.

Ishmael   Served in Capt. Greene's Co. in 1757, in Capt. Russell's Co. in 1760, and as Ensign of Capt. Fry's Co. in 1762.

Jeoffrey, Jr.   Ensign of Capt. Greene's Co. in 1757, 2nd Lieut. of Capt. Russell's Co. in 1760, and Captain Lieutenant of Col. Rose's Co. in 1762.

Jerem'y   Served in Capt. Russell's Co. in 1760.

Job   Served in Capt. J. Whiting's Co. in 1757.

Thomas   Served in Capt. Potter's Co. in 1755, and in Capt. Wall's Co. in 1757.

William of Little Compton   Marched on alarm of Aug. 1757, and served in campaign of 1762.

WILES, see WILL.

WILKEY, John   Served in Col. Rose's Regt. in 1762.

Thomas of Exeter   Marched on alarm of Aug. 1757.

WILKINSON, John   Served in Lt. Col. Hargill's Co. at Havana in 1762.

Samuel   Served on Privateer Providence, and died at Port Morant in 1758.

WILKS, George   Gunner on Privateer General Johnson in 1757.

WILL,

WILES, John of Newport   Marched on alarm of Aug. 1757,

enlisted for campaign of 1762, and in H. M. regular army in 1762.

WILLARD, Charles   Served in Capt. Fry's Co. in 1761, and in Capt. Fry's Co. at Havana in 1762.

WILLIAMS, David   Served as a seaman at Oswego in 1756 and was taken prisoner.

John   Served on Privateer Defiance of Newport in 1756.

Peleg of Providence   Served in Capt. Jenckes' Co. in 1756, marched on alarm of Aug. 1757, and served in campaigns of 1758 and 1759.

Peter   Served in Capt. J. Whiting's Co. in 1757.

Peter   Served on Privateer George of Newport in 1758.

Robert   Served in campaigns of 1758 and 1759.

Samuel   Enlisted at Newport for campaign of 1762.

Theophilus of Providence   Volunteered on alarm of Aug. 1757.

Thomas   Served in Capt. Jenckes' Co. in 1757, and in campaign of 1758.

Timothy   Served in Capt. Jenckes' Co. in 1757, and in campaigns of 1758 and 1760.

Zebedee   Served in Col. Harris' Regt. in 1760.

WILLIAMSON, John   Served in campaign of 1759.

WILLIE,

WYLLIE, Benjamin   Served in Capt. J. Whiting's Co. in 1757, and enlisted in H. M. regular army in 1762.

WILLIS, Charles   Served in Capt. Greene's Co. in 1757.

Henry   Served in Capt. J. Whiting's Co. in 1757.

WILLISTON, John of Little Compton   Marched as Capt. on alarm of Aug. 1757.

WILLS, Henry   Served in Capt. Brown's Co. in 1759.

Peter   Served in Capt. Wall's Co. in 1757.

See WILL.

WILMARTH, Thomas   Served in Major Peck's Co. in 1762.

Timothy   Served in campaign of 1758.

WILSON, Elisha   Served in Col. Harris' Regt. in 1760.

James   Served as boat-builder at Oswego in 1756 and was taken prisoner.

James   Enlisted in H. M. regular army in 1762.

WILSON

John   Served in Capt. Wall's Co. in 1757.

Joseph   Served in Capt. Jenckes' Co. in 1756.

WINDSOR, Joseph of Providence   Appointed Captain of special company in Sept. 1756; appointed and served as Captain of Sixth Co. of Col. Hopkins' Regt. in Oct. 1756, and volunteered on alarm of Aug. 1757.

WINGOOD, Samuel   Served as ordinary seaman on H. M. S. Pembroke in 1759 and 1760.

WINMAN, Richard   Served in Capt. Wall's Co. in 1757, in Col.
WINDMAN,   Harris' Regt, in 1760, and in Col. Rose's Regt. in 1762.

WINRIGHT, Thomas of E. Greenwich   Served in Capt. Wall's
WAINWRIGHT,   Co. in 1757.

WOID, Abner   Served in Major Burkett's Co. in 1760.

WOLLARD, Richard   Served in Capt. Belcher's Co. in 1756, and in Col. Babcock's Co. in 1758 and 1759.

WONKUM, Ebenezer   Served in Capt. J. Whiting's Co. in 1757.

WOOD, Benjamin of Warwick   Served in Capt. Wall's Co. in 1757, and in Col. Harris' Regt. in 1760.

George of Little Compton   Marched on alarm of Aug. 1757.

Henry of Little Compton   Marched as Ensign on alarm of Aug. 1757.

John   Served in Capt. J. Whiting's Co. in 1757, in Capt. E. Whiting's Co. in 1758 and 1759, in campaign of 1760, and in Capt. Russell's Co. at Havana in 1762.

John   Served in Capt. Fry's Co. at Havana in 1762.

Nathan   Served in campaign of 1760, and in Capt. Kimball's Co. in 1761.

Thomas of Newport   Served in Col. Hopkins' Regt. in 1756, and in campaign of 1762.

William of Warwick   Marched on alarm of Aug. 1757.

William, Jr., of Warwick   Marched on alarm of Aug. 1757.

Zebulon of Coventry   Served in Capt. Wall's Co. in 1757, and in Capt. Fry's Co. at Havana in 1762.

WOODBURY, Ebenezer of Newport   Marched on alarm of Aug. 1757.

Woodbury

(husband of Hannah)   Served in campaign of 1755.
Woodin, John   Served in campaign of 1758.
Woodman, Thomas   Served in Capt. E. Whiting's Co. in 1757.
Woodward, Elijah   Served in Capt. Hawkins' Co. in 1762.
Hezekiah   Served in Col. Babcock's Co. in 1758 and 1759.
John   Served in campaign of 1762.
Jonas   Served in Capt. Brown's Co. in 1758 and 1759.
Robert   Served in Capt. Hawkins' Co. in 1762.
Zephaniah   Served in Capt. Hawkins' Co. in 1762.
Woodworth, Nathaniel   Served in Capt. E. Whiting's Co. in 1757.
Worden, Nathaniel   Served in Capt. Brown's Co. in 1759.
William   Served in Capt. E. Whiting's Co. in 1757.
Worry, John   Served in Capt. Rose's Co. in 1758.
Worris, William   Served in Capt. E. Whiting's Co. in 1757.
Worth, Lillibridge   Served in Capt. Belcher's Co. in 1756.
Wright, John of Newport   Volunteered and marched as Captain on alarm of Aug. 1757.
Stephen   Served in campaigns of 1758, 1759 and 1760.
William   Served in Capt. Kimball's Co. in 1761.
Wyatt, John   Served on Privateer Defiance of Newport in 1756, and on Privateer George of Newport in 1758.
Newport   Served on Privateer Defiance of Newport in 1756.
William of Newport   Marched on alarm of Aug. 1757.
Wyllye, see Willie.
Wyllys, see Willis.

Yaw, William   Served in Capt. Jenckes' Co. in 1758.
Yates, Benedict   Served on Privateer George of Newport in 1758.
William   Served in campaign of 1762.
Yeoman, Ezekiel of Newport   Marched on alarm of Aug. 1757.
York, Moses   Enlisted at Newport for campaign of 1762.
Thomas   Served in Capt. E. Whiting's Co. in 1757.

YOUNG, Andrew   Served in campaign of 1761.
 Benjamin   Served in Col. Rose's Regt. in 1762.
 James of Newport   Commander of Privateer Skip Jack
  of Newport in 1756.
 James   Served in campaigns of 1760 and 1762.
 John   Served in Capt. J. Whiting's Co. in 1757.
 Joseph   Served in Col. Hopkins' Regt. in 1756.
 Nathaniel   Served in campaign of 1759.
 Richard of Providence   Marched on alarm of Aug. 1757.
 Samuel of Newport   Served in Capt. Belcher's Co. in
  1756, and marched on alarm of Aug. 1757.
 William of Coventry   Marched on alarm of Aug. 1757,
  and served in campaign of 1760.
YOUNGMAN, Cornelius   Served in Capt. Jenckes' Co. in 1758,
  in campaign of 1759, and in Col. Harris' Regt. in 1760.
Yows, John   Served in Capt. J. Whiting's Co. in 1757.